PSYCHOLOGICAL CAPITAL

PSYCHOLOGICAL CAPITAL

Developing the Human Competitive Edge

FRED LUTHANS

CAROLYN M. YOUSSEF

BRUCE J. AVOLIO

OXFORD
UNIVERSITY PRESS

2007

OXFORD
UNIVERSITY PRESS

Oxford University Press, Inc., publishes works that further
Oxford University's objective of excellence
in research, scholarship, and education.

Oxford   New York
Auckland   Cape Town   Dar es Salaam   Hong Kong   Karachi
Kuala Lumpur   Madrid   Melbourne   Mexico City   Nairobi
New Delhi   Shanghai   Taipei   Toronto

With offices in
Argentina   Austria   Brazil   Chile   Czech Republic   France   Greece
Guatemala   Hungary   Italy   Japan   Poland   Portugal   Singapore
South Korea   Switzerland   Thailand   Turkey   Ukraine   Vietnam

Published by Oxford University Press, Inc.
198 Madison Avenue, New York, New York 10016

www.oup.com

Library of Congress Cataloging-in-Publication Data
Luthans, Fred.
Psychological capital : developing the human competitive edge / Fred Luthans, Carolyn M. Youssef,
and Bruce J. Avolio.
p. cm.
Includes bibliographical references and index.
ISBN 978-0-19-518752-6
1. Employee competitive behavior.   2. Employee motivation.   3. Employees—Psychology.   4. Human
capital—Psychological aspects.   5. Management—Psychological aspects.   I. Youssef, Carolyn M.
II. Avolio, Bruce J.   III. Title.
HF5549.5.C7L88 2007
658.3'14—dc22   2006005346

9 8 7 6

Printed in the United States of America
on acid-free paper

To our spouses, children, other family members, friends, mentors, colleagues, and students who have modeled and nurtured our psychological capital development journey

Thank you!

Fred, Carolyn, and Bruce

PREFACE

THIS BOOK INTEGRATES our recent theory-building, empirical findings, and practical applications on positively oriented human resource strengths and psychological capacities. We only include those capacities that can be measured, developed, and effectively managed for performance improvement in today's workplace. This interest in positivity in the workplace was fueled by the still-emerging positive psychology movement. Positive psychology has broadened the perspective beyond what is wrong with people toward optimal functioning, flourishing, and reaching human potential. Although not as evident in the field of organizational behavior and human resource management, unfortunately, negativity has too often also prevailed when applied to the workplace. Leaders at all levels and types of organizations and organizational behavior scholars have tended to focus on what is wrong with human resources and how to fix its weaknesses and problems. However, similar to positive psychology, we do feel that, following our call from a few years ago in some published articles on positive organizational behavior (POB), the pendulum has started to swing in a more positive direction for both research and practice.

Few would argue that effectively managing today's organizations requires a shift to a new paradigm where excellence and sustainable competitive advantage can no longer be founded on traditional, scarce resources (e.g., physical, financial, or technological resources). Starting with human and social capital as the point of departure, we propose that what we call *psychological capital* (or, simply, *PsyCap*) can be invested and developed for sustainable competitive advantage through people. What sets PsyCap apart from longtime popular perspectives such as "the power of positive thinking" and many best-selling, positively oriented personal development books is its foundation in theory and research. We are fully aware that both researchers and practitioners have grown weary of management fads, unsubstantiated claims, and short-term results. Instead, we base our core construct of PsyCap on rich theory and methodologically sound measures and research findings.

Aside from the foundation of theory and research evidenced in this book, the other overriding feature of PsyCap is that, unlike most positive psychology and organizational behavior constructs, PsyCap is open to development and change. As will be seen in this book, PsyCap can be enhanced in the workplace through relatively brief and highly focused interventions. In today's turbulent work environment, managers need to see results, and to see them fast. The developmental nature of PsyCap, as well as its demonstrated performance impact, fits the fast-paced workplace that demands results, now. The book will show how organizational leaders can utilize both planned interventions and unplanned positive and negative events to facilitate and trigger their own and their associates' PsyCap. This development effort can create ripple effects where positivity and authenticity can become contagious throughout an organization.

It is our sincere hope that this book will inform and stimulate you to join us in our journey to better understand and apply the core construct of PsyCap in making ourselves, organizational leaders, and the management of human resources more effective and collaborative in meeting the challenges that lie ahead.

CONTENTS

PSYCHOLOGICAL CAPITAL

CHAPTER 1

Introduction to Psychological Capital

WHAT WILL MAKE a real difference in having a true competitive advantage in the global "market space" of tomorrow? How can organizations and individuals ready themselves to achieve distinct competitive advantages? This book serves as your guide to a newly emerging answer to gaining competitive advantage through people. We call for the investment and development of psychological capital. We define psychological capital, or what we refer to throughout this book simply as *PsyCap*, as follows:

> PsyCap is an individual's positive psychological state of development and is characterized by: (1) having confidence (self-efficacy) to take on and put in the necessary effort to succeed at challenging tasks; (2) making a positive attribution (optimism) about succeeding now and in the future; (3) persevering toward goals and, when necessary, redirecting paths to goals (hope) in order to succeed; and (4) when beset by problems and adversity, sustaining and bouncing back and even beyond (resiliency) to attain success.

Much has been written on the exponential increase in the range, intensity, and variety of the challenges facing today's organizations. Although counterintuitive, given the frequent newsworthy events of downsizing resulting in massive layoffs, fighting and winning the so-called "war for talent" is one such prominent challenge (Axelrod, Handfield-Jones, & Welsh, 2001; Fishman, 1998; Michaels, Handfield-Jones, & Axelrod, 2001; Pfeffer,

3

2001). Indeed, the challenge is not only finding creative sources of needed talent; even more important but too often slighted in this war, we would argue, is finding innovative ways of capitalizing on and developing human, social, and especially the psychological capacities of human resources for sustained competitive advantage.

As shown by the comprehensive definition of PsyCap above and by our research support so far (e.g., Luthans, Avey, Avolio, Norman, & Combs, 2006; Luthans, Avolio, Avey, & Norman, 2006; Luthans, Avolio, Walumbwa, & Li, 2005), PsyCap is a higher order positive construct comprised of the four-facet constructs of self-efficacy/confidence, optimism, hope, and resiliency. This PsyCap is open to development that we propose can pick up where the war perspective leaves off in meeting today's—and tomorrow's—challenges.

After first outlining some of the parameters and limitations of a war-for-talent perspective, this introductory chapter provides the background and meaning of PsyCap, including the need for this new approach; the contribution of positive psychology, positive organizational scholarship (POS), and positive organizational behavior (POB); the criteria of inclusion; and, finally, the theoretical, measurement, and developmental frameworks for the rest of the book.

THE WAR-FOR-TALENT PERSPECTIVE

A number of best practices have been proposed as effective ways for attracting and managing talent, including job design, pay and benefits, growth opportunities, work-life balance programs, and others (e.g., Barnett & Hall, 2001; Johnson, 2004; Lance, 2005; Olson, 2003). There is no question that meeting and exceeding performance requirements in today's hypercompetitive environment are becoming increasingly difficult as organizations vie for the same pool of talented human resources, especially with readily accessible information flows across organizations and even industries (Goodwin, 2005; Wilkinson, 2005). Further challenges are encountered as the precise requirements of highly specialized jobs and the diverse needs of talented employees call for customization and an increased emphasis on person-organization fit (Ng & Burke, 2005; Trank, Rynes, & Bretz, 2002). Perhaps even more importantly, with 70 million baby boomers readying to retire, the competition for the pool of employees that remain may be unprecedented in the history of the United States, a pattern we see replicated in other Western nations and Japan, which face similarly aging working populations.

To further complicate the current situation, a new psychological contract has emerged from the turbulent corporate landscape characterized by downsizing and a lack of personal identity. Neither employers nor employees are willing or able to sustain their mutual commitment and loyalty, at least in the traditional sense, for extended periods of time. Lifetime employment, seniority-based human resources practices, union-negotiated working conditions, and attitudes of entitlement have given way to what has been termed "career resiliency" (Waterman, Waterman, & Collard, 1994). At a time when organizations likely need to build a greater sense of ownership among their employees to take charge of their workspace and their careers, the conditions for feeling like an owner are at best challenging and at worst dire.

Psychological ownership has been defined as "the state in which individuals feel as though the target of ownership or a piece of that target is 'theirs'" (Pierce, Kostova, & Dirks, 2003, p. 86). Specifically, they feel responsible for a particular target and experience feelings of concern for the target, which in this case can be their job or their organization (Parker, Wall, & Jackson, 1997).

Vandewalle, Van Dyne, and Kostova (1995) have shown that psychological ownership was positively related to extra role/organizational citizenship behaviors. Wagner, Parker, and Christiansen (2003) provided further support showing a positive connection between individuals' beliefs about their ownership and the financial performance of the organization. Van Dyne and Pierce (2004) also found that psychological ownership for the organization was positively related with employee levels of organizational commitment, job satisfaction, and organization-based self-esteem, as well as work behavior and performance.

In this new psychological contract, employees are expected to take charge of strategic management of their own careers or, in essence, take ownership. This self-management involves keeping their skills and competencies current in relation to their employers' needs, as well as making strategic moves across employers when necessary. On the other hand, employers' responsibility toward their employees has become more of a "service provider" mode, which is limited to the duration and capacity of where the costs can be justified.

The best places to work are no longer those that promise lifetime employment but, rather, those that provide their participants with the opportunities, resources, and flexibility for sustainable growth, learning, and development. Today's talented employees are looking for employers that can contribute to sustaining their career progress, either within or beyond the specific organizational context—where they even become what some progressive-thinking employers have dubbed alumni of the organization.

Adding to the complex equation of today's competitive battles for talent and market share are the challenges of a global economy with borderless and ever-changing political, economic, technological, social, and ethical climates. This uncertain environment takes its toll on leaders and employees as they make important personal or organizational decisions or even in their routine, day-to-day activities. Perceptions of "losing control" can strip organizational members of their self-confidence, causing them to feel hopeless and pessimistic about the future and eventually weakening their resiliency. This, in turn, can result in unfavorable organizational outcomes, such as decreased performance and morale, as well as adverse personal and social implications, such as decreased physical and psychological engagement, health, and well-being.

LIMITATIONS OF THE WAR PERSPECTIVE

As a by-product of the call for the war for talent, considerable attention has been given to negatively oriented constructs, such as emotional labor, stress, burnout, conflict, and disengagement, as well as more positive, traditional organizational behavior constructs, such as self-esteem, reinforcement, goal-setting, positive affectivity, pro-social/citizenship behaviors, empowerment, engagement, and participation (e.g., see Locke, 2000; Luthans, 2005, for comprehensive reviews of this body of knowledge).

Although this traditional approach to managing talent remains necessary, we would argue that it is not sufficient. We propose that the answers to today's and the future's challenges require more than just doing what we already know how to do well. We believe that organizational behavior theory, research, and practice are each on the verge of a paradigm shift that requires immediate attention and action. The competitive war perspective, on which the past 10 to 15 years of research and practice have been built, may no longer be adequate for at least two major reasons: (1) the need for unique, new-paradigm thinking when it comes to developing and managing human resources; and (2) the need for positive, cross-disciplinary research support for more effective, sustainable growth and performance. Short-term growth that is not sustainable in a market of diminishing human talent portends disaster for organizations in markets that have the potential for growth. Growth may actually turn out to be a more potent killer of organizations than decline.

THE NEED FOR A NEW APPROACH

Simply concentrating and accumulating more of the traditional resources once considered vital for organizational success have proven insufficient for attaining sustainable sources of competitive advantage. Examples of such traditional resources include economic and financial capital, advanced technology, and proprietary information. Competitive strategies that rely on raising entry barriers are also no longer effective in creating sources of distinct advantage that can be sustained in the long run. We would argue that now sustainable competitive advantage can best be accomplished through context-specific, cumulative, renewable, and thus hard-to-imitate factors, even given the continued presence of traditional material resources (Drucker, 1994; Luthans & Youssef, 2004). We propose that such advantage can be gained through investing, leveraging, developing, and managing psychological capital (PsyCap).

This new PsyCap approach to gaining competitive advantage is based on the generally accepted fact that most organizations today are not realizing the full potential of their human resources (Avolio, 2005). They do not truly believe in the value of their human resources and thus neither invest in them nor effectively develop and manage them. Although they may occasionally apply some of the latest high-performance work practices (HPWPs) such as 360-degree feedback systems or self-managed teams, they do not truly understand their implications on and interactions with other core organizational values and practices (e.g., see Pfeffer, 1998). As a result, too often human resource management practices become highly inconsistent and incoherent, subject to management fads, resource availability, and organizational politics.

From the war perspective, we would agree that most of today's recognized human resource practices may be adequate for attracting talent but not for creating unique, new paradigm thinking for how to develop and manage human resources for competitive advantage over the long-term. For example, extensive investments in technical training may be easily imitable by competitors at a fraction of the cost through off-the-shelf, on-line, self-paced alternatives, and they are usually subject to obsolescence. Similarly, creative pay and benefit packages may not necessarily matter in today's world of alternative work arrangements, and when they do, they become the standard through benchmarking efforts in today's copycat environment. Team-building, decision-making, and other notable "competencies" or "best practices" have become the norm across competitors and industries. Management consultants have commonly replaced customized, organizational-specific solutions with faster, more profitable packaged programs and approaches. Consequently, there is a strong need not only for more consistent and integrated human resource practices but also for an expanded framework that selectively and adaptively employs various practices for the investment in and development of unique approaches, such as our proposed PsyCap.

THE NEED FOR A POSITIVE APPROACH

Decades of relentless research on negatively oriented perspectives and problems in foundational disciplines to organizational behavior and human resources management (HRM) such as psychology or even sociology did not result in a better understanding of human strengths, flourishing, and optimal functioning. Unfortunately, this negativity has also penetrated into the organizational behavior and HRM fields and accompanied the war perspective. This negativity exposes individuals and organizations to the danger of shifting to a fight-or-flight mode, where scarce time, energy, and resources are only invested in basic tried-and-true survival mechanisms. A negative approach also focuses on minimizing what is wrong or a deficit reduction model of human and organizational development. Richer, more positive alternatives with potentially higher returns are shunned as too risky, too soft, or too time consuming considering the critical nature of the situation at hand.

The field of psychology is a case in point. Prior to World War II, psychologists were charged with a three-pronged mission: healing mental illness, helping healthy people become happier and more productive, and actualizing human potential. However, as the war concluded, tremendous needs existed for reparative psychological treatment, and substantial resources were allocated to damage-control and weakness-fixing mechanisms at the expense of psychology's other two missions. As a result of this real-war model (i.e., the aftermath of World War II), until the turn of the century, little attention was devoted to human strengths. Even the prevention of psychological problems, beyond philosophical discourses and scattered extrapolations from research findings based on proactive applications of the same disease-oriented paradigm, was largely absent (Keyes & Haidt, 2003; Seligman & Csikszentmihalyi, 2000).

Similar to what happened in psychology, we propose that the short-term-oriented, crisis-management model that characterizes today's war perspective has also resulted in a negative perspective. This prevailing approach largely precludes the potential for building sustainable competitive advantage through a new positive approach. Notable exceptions certainly exist, such as Gallup's strengths-based management approach, in which individuals are selected, developed, and managed along their strengths rather than their weaknesses (e.g., Buckingham & Clifton, 2001; Buckingham & Coffman, 1999). But it was the positive psychology movement and its applications to the workplace in terms of positive organizational scholarship (POS) and especially positive organizational behavior (POB) that provided a foundation for our proposed core construct of PsyCap to help meet the need for a new, positive approach.

THE CONTRIBUTION OF POSITIVE PSYCHOLOGY AND POS

At the turn of the twenty-first century, psychologists led by Martin Seligman, a well-known researcher in the traditional negative approach (e.g., learned helplessness) and former president of the American Psychological Association (APA), took inventory of their achievements under the disease model for over five decades in the post–World War II era. Despite recognized accomplishments in finding effective treatments for mental illness and dysfunctional behavior, psychology as a whole had paid relatively very little attention to healthy individuals in terms of growth, development, and self-actualization. The call by Seligman and a few others for redirecting psychological research toward psychology's two forgotten missions of helping healthy people become happier and more productive and actualizing human potential has resulted in not only a surge of interest but also theory-building and empirical research, in what is now known as positive psychology (e.g., see the January 2000 and March 2001 special issues of *American Psychologist*, as well as Aspinwall & Straudinger, 2003; Carr, 2004; Compton, 2005; Keyes & Haidt, 2003; Linley & Joseph, 2004; Lopez & Snyder, 2003; Peterson & Seligman, 2004; Snyder & Lopez, 2002).

Under the leadership of these researchers, positive psychology bases its conclusions on science rather than philosophy, rhetoric, conventional wisdom, gurus, or personal opinion. It is noteworthy that the theory and research requirements of positive psychology were intended and indeed have differentiated it from the plethora of popular literature on the power of positive thinking and from much of positively oriented humanistic psychology and the human potential movement. This scientific basis also serves as an important precedent and has become a prerequisite for our proposed application of positivity to the workplace in the form of PsyCap.

Besides positive psychology, organizational theory and behavior scholars have recently recognized the untapped potential of a science-based, positively oriented approach, which has resulted in two major parallel, and complementary, movements. These are commonly referred to as positive organizational scholarship (POS), emanating primarily from a research group at the University of Michigan (see Cameron, Dutton, & Quinn, 2003), and our positive organizational behavior (POB), arising from the University of Nebraska's Gallup Leadership Institute (Luthans, 2002a, 2002b, 2003; Luthans & Avolio, 2003). Both approaches definitely complement each other, but POS tends to concentrate more on the macro, organizational level, while POB at least has started out at the more micro, individual level. Other distinguishing features are that POS deals with constructs such as compassion and virtuousness that may or may not be open to development and/or relate to performance impact (e.g., see Cameron, Bright, & Caza, 2004; Cameron & Caza, 2004), while to be included in POB the construct must meet the criteria of being state-like, and thus open to development, and related to performance outcomes (Luthans, 2002a, 2002b, 2003; Luthans & Avolio, 2003). PsyCap is derived from the POB foundation and criteria (Avolio & Luthans, 2006; Luthans, Luthans, & Luthans, 2004; Luthans & Youssef, 2004).

POSITIVE ORGANIZATIONAL BEHAVIOR (POB)

Positive organizational behavior (POB) was first defined as "the study and application of positively oriented human resource strengths and psychological capacities that can be measured, developed, and effectively managed for performance improvement in today's workplace" (Luthans, 2002b, p. 59; see also Cooper & Nelson, 2006; Wright, 2003). Thus, for a psychological strength or capacity to be included in our conception of POB, it must be positive and relatively unique to the field of organizational behavior, but most importantly, it must meet the scientific criteria of being theory- and research-based, measurable, state-like or developmental, and related to work performance outcomes. The approach we have chosen is very much in line with a growing trend in both medicine and in the organizational sciences for evidence-based practices (Pfeffer & Sutton, 2006).

The above set of POB criteria serves vital purposes that go beyond mere branding and marketing of a new research stream or human resource management fad. In a manner similar to positive psychology, we recognize the continued importance of studying negatively oriented constructs and approaches, but we also propose that POB can represent a paradigm shift that has the potential to transform organizational behavior and human resource management research and practice. Thus, we dedicate the balance of this section to a more detailed discussion and rationale behind each of the POB inclusion criteria.

The Positivity Criterion of POB

The deficits-and-disease model prominently used in clinical psychology fails to recognize and enhance our understanding and appreciation of well-being. Analogously, but perhaps not to the same degree, traditional negatively oriented organizational behavior theories and approaches have emphasized ineffective leaders, unethical employees, stress and conflict, dysfunctional attitudes and behaviors, and counterproductive organizational structures, strategies, and cultures. We would argue that such a negative approach has greatly contributed to the generally recognized lack of truly superior performance, continuous learning and development, and proactive, strategic change and adaptation. At best, the existing equivalent to the war model discussed at the beginning of the chapter can only equip organizations and their members with some survival skills that may help them sustain average performance for a reasonable period of time by reducing that which is wrong versus enhancing and building on what is right. However, average performance is no longer adequate for sustainability in today's highly competitive environment (Avolio & Luthans, 2006; Sutcliffe & Vogus, 2003).

A valid question for today's environment and the state of the organizational behavior field becomes: Can we just extrapolate from the findings of the negative approach to better understand positivity? Unfortunately, the answer is far from that simple. For example, many years ago, Frederick Herzberg pointed out that reducing job dissatisfaction is not necessarily conducive to increased job satisfaction, as those two attitudes may be influenced by different factors (Herzberg, Mauesner, & Snyderman, 1959). In other words, positive and negative constructs are not necessarily opposite sides of a single continuum. Rather, positive and negative are divergent constructs, each with its own continuum, antecedents, dimensions, and outcomes (Peterson & Chang, 2002). With POB, we are simply trying to recognize and emphasize the largely untapped power that positivity may have in contemporary and future workplaces with a specific emphasis on criteria meeting psychological capacities.

Theory- and Research-Based Criteria of POB

In response to the apparent inadequacy of a negative approach, the intuitive appeal of positivity has led to a proliferation of positively oriented popular self-help literature such as Kenneth Blanchard's *One Minute Manager*, Steven Covey's *Seven Habits of Highly Effective People*, and Spencer Johnson's *Who Moved My Cheese?* Although filling a significant void and promoting positivity, these best-sellers provide very limited, if any, scientific theory or research backup and are thus not evidence based. Even when descriptive findings are reported, they lack the minimal criteria of scientific rigor and meaningful, sustainable knowledge to know what has caused what. When these books offer self-assessment questionnaires, they may have face validity, be creative, and be fun to complete, but they lack any empirically derived construct validity and/or evidence for cause and effect. When applications to the workplace are provided, serious internal and external validity threats exist, and findings are often extrapolated out of context.

For example, oftentimes practitioners who are touting a particular intervention that may have legitimately worked fail to realize that what works in one setting may not generalize to another. More importantly, the fact that the intervention occurred does not necessarily mean that it caused the changes observed. This can only be ascertained by conducting experimental research. As noted by Pfeffer and Sutton (2006), managers are often quite ignorant about which prescriptions work and do not work and have little motivation to find out. Many managers yearn for remedies without sufficient evidence to warrant their continued use in organizations.

Using positive psychology instead of these popular books as the standard, POB is committed to a scientific approach for inclusion and for accumulating a sustainable, impactful body of knowledge for leadership and human resources development and performance impact. This is the way that we can assure we are working with the right constructs that contribute over time to sustainable growth and performance.

Valid Measurement Criterion of POB

Measurement has always been at the core of scientific research and application. The existence of reliable and valid instruments for measuring work-related constructs has raised organizational behavior in general, and POB in particular, into the realm of science. With valid measurement, systematic analysis, prediction, and control become possible. Again, following the lead of positive psychology (e.g., see Lopez & Snyder, 2003, for a comprehensive summary of a number of positive psychological assessments), POB requires that for a construct to be included, there must be reliable and valid measures. This criterion excludes many interesting but highly philosophical metaconstructs that do not lend themselves to operationalization and assessment, as well as the "soft" qualities and positive characteristics that the popular best-sellers advocate for success. In the concluding chapter, chapter 8, we include our recently developed Psychological Capital Questionnaire (PCQ), and in other chapters we discuss possible additions that may be included in the future as PsyCap constructs.

The State-Like Criterion of POB

There is a wide variety of research-based selection tools in human resource management. For example, there are a large number of personality traits with demonstrated relationships with performance and attitudinal work outcomes. These are legally defensible for use as selection tools. Examples include the "Big Five" personality traits (Barrick & Mount, 1991), core self-evaluations (Judge & Bono, 2001), Gallup's talents and strengths (Buckingham & Clifton, 2001; Buckingham and Coffman, 1999), and cognitive mental abilities (Schmidt & Hunter, 2000).

Similarly, the positive psychology movement is dominated by trait-like character strengths and virtues that tend to exhibit considerable stability over time (Peterson & Seligman, 2004; Snyder & Lopez, 2002). Unlike genetically determined factors, positive psychological traits show some malleability and thus may be able to experience some growth and development over one's lifespan, given optimal situational factors, certain trigger moments, jolts, or extensive psychotherapy (Avolio & Luthans, 2006; Linley & Joseph, 2004). However, little change is likely in the short term, and thus these positive traits are difficult to develop and change in human resource management.

In today's environment, which is characterized by high turnover rates and emphasis on continuous improvement and sharp learning curves, most long-term initiatives for creating or nurturing job-related talents, character strengths, positive virtues, and other relatively stable personality traits is not cost effective or, in most instances, even possible. The importance of coming to the workplace prepared with such enduring talents, strengths, and especially personality traits, as well as the relatively early age at which they are developed, has led such initiatives to be mostly transferred to educational institutions. Thus, within the domain of the workplace, human resources' traits have been the focus for effective recruitment, selection, and placement "fit" initiatives.

We certainly believe that selecting the right people and placing them in the right roles (i.e., the right fit) are necessary for effective human resource management, but once again, they are not sufficient. We believe human development/potential is far more elastic than has been previously assumed. By the same token, developing knowledge, skills, and technical abilities is no longer enough. In our proposed POB, we only include positive psychological capacities that are state-like and malleable. Being state-like (rather than trait-like), these positive capacities are open to development and improvement using relatively brief training programs, on-the-job activities, and short, highly focused "microinterventions" (Luthans, Avey, et al., 2006). The model we have recently developed for our PsyCap Intervention (PCI) is given detailed attention in chapter 8. The state-like criterion of POB is perhaps the biggest differentiator from positive psychology and POS, which tend to be more dominated by dispositional trait-like constructs.

In addition to the fit of developmental states within the context of the workplace, it is also important to note that POB expands the domain of positive psychological capacities beyond just the prediction of performance and into support of a causal relationship between POB states and desired performance outcomes. As noted above with regard to evidence-based management, only through the manipulation of POB factors in an experimental intervention study can such causal conclusions be firmly established. The measurement of the state before and after a microintervention to develop it (especially when compared to a randomly assigned or matched control group that either did not receive the developmental intervention or, better yet, received the next best alternative) can demonstrate that the state can be developed. Chapter 8 reports that such development of PsyCap has indeed been demonstrated through our microintervention studies (see Luthans, Avey, et al., 2006).

If performance measures are taken pre- and postintervention in both the experimental and control groups of these PsyCap microinterventions, a case can be made that the state caused the performance outcome. By contrast, the stability of personality traits limits their explanatory power in the workplace. Although stable traits are desirable for various reasons, including career planning or performance management, the value of developable states such as found in PsyCap has been generally overlooked. By emphasizing states rather than traits, POB creates new opportunities and dimensions for human resource development and performance management.

The Performance Impact Criterion of POB

Quantifying the dollar return on human resource investments has become of vital importance to organizational decision-makers (e.g., Cascio, 1991; Cascio & Ramos, 1986; Hunter & Schmidt, 1983; Huselid, 1995; Kravetz, 2004). As various attractive investments compete for the scarce resources in an organization, an adequate return becomes one of the most critical factors in determining the extent to which human resource development initiatives receive organizational support. It is generally acknowledged that many human resource investments have a high potential for yielding above average returns. However, the questionable assumptions and difficulties associated with quantifying these returns may channel resources away from such worthwhile investments and instead toward the accumulation of more traditional assets such as physical, financial, and technological capital.

In selecting only positive psychological capacities that meet the criterion of being related to performance, POB is fully expected to have a significant impact on work outcomes. We anticipate that this performance orientation and bottom-line relevance will warrant the attention and buy-in of both public and private organizations. It is also important to note that other positive, scientific, work-related initiatives, such as those coming out of positive organizational scholarship (e.g., Cameron, et al., 2004; Cameron, et al., 2003) may also have a positive performance impact. However, as we pointed out, a major distinction between POB and such initiatives is that POB is restricted to only those positive capacities that impact performance, whereas most of the POS constructs have not yet been demonstrated to relate to performance.

POB CRITERIA MEETING PSYCHOLOGICAL CAPACITIES

Since the above criteria were established for POB, several positive psychological capacities have been considered for inclusion, studied, and empirically tested in the context of the workplace. Those that we have determined best meet the POB inclusion criteria are self-efficacy, hope, optimism, and resiliency (e.g., see Luthans, 2002a; Luthans & Avolio, 2003; Luthans, Avolio, et al., 2006; Luthans & Jensen, 2002; Luthans, et al., 2004; Luthans, Vogelgesang, & Lester, 2006; Luthans & Youssef, 2004; Peterson & Luthans, 2003). We only briefly introduce each of these four capacities since an in-depth discussion of each is presented in the following four chapters.

Founded on the extensive work of Albert Bandura (1997) and specifically his social cognitive theory, *self-efficacy* can be defined as: "an individual's conviction (or confidence) about his or her abilities to mobilize the motivation, cognitive resources, and courses of action needed to successfully execute a specific task within a given context" (Stajkovic & Luthans, 1998b, p.66). Meta-analytical findings support a highly significant positive correlation between such self-efficacy and work-related performance (Stajkovic & Luthans, 1998a).

Of the four capacities that we determined meet our POB definitional criteria, self-efficacy has the most established theoretical foundation and empirical research base, particularly in the workplace. Self-efficacy development approaches have also been well established in the research literature. These include mastery experiences, vicarious learning/modeling, social persuasion, and physiological and psychological arousal (Bandura, 1997). We have devoted chapter 2 of this book to this powerful positive psychological capacity.

Based on C. Rick Snyder's (2000) extensive theory-building and research, *hope* is defined as "a positive motivational state that is based on an interactively derived sense of successful (1) agency (goal-directed energy) and (2) pathways (planning to meet goals)" (Snyder, Irving, & Anderson, 1991, p. 287). The agency (or willpower) and pathways (or waypower) components of hope make it particularly relevant to the emphasis in today's workplace on self-motivation, autonomy, and contingency actions. Hope has been recently shown to relate conceptually and empirically to performance in various domains, including the workplace (Adams, et al., 2003; Curry, Snyder, Cook, Ruby, & Rehm, 1997; Jensen & Luthans, 2002; Luthans, Avolio, et al., 2006; Luthans, Avolio, Walumbwa, et al., 2005; Luthans & Jensen, 2002; Luthans, Van Wyk, & Walumbwa, 2004; Luthans & Youssef, 2004; Peterson & Luthans, 2003; Snyder, 1995; Youssef & Luthans, 2005b, 2006).

Although hope can be conceived as trait-like, importantly, hope is also recognized as a developmental state (Snyder, et al., 1996). Practical approaches for developing hope include setting challenging "stretch" goals, contingency planning, and regoaling when necessary to avoid false hope. Hope is fully discussed in chapter 3.

A third positive psychological capacity that meets our POB definitional criteria is optimism. According to Seligman (1998), optimism is an attributional style that explains positive events in terms of personal, permanent and pervasive causes, and negative events as external, temporary and situation-specific. Like hope, although sometimes portrayed as dispositional, an optimistic explanatory style can be learned and developed, and its potential contributions to work performance have been empirically demonstrated (Luthans, Avolio, et al, 2006; Luthans, et al., 2005; Seligman, 1998). Particularly relevant to the workplace is realistic (Schneider, 2001), flexible (Peterson, 2000) optimism, which equips organizational leaders and employees with the ability to discern when to use optimistic versus pessimistic explanatory styles, as well as the capacity to adapt those styles realistically to the situations at hand. Chapter 4 presents a detailed discussion of such realistic, flexible optimism.

Fourth is the positive psychological capacity of *resiliency*, which we define as "the developable capacity to rebound or bounce back from adversity, conflict, and failure or even positive events, progress, and increased responsibility" (Luthans, 2002a, p. 702). Factors drawn from clinical and positive psychology that have been found to contribute or hinder resiliency include one's inventory of physiological, cognitive, affective and social assets; risks encountered; adaptational processes utilized to balance the use of assets in facing risks; and underlying value systems (Coutu, 2002; Masten, 2001; Masten & Reed, 2002). We have also drawn from this literature and from developmental psychology to make the case for resiliency as relevant and necessary in today's workplace, and we have shown empirically that it relates to performance outcomes (Luthans, Avolio, et al., 2006; Luthans, et al., 2005; Youssef & Luthans, 2005b). Resiliency is given detailed attention in chapter 5.

It is important to note that both positive psychology and POS have triggered a vast body of emerging research on a number of positive constructs beside the four we have determined best meet our POB inclusion criteria. Some of these other capacities meet our definitional criteria to varying degrees and thus have a high potential for inclusion into our POB stream of theory-building and research in the near future. We devote chapters 6 and 7 to the careful assessment of such potential POB criteria-meeting psychological capacities. Specifically, we recognize the cognitive capacities of creativity and wisdom, as well as the affective capacities of subjective well-being, flow, and humor, which are discussed and evaluated in chapter 6. The social capacities of gratitude, forgiveness, and emotional intelligence, as well as the higher order capacities of spirituality, authenticity, and courage, are also possible candidates for the future and are discussed in chapter 7.

PSYCHOLOGICAL CAPITAL (PSYCAP)

With POB and its specific criteria serving as the foundation, we have not only studied and assessed additional individual positive psychological capacities for potential inclusion, but most attention has been devoted to the underlying conceptual framework researching the propositions, developing the measure, and translating for actual practice. The result of this effort is what we call psychological capital (PsyCap; Luthans, Luthans, & Luthans, 2004; Luthans & Youssef, 2004). We formally defined PsyCap at the beginning of the chapter as being made up of the POB criteria meeting capacities of self-efficacy, optimism, hope, and resiliency. However, importantly, we propose, and our research to date supports, that PsyCap goes beyond just the categories of these capacities.

Specifically, PsyCap is a higher order core construct that integrates the various POB criteria–meeting capacities, not only additively but also perhaps, synergistically. Thus, the resulting impact of investing in, developing, and managing overall PsyCap on performance and attitudinal outcomes is expected to be larger than the individual, positive psychological capacities that comprise it. In other words, the whole (PsyCap) may be greater than the sum of its parts (self-efficacy, optimism, hope, and resiliency).

An example of how the factors of PsyCap interact would be that hopeful persons who possess the agency and pathways to achieve their goals will be more motivated to and capable of overcoming adversities and, thus, be more resilient. Confident persons will be able to transfer and apply their hope, optimism, and resiliency to the specific tasks within specific domains of their lives. A resilient person will be adept in utilizing the adaptational mechanisms necessary for realistic and flexible optimism. PsyCap self-efficacy, hope, and resiliency can in turn contribute to an optimistic explanatory style through internalized perceptions of being in control. These are just representative of the many positive outcomes that may result from the interaction among the PsyCap factors.

In more analytical terms, it is through the discriminant validity across the individual PsyCap capacities (e.g., see Bryant & Cvengros, 2004; Carifio & Rhodes, 2002; Luthans, Avolio, et al., 2006; Magaletta & Oliver, 1999) that each capacity adds unique variance and becomes additive to PsyCap overall. Furthermore, both conceptual developments (e.g., see Avolio & Luthans, 2006; Bandura & Locke, 2003; Gillham, 2000; Luthans & Youssef, 2004; Luthans, Youssef, et al., 2006; Snyder, 2000) and our emerging basic research on PsyCap (Luthans, et al., 2005; Luthans, Avey, et al., 2006; Luthans, Avolio, et al., 2006; Youssef, 2004) provide substantial evidence for the convergent validity of our four POB criteria-meeting capacities of self-efficacy, hope, optimism, and resiliency. The theory and research so far supports an underlying PsyCap core construct to which the individual capacities contribute.

A TYPE OF RESOURCE THEORY

To provide further support for our proposed PsyCap as a core construct, we can also draw from psychological resource theories (e.g., see Hobfoll, 2002, for a review). These widely recognized theories emphasize the necessity of treating individual resources (in this case, the POB capacities) as manifestations of an underlying core construct or an integrated resource set (in this case PsyCap) rather than in isolation. For example, key resource theories (e.g., Thoits, 1994) have identified individual-level resources such as self-efficacy, optimism, resiliency, and degree of goal pursuit (an integral component of hope) as essential foundational resources for managing and adapting other resources to achieve favorable outcomes. Such key resources have been empirically supported as interactive and synergistic (Cozzarelli, 1993; Rini, Dunkel-Schetter, Wadhwa, & Sandman, 1999).

Similarly, multiple-component resource theories support resource synergies, in which the whole is greater than the sum of the constituent parts. Examples of such theories include the theory of sense of coherence (Antonovsky, 1979), which is conceptually similar to PsyCap optimism, as well as the well-known construct of hardiness (Kobasa, 1979), which in many ways parallels PsyCap resiliency (see Hobfoll, 2002). In other words, resource theory could be used to support our theory-building and initial research that synergies may exist both within the components of individual PsyCap capacities, as well as between the capacities that constitute PsyCap as a core construct.

BEYOND HUMAN AND SOCIAL CAPITAL

Besides framing PsyCap as a type of resource theory, another way to provide understanding of PsyCap as a core construct is that in our theory-building, we propose that it goes beyond established human and social capital. PsyCap recognizes, builds upon, and goes beyond the existing established theory and research on *human capital,* that is, "what you know," and *social capital,* that is, "who you know" (e.g., see Adler & Kwon, 2002; Coleman, 1988; Hitt & Ireland, 2002; Wright & Snell, 1999). Specifically, PsyCap is concerned with "who you are" and, in the developmental sense, "who you are becoming" (Avolio & Luthans, 2006; Luthans, Luthans, et al., 2004; Luthans & Youssef, 2004). PsyCap can include knowledge, skills, technical abilities, and experience because this is also "who you are." The same is true of social capital. PsyCap can include group-level metaconstructs, such as social support and the network of relationships, that are part of "who you are," particularly in times of psychological stress (Sarason, Sarason, Shearin, & Pierce, 1987). However, how *PsyCap goes beyond* is found in the psychological capacities, which have generally been ignored in human and social capital, and especially the developmental piece of PsyCap of "what you are becoming." That is, PsyCap recognizes moving (developing) from the actual self (human, social, and psychological capital) to the possible self (see Avolio & Luthans, 2006).

Instead of just introducing yet another set of "competencies" or "best practices" for organizational behavior researchers and human resources practitioners to use, either individually or in combination, we propose that PsyCap offers a more comprehensive, higher order conceptual framework for understanding and capitalizing on human assets in today's organizations (Avolio & Luthans, 2006; Luthans, Luthans, et al., 2004; Luthans & Youssef, 2004; Luthans, Youssef, et al., 2006). We believe that synergistically integrating human, social, and psychological capital is central to actualizing human potential (i.e., attaining the possible self) in today's workplace. For example, many of the assets necessary for building and maintaining resiliency in the face of hardships are in fact integral elements of human capital, such as knowledge, skills, abilities, and experiences. Assets that are antecedents to resiliency also include vital elements of social capital, such as relationships and social networks. Similarly, integral to self-efficacy development is the presence of effective role models and source of socially persuading positive feedback, that is, social capital. However, like the individual capacities, when in interaction, we propose that PsyCap has a greater impact than human or social capital by themselves and that the whole (PsyCap) is greater than the sum of its parts (human and social capital).

PSYCAP MEASUREMENT AND DEVELOPMENT

Still another contribution to PsyCap as a core construct worth highlighting is its unique measurement. In our earlier work on POB, we utilized existing standardized measures of self-efficacy (Parker, 1998), hope (Snyder, et al., 1996), optimism (Scheier & Carver, 1985), and resiliency (Wagnild

& Young, 1993) with very minor adaptations. However, the emergence of PsyCap as a higher order, core construct triggered our efforts to develop and validate a unique, work-related instrument for PsyCap measurement (Luthans, Avolio, et al., 2006; Luthans, Youssef, et al., 2006). In chapter 8, we discuss this measure development and, as said before, present our 24-item PsyCap Questionnaire (PCQ) in the appendix.

Finally, using our developing PsyCap theoretical framework as presented in this book, we have been able to introduce successful microinterventions for PsyCap development in the workplace (Luthans, Avey, et al., 2006). Utilizing our PsyCap Questionnaire, we have been able to demonstrate that PsyCap development can yield a very high (over 200%) return on investment (Luthans, Avey, et al., 2006). We present this microintervention and offer practical tools for calculating the potential return on PsyCap investment, or what we prefer to call return on development (ROD), under various conditions and applications in chapter 8.

FUTURE IMPLICATIONS AND DIRECTIONS FOR PSYCAP RESEARCH AND PRACTICE

While many workplace constructs are generalizable across organizational levels, we believe that PsyCap presents remarkable opportunities that are particularly relevant for authentic leadership development (ALD; Avolio & Luthans, 2006; Luthans & Avolio, 2003). Specifically, when PsyCap development efforts are introduced within a positive organizational context in which planned and unplanned trigger events are integrated, developing leaders can enhance their self-awareness, self-regulation, and self-development. The result is not only leaders with higher PsyCap but also more authentic leaders. And if the leaders are both higher in PsyCap and also more authentic, we expect the same will be true in terms of the development of followers (Avolio, Gardner, Walumbwa, Luthans, & May, 2004; Gardner, Avolio, Luthans, May, & Walumbwa, 2005)

In addition to self-development, one of the primary characteristics of authentic leaders is that they are capable of and motivated to develop their followers. The integrity, trust, and transparency of the authentic leader can encourage reciprocity from followers and an organizational culture in which openness, sharing, and ongoing PsyCap development become the norm. Indeed, the possibility that positivity may exhibit both downward and upward spirals and contagion effects has been consistently utilized as a backdrop in recent psychological research (Cameron, Dutton & Quinn, 2003; Fredrickson, 2001). We have begun to integrate such notions conceptually in our recent work (Luthans, Norman, & Hughes, 2006; Youssef & Luthans, 2005b). PsyCap theory-building and empirical testing that take into consideration the possibility of such multiple levels of analysis are needed for the future.

Standing in contrast to the upward spirals and positive contagion effects, resource theories, such as the conservation of resources (COR) theory (Hobfoll, 1989) and the selective optimization with compensation (SOC) theory (Baltes, 1997), have primarily focused on the dynamics through which people deal with losses and deterioration of resources. A valid question for PsyCap becomes whether previously built PsyCap can deteriorate over time. Since PsyCap capacities are states rather than enduring traits, we would expect them to fluctuate over time, increasing or decreasing depending on the existing conditions at the time of their assessment. For example, since self-efficacy is a domain-specific capacity, an employee who has been recently promoted to a more demanding job with unfamiliar and/or uncertain responsibilities will likely exhibit at least a temporary drop in self-efficacy. Thus, ongoing self-efficacy development efforts will be necessary to maintain a high level of self-efficacy in today's constantly changing work environment. Similarly, a manager who may have been very effective when operating locally may appear to lose personal resiliency when sent as an expatriate on an international assignment. This loss of resilience may result because significant sources of social support have been withdrawn. On the other hand, through ongoing mentoring and support by the home office, as well as the manager's involvement establishing new relationships and connections in the new locale, resiliency can be rebuilt, perhaps at an accelerated rate.

Despite these potential problems and limitations, we contend that, unlike traditional human and social capital or even the individual psychological capacities, our proposed PsyCap offers a dynamic resource potential that can grow and be sustainable over time. For example, the expatriate whose resiliency may become threatened by losses of social assets can capitalize on PsyCap hope pathways to find new ways to overcome and bounce back from obstacles faced. This ex-pat may draw upon and enhance personal relationships with an accompanying spouse or partner, children, and new coworkers, which may result in long-term resource gains rather than losses. The manager may also establish a new social network through friendships and activities within the community, which will likely reflect on the reputation of the organization, as well as on the ex-pat's well being and followers' responsiveness and cooperation.

Similarly, the ex-pat in this example may capitalize on previously built self-efficacy if successful in other international assignments. The manager can also capitalize on optimism by explaining initial negative events using causes that are external (e.g., "It is natural for anyone in my culture-shock situation to feel that way at the beginning"), temporary (e.g., "This is only for a while, but everything will eventually be fine"), and situation specific (e.g., "I must be feeling this way because my first meeting with the staff did not go very well"). Such approaches can help the expatriate maintain, or even enhance, personal resiliency, bouncing back to an even higher level of performance and well-being.

This example points to one of the reasons that we prefer to refer to the factors of PsyCap as positive psychological capacities rather than resources, as in psychological resource theory. Under the war-for-talent paradigm used in the introductory discussion, the emphasis is on competing for scarce, nonrenewable resources that are subject to obsolescence, depletion, or loss to competition. On the other hand, PsyCap capacities are renewable, complementary, and may even be synergistic. Individuals with high PsyCap can flexibly and adaptively "act with different capacities" to meet the dynamic demands of their jobs, while their PsyCap at the same time helps them experience higher levels of competence and well-being. This is in contrast to the stress and strain traditionally associated with resource acquisition processes (e.g., hours of technical training to acquire human capital and/or impression management and political maneuvering to build social capital).

This new PsyCap position does not negate the need for some resource sacrifices throughout the PsyCap development process (e.g., time, energy, and even financial resources). However, as we show in chapter 8, these sacrifices should be viewed as investments with very high potential returns (a balance sheet perspective) rather than as losses (a short-term, income statement mentality). High-return investments are proactively pursued not only because they are desirable from a financial perspective but also because they are motivating and exciting. By the same token, losses tend to be feared and avoided or reactively and passively handled, as necessary. PsyCap is certainly better aligned with the positive reactions and well-being at all levels (leaders, associates, and the overall organization) rather than the negativity and downward spiral associated with stagnation and losses.

Also relevant to future directions are cross-cultural applications of PsyCap. Since PsyCap is developmental, it will be influenced by cultural contexts. Cultural differentiation is in line with Hobfoll's (2002, p. 312) notion of "resource caravans" that influence the resource sets that people acquire over their life spans. For example, since self-efficacy and hope are more self-based, while optimism and resiliency are also more dependent on others and the external environment, there may be resulting differences between individualistic and collectivistic cultures to the extent to which the development of these PsyCap capacities is encouraged. Our work to date supports the relevance of PsyCap for diverse cultural backgrounds in general (Youssef & Luthans, 2003), as well as in specific countries such as China (Luthans, et al., 2005), South Africa (Luthans, Van Wyk, et al., 2004), and the Middle East (Youssef & Luthans, 2006). At this stage of development, we believe that PsyCap represents a high-potential construct for both domestic and cross-cultural research and applications.

To conclude this opening chapter, we strongly encourage maintaining a big-picture PsyCap perspective as each of the succeeding chapters take a deeper dive into the four main (self-efficacy, hope, optimism, and resiliency) POB criteria meeting capacities and also explore some of the other potential PsyCap capacities. It should be remembered that PsyCap may be greater than the sum of its parts. We hope you will not be satisfied with learning about one or two capacities that may be of interest to you for academic or practical purposes. Our intent is to encourage and to keep exploring new psychological capacities, continually build theory, conduct on-going research, and apply to practice. By the end of the book, there should be the realization that much has been learned not only about PsyCap as a whole and the dramatic impact it can have on who you are but also, more importantly, who you (and your people) can become. This book can help in your self-awareness and development, but it can also serve as a new paradigm for developing and managing human resources for performance improvement and competitive advantage.

REFERENCES

Adams, V. H., Snyder, C. R., Rand, K. L., King, E. A., Sigmon, D. R., & Pulvers, K. M. (2003). Hope in the workplace. In R. Giacolone & C. Jurkiewicz (Eds.), *Handbook of workplace spirituality and organizational performance* (pp. 367–377). New York: Sharpe.
Adler, P. S., & Kwon, S. (2002). Social capital: Prospects for a new concept. *Academy of Management Review, 27,* 17–40.

Antonovsky, A. (1979). *Health, stress, and coping.* San Francisco: Jossey-Bass.

Aspinwall, L., & Staudinger, U. (Eds.). (2003). *A psychology of human strengths: Fundamental questions and future directions for a positive psychology.* Washington, DC: American Psychological Association.

Avolio, B. J. (2005). The chief integrative leader: Moving to the next economy's HR leader. In M. Losey, S. Meisenger, & D. Ulrich (Eds.), *The future of human resource management: 63 thought leaders explore the critical HR issues of today and tomorrow* (pp. 95–102). Washington, DC: Society of Human Resource Management.

Avolio, B. J., Gardner, W. L., Walumbwa, F. O., Luthans, F., & May, D. R. (2004). Unlocking the mask: A look at the process by which authentic leaders impact follower attitudes and behaviors. *Leadership Quarterly, 15,* 801–823.

Avolio, B.J., & Luthans, F. (2006). *The high impact leader: Moments matter in accelerating authentic leadership development.* New York: McGraw-Hill.

Axelrod, E., Handfield-Jones, H., & Welsh, T. (2001). War for talent, part two. *The McKinsey Quarterly, 2,* 9–12.

Baltes, P. (1997). On the incomplete architecture of human ontogeny: Selection, optimization, and compensation as foundation of development theory. *American Psychologist, 52,* 366–380.

Bandura, A. (1997). *Self-efficacy: The exercise of control.* New York: Freeman.

Bandura, A., & Locke, E. A. (2003). Negative self-efficacy and goal effects revisited. *Journal of Applied Psychology, 88,* 87–99.

Barnett, R., & Hall, D. (2001). How to use reduced hours to win the war for talent. *Organizational Dynamics, 29*(3), 192–210.

Barrick, M. R., & Mount, M. K. (1991). The Big Five personality dimensions and job performance: A meta-analysis. *Personnel Psychology, 44,* 1–26.

Bryant, F. B., & Cvengros, J. A. (2004). Distinguishing hope and optimism. *Journal of Social and Clinical Psychology, 23,* 273–302.

Buckingham, M., & Clifton, D. (2001). *Now, discover your strengths.* New York: Free Press.

Buckingham, M., & Coffman, C. (1999). *First, break all the rules: What the world's greatest managers do differently.* New York: Simon & Schuster.

Cameron, K., Dutton, J., & Quinn, R. (Eds.). (2003). *Positive organizational scholarship.* San Francisco: Berrett-Koehler.

Cameron, K. S., Bright, D., & Caza, A. (2004). Exploring the relationships between organizational virtuousness and performance. *American Behavioral Scientist, 47,* 766–790.

Cameron, K. S., & Caza, A. (2004). Contributions to the discipline of positive organizational scholarship. *American Behavioral Scientist, 47,* 731–739.

Carifio, J., & Rhodes, L. (2002). Construct validities and the empirical relationships between optimism, hope, self-efficacy, and locus of control. *Work, 19,* 125–136.

Carr, A. (2004). *Positive psychology.* New York: Brunner-Routledge.

Cascio, W. F. (1991). *Costing human resources: The financial impact of behavior in organizations* (3rd ed.). Boston: PWS-Kent.

Cascio, W. F., & Ramos, R. A. (1986). Development and application of a new method for assessing job performance and behavioral/economic terms. *Journal of Applied Psychology, 71*, 20–28.

Coleman, J. S. (1988). Social capital in the creation of human capital. *American Journal of Sociology, 94*, S95–120.

Compton, W. C. (2005). *Introduction to positive psychology.* Belmont, CA: Thompson Wadsworth.

Cooper, C. L., & Nelson, D. L. (Eds.). (2006). *Positive organizational behavior: Accentuating the positive at work.* Thousand Oaks, CA: Sage.

Coutu, D. L. (2002). How resilience works. *Harvard Business Review, 80*(3), 46–55.

Cozzarelli, C. (1993). Personality and self-efficacy as predictors of coping with abortion. *Journal of Personality and Social Psychology, 65*, 1224–1237.

Curry, L. A., Snyder, C. R., Cook, D. I., Ruby, B. C., & Rehm, M. (1997). The role of hope in student-athlete academic and sport achievement. *Journal of Personality and Social Psychology, 73*, 1257–1267.

Drucker, P. (1994). The theory of business. *Harvard Business Review, 72*(5), 95–104.

Fishman, C. (1998, August). The war for talent. *Fast Company, 16*, 104.

Fredrickson, B. L. (2001). The role of positive emotions in positive psychology: The broaden-and-build theory of positive emotions. *American Psychologist, 56*, 218–226.

Gardner, W. L., Avolio, B. J., Luthans, F., May, D. R., & Walumbwa, F. O. (2005). "Can you see the real me?" A self-based model of authentic leader and follower development. *Leadership Quarterly, 16*, 343–372.

Gillham, J. (Ed.). (2000). *The science of optimism and hope.* Radnor, PA: Templeton Foundation.

Goodwin, B. (2005, February 1). IT departments to face 'war of talent' as firms vie for scarce skills. *Computer Weekly, 5.*

Herzberg, F., Mauesner, B., & Snyderman, B. (1959). *The motivation to work* (2nd ed.). New York: Wiley.

Hitt, M. A., & Ireland, D. (2002). The essence of strategic management: Managing human and social capital. *Journal of Leadership and Organizational Studies, 9*(1), 3–14.

Hobfoll, S. (1989). Conservation of resources: A new attempt at conceptualizing stress. *American Psychologist, 44*, 513–524.

Hobfoll, S. (2002). Social and psychological resources and adaptation. *Review of General Psychology, 6*, 307–324.

Hunter, J. E., & Schmidt, F. L. (1983). Quantifying the effects of psychological interventions on employee job performance and work-force productivity. *American Psychologist, 38*, 473–478.

Huselid, M. A. (1995). The impact of human resource management practices on turnover, productivity, and corporate financial performance. *Academy of Management Journal, 38*, 635–672.

Jensen, S. M., & Luthans, F. (2002). The impact of hope in the entrepreneurial process:

Exploratory research findings. In *Decision Sciences Institute Conference Proceedings,* San Diego, CA.

Johnson, M. (2004, June 29). Life-work balance should be the real issue in war for talent. *Personnel Today,* 3.

Judge, T. A., & Bono, J. E. (2001). Relationship of core self-evaluations traits—self-esteem, generalized self-efficacy, locus of control, and emotional stability—with job satisfaction and job performance: A meta-analysis. *Journal of Applied Psychology, 86,* 80–92.

Keyes, C., & Haidt, J. (Eds.). (2003). *Flourishing: Positive psychology and the life well-lived.* Washington, DC: American Psychological Association.

Kobasa, S. (1979). Stressful life events, personality and health: An inquiry into hardiness. *Journal of Personality and Social Psychology, 37,* 1–11.

Kravetz, D. (2004). *Measuring human capital: Converting workplace behavior into dollars.* Mesa, AZ: KAP.

Lance, R. (2005, March 8). Benefits packages play key role in war for talent. *Personnel Today,* 17.

Linley, P., & Joseph, S. (Eds.). (2004). *Positive psychology in practice.* Hoboken, NJ: John Wiley & Sons.

Locke, E. (Ed.). (2000). *The Blackwell handbook of principles of organizational behavior.* Oxford, UK: Blackwell.

Lopez, S., & Snyder, C. R. (Eds.). (2003). *Positive psychological assessment: A handbook of models and measures.* Washington, DC: American Psychological Association.

Luthans, F. (2002a). The need for and meaning of positive organizational behavior. *Journal of Organizational Behavior, 23,* 695–706.

Luthans, F. (2002b). Positive organizational behavior: Developing and managing psychological strengths. *Academy of Management Executive, 16*(1), 57–72.

Luthans, F. (2003). Positive organizational behavior (POB): Implications for leadership and HR development and motivation. In R. M. Steers, L. W. Porter, & G. A. Begley (Eds.), *Motivation and leadership at work* (pp.187–195). New York: McGraw-Hill/Irwin.

Luthans, F. (2005). *Organizational behavior.* New York: McGraw-Hill/Irwin.

Luthans, F., Avey, J. B., Avolio, B. J., Norman, S. M., & Combs, G. J. (2006). Psychological capital development: Toward a micro-intervention. *Journal of Organizational Behavior, 27,* 387–393.

Luthans, F., & Avolio, B. (2003). Authentic leadership: A positive development approach. In K. S. Cameron, J. E. Dutton, & R. E. Quinn (Eds.), *Positive organizational scholarship* (pp. 241–258). San Francisco: Berrett-Koehler.

Luthans, F., Avolio, B., Avey, J., & Norman, S. (2006). Psychological capital: Measurement and relationship with performance and satisfaction (Working Paper No. 2006–1). Gallup Leadership Institute, University of Nebraska–Lincoln.

Luthans, F., Avolio, B. J., Walumbwa, F. O., & Li, W. (2005). The psychological capital of Chinese workers: Exploring the relationship with performance. *Management and Organization Review, 1,* 247–269.

Luthans, F., & Jensen, S. M. (2002). Hope: A new positive strength for human resource development. *Human Resource Development Review, 1,* 304–322.

Luthans, F., Luthans, K., & Luthans, B. (2004). Positive psychological capital: Going beyond human and social capital. *Business Horizons, 47*(1), 45–50.

Luthans, F., Norman, S. M., & Hughes, L. (2006). Authentic leadership. In R. Burke & C. Cooper (Eds.), *Inspiring leaders* (pp.84–104). London: Routledge, Taylor & Francis.

Luthans, F., Van Wyk, R., & Walumbwa, F. O. (2004). Recognition and development of hope for South African organizational leaders. *Leadership and Organization Development Journal, 25,* 512–527.

Luthans, F., Vogelgesang, G. R., & Lester, P. B. (2006). Developing the psychological capital of resiliency. *Human Resource Development Review, 5,* 25–44.

Luthans, F., & Youssef, C. M. (2004). Human, social, and now positive psychological capital management: Investing in people for competitive advantage. *Organizational Dynamics, 33*(2), 143–160.

Luthans, F., Youssef, C. M., & Avolio, B. J. (2006). Psychological capital: Investing and developing positive organizational behavior. In C. L. Cooper & D. Nelson (Eds.), *Positive organizational behavior: Accentuating the positive at work.* Thousand Oaks, CA: Sage.

Magaletta, P. R., & Oliver, J. M. (1999). The hope construct, will and ways: Their relations with self-efficacy, optimism and well-being. *Journal of Clinical Psychology, 55,* 539–551.

Masten, A. S. (2001). Ordinary magic: Resilience processes in development. *American Psychologist, 56,* 227–239.

Masten, A. S., & Reed, M. G. J. (2002). Resilience in development. In C. R. Snyder & S. J. Lopez (Eds.), *Handbook of positive psychology* (pp. 74–88). Oxford, UK: Oxford University Press.

Michaels III, E., Handfield-Jones, H., & Axelrod, E. (2001). *The war for talent.* Boston: Harvard Business School Press.

Ng, E., & Burke, R. (2005). Person-organization fit and the war for talent: Does diversity management make a difference? *International Journal of Human Resource Management, 16,* 1195–1210.

Olson, J. (2003). A powerful weapon in the war for talent. *National Underwriter/Life & Health Financial Services, 107*(25), 5–6.

Parker, S. (1998). Enhancing role-breadth self efficacy: The roles of job enrichment and other organizational interventions. *Journal of Applied Psychology, 83,* 835–852.

Parker, S. K., Wall, T. D., & Jackson, P. R. (1997). "That's not my job": Developing flexible employee work orientations. *Academy of Management Journal, 40,* 899–929.

Peterson, C. (2000). The future of optimism. *American Psychologist, 55,* 44–55.

Peterson, C., & Chang, E. (2002). Optimism and flourishing. In C. Keyes & J. Haidt (Eds.), *Flourishing: Positive psychology and the life well-lived* (pp. 55–79). Washington, DC: American Psychological Association.

Peterson, C., & Seligman, M. (2004). *Character strengths and virtues: A handbook and classification.* New York: Oxford University Press.

Peterson, S. J., & Luthans, F. (2003). The positive impact and development of hopeful leaders. *Leadership and Organization Development Journal, 24*(1), 26–31.

Pfeffer, J. (1998). *The human equation.* Boston: Harvard Business School Press.

Pfeffer, J. (2001). Fighting the war for talent is hazardous to your organization's health. *Organizational Dynamics, 29*(4), 248–259.

Pfeffer, J., & Sutton, R. I. (2006). Evidenced-based management. *Harvard Business Review, 84*(1), 63–74.

Pierce, J. L., Kostova, T., & Dirks, K. T. (2003). The state of psychological ownership: Integrating and extending a century of research. *Review of General Psychology, 7,* 84–107.

Rini, C. K., Dunkel-Schetter, C., Wadhwa, P. D., & Sandman, C. A. (1999). Psychological adaptation and birth outcomes: The role of personal resources, stress, and sociocultural context in pregnancy. *Health Psychology, 18,* 333–345.

Sarason, I., Sarason, B., Shearin, E., & Pierce, G. (1987). A brief measure of social support: Practical and theoretical implications. *Journal of Social and Personal Relationships, 4,* 497–510.

Scheier, M. F., & Carver, C. S. (1985). Optimism, coping, and health: Assessment and implications of generalized outcome expectancies. *Health Psychology, 4,* 219–247.

Schmidt, F., & Hunter, J. (2000). Select on intelligence. In E. Locke (Ed.), *The Blackwell handbook of principles of organizational behavior* (pp. 3–14). Oxford, UK: Blackwell.

Schneider, S. L. (2001). In search of realistic optimism. *American Psychologist, 56,* 250–263.

Seligman, M. E. P. (1998). *Learned optimism.* New York: Pocket Books.

Seligman, M. E. P., & Csikszentmihalyi, M. (2000). Positive psychology. *American Psychologist, 55,* 5–14.

Snyder, C. R. (1995). Managing for high hope. *R&D Innovator, 4*(6), 6–7.

Snyder, C. R. (2000). *Handbook of hope.* San Diego: Academic Press.

Snyder, C. R., Irving, L., & Anderson, J. (1991). Hope and health: Measuring the will and the ways. In C. R. Snyder & D. R. Forsyth (Eds.), *Handbook of social and clinical psychology* (pp. 285–305). Elmsford, NY: Pergamon.

Snyder, C. R., & Lopez, S. (Eds.). (2002). *Handbook of positive psychology.* Oxford, UK: Oxford University Press.

Snyder, C. R., Sympson, S. C., Ybasco, F. C., Borders, T. F., Babyak, M. A., & Higgins, R. L. (1996). Development and validation of the state hope scale. *Journal of Personality and Social Psychology, 70,* 321–335.

Stajkovic, A. D., & Luthans, F. (1998a). Self-efficacy and work-related performance: A meta-analysis. *Psychological Bulletin, 124,* 240–261.

Stajkovic, A. D., & Luthans, F. (1998b). Social cognitive theory and self-efficacy: Going beyond traditional motivational and behavioral approaches. *Organizational Dynamics, 26,* 62–74.

Sutcliffe, K. M., & Vogus, T. (2003). Organizing for resilience. In K. S. Cameron, J. E. Dutton, & R. E. Quinn (Eds.), *Positive organizational scholarship* (pp. 94–110). San Francisco: Berrett-Koehler.

Thoits, P. (1994). Stressors and problem solving: The individual as a psychological activist. *Journal of Health and Social Behavior, 35,* 143–160.

Trank, C., Rynes, S., & Bretz, R. (2002). Attracting applicants in the war for talent: Differences in work preferences among high achievers. *Journal of Business & Psychology, 16,* 331–345.

Vandewalle, D., Van Dyne, L., Kostova, T. (1995). Exploring psychological ownership: An empirical examination of its consequences. *Group and Organization Management, 20,* 210–226.

Van Dyne, L., & Pierce, J. L. (2004). Psychological ownership and feelings of possession: Three field studies predicting employee attitudes and organizational citizenship behavior. *Journal of Organizational Behavior, 25,* 439–459.

Wagner, S. H., Parker, C. P., Christiansen, N. D. (2003). Employees that think and act like owners: Effects of ownership beliefs and behaviors on organizational effectiveness. *Personnel Psychology, 56,* 847–871.

Wagnild, G. M., & Young, H. M. (1993). *Journal of Nursing Management, 1*(2), 165–178.

Waterman, R. H., Waterman, J. A., & Collard, B. A. (1994). Toward a career-resilient workforce. *Harvard Business Review, 72*(4), 87–95.

Wilkinson, J. (2005). Distribution: A war for talent. *Money Management, 19*(26), 20–23.

Wright, R. M., & Snell, S. A. (1999). Social capital and strategic HRM: It's who you know. *Human Resource Planning, 22,* 62–65.

Wright, T. A. (2003). Positive organizational behavior: An idea whose time has truly come. *Journal of Organizational Behavior, 24,* 437–442.

Youssef, C. M. (2004). *Resiliency development of organizations, leaders, and employees: Multi-level theory building and individual-level, path-analytical empirical testing.* Unpublished doctoral dissertation, University of Nebraska–Lincoln.

Youssef, C. M., & Luthans, F. (2003). Immigrant psychological capital: Contribution to the war for talent and competitive advantage. *Singapore Nanyang Business Review, 2*(2), 1–14.

Youssef, C. M., & Luthans, F. (2005a). A positive organizational behavior approach to ethical performance. In R. Giacalone, C. Jurkiewicz, & C. Dunn (Eds.), *Positive psychology in business ethics and corporate social responsibility* (pp. 1–22). Greenwich, CT: Information Age.

Youssef, C. M., & Luthans, F. (2005b). Resiliency development of organizations, leaders, and employees: Multi-level theory building for sustained performance. In W. Gardner, B. Avolio, & F. Walumbwa (Eds.), *Monographs in leadership and management: Volume 3. Authentic leadership theory and practice: Origins, effects and development* (pp. 303–343). Oxford, UK: Elsevier.

Youssef, C. M., & Luthans, F. (2006). Time for positivity in the Middle East: Developing hopeful Egyptian organizational leaders. In W. Mobley & E Weldon (Eds.), *Advances in global leadership* (Vol. 4). Oxford, UK: Elsevier/JAI.

CHAPTER 2

PsyCap Efficacy

Confidence to Succeed

Do you believe in yourself? Do you know that you have what it takes to be successful? Do you believe it is all within you? These questions could also be lead-ins for our other chapters on hope and optimism, but they are especially relevant to this chapter on PsyCap efficacy.

Underlying each of our capacities to engage in activities is motivation that we have based on the probability that we believe we will be successful in our endeavors. Albert Bandura (1997) referred to the probability that people estimate that they can take on a particular task as an estimate of their self-efficacy. For example, one can ask a leader how able she is to inspire others to work or to get others to think about problems and issues in new ways. The probability that the individual associates with being able to do just that is the level of self-efficacy. Although originally described as applying to a very specific domain of activity, there is increasing recognition that individuals can also have a "generalized" level of self-efficacy across a common domain of challenges and tasks, such as the workplace (Parker, 1998).

There is increasing evidence that the answers to the questions posed above are not just found in your knowledge, skills, or abilities, not just in your IQ (or EQ, emotional intelligence) or your personality traits, although these all can help, too. We have argued in the introductory chapter that your PsyCap makes a large input into who you are, what you believe you can do, what you do, and who you can become. In particular, perhaps the strength and psychological capacity that best meets the PsyCap criteria outlined in the last chapter of being theory- and research-based, state-like and open to development, and related to performance impact is PsyCap self-efficacy. So a good answer to the opening questions is your level of self-efficacy. It motivates you to choose and welcome challenges and to use your strengths and your skills to meet those challenges. It encourages and energizes you to pursue your goals and invest the time and hard work that may be necessary to accomplish them. It helps you to persevere when you are faced with obstacles that may otherwise lead you to give up, and thus, it also relates to your hope, optimism, and resiliency. It is something you have learned about yourself and developed over time. It is an aspect of your self and your awareness about who you are that can be positively changed or developed with relatively short interventions to spur you on to what you can become.

You may think of yourself as a very confident person, or otherwise. However, in order to accurately assess your level of PsyCap efficacy, you need to analyze what it is that you are confident about. People tend to have comfort zones, areas that they have mastered and thus feel very confident about. Most people also have new domains that they are interested in venturing into someday. However, this only happens if they can overcome their fears and resistance to change, raise their confidence level beyond a certain threshold, and take that important first step.

As a way to get you as the reader more personally engaged in the understanding of each of the four major components of PsyCap, we will start off this and the subsequent three chapters on hope, optimism, and resiliency with an exercise and case example. We feel that this will not only get you more involved in the learning process but will also cause you to reflect on your own PsyCap development and give more meaning to the academically based discussion of the PsyCap constructs in the balance of the chapters.

So, after the following brief reflection exercise, this chapter will present an in-depth discussion of the meaning, process, and development of the important confidence component of PsyCap.

PERSONAL REFLECTIONS EXERCISE ON PSYCAP EFFICACY

As part of this opening reflection exercise for PsyCap efficacy, we ask you to choose a specific domain of your life that you feel very confident about. It can be your job, your education, your family, your friendships, a favorite sport, a leadership role, or a hobby. Then, carefully note the various tasks that you need to perform in this domain in order to achieve success. For example, at work, you may need to utilize your analytical skills to solve problems or make decisions, especially if you are in a leadership role. Most managers and employees also need to use their communication skills in interacting with others and with customers. For example, those in marketing or sales often capitalize on their presentation skills. Your job may also involve some written communication, in which your writing skills can become vital. If you are in an administrative role, organization and coordination skills are important. Other positions may require negotiation skills, creativity, or use of computers. The list can become quite lengthy when you break it down into the specific tasks within the larger domain of inquiry.

Next, prioritize your list: focus on the most critical three or four tasks, that is, those that have the biggest impact on overall success. Then, on a scale of 0–100%, determine how confident you are that you can do the following.

- At least get by on these tasks?
- Meet your own and others' expectations in performing these tasks?
- Excel in accomplishing these tasks?

Next, we ask you to leave your comfort zone and areas of mastery and to start focusing on your dreams and aspirations. Choose any domain of life that you have always wanted to try or to be better at. Using similar analysis, try to break that area down into its critical tasks or components. Then, use the above three questions again as guidelines for assessing your level of confidence regarding each of your identified tasks or components.

What were some of your key discoveries with the exercise above? How far from the mastery set of domains did you choose on which to focus your energies? In other words, did you step outside your "comfort box"? Was the challenge you identified related to your strengths, or was it an area that had no previous linkages to what you felt confident in being able to do?

FIVE KEY DISCOVERIES OF PSYCAP EFFICACY

As you go through the above reflection exercise, you are likely to experience at least five important discoveries about PsyCap efficacy. These illuminating discoveries should help you understand the nature of your own PsyCap efficacy and will hopefully not only guide your journey of further developing and nurturing your own confidence level in various life domains but also serve as a platform and point of departure for better understanding the more academic-based discussion of PsyCap confidence and self-efficacy that follows.

Discovery 1: PsyCap Efficacy Is Domain-Specific

Based on your reflective analysis, you should begin to realize that no matter how confident you are in some areas of your life, you may be very unsure about other areas. In other words, your PsyCap efficacy is specific to the domain being analyzed. Thus, previously built confidence in one domain may not be readily transferable to other domains that you are either familiar with or not familiar with. For example, as a leader, you may be highly confident in being a great one-to-one developer. However, being an inspirational platform speaker may be far outside your comfort zone and have only a small overlap with your ability to read and develop individuals.

Discovery 2: PsyCap Efficacy Is Based on Practice or Mastery

It is likely that the tasks that you are most confident about are the ones that you have repeatedly practiced and mastered. Tasks that you are not confident about are likely to be ones that you tend to avoid or with which you have little experience. Efficacy is based on your estimate of your future probability of success, and therefore, it requires that you have some experience to come up with a positive estimate of self-efficacy. However, as we said earlier, some people can generalize positive experiences from one domain to another in judging their self-efficacy, leading to a more positive sense of generalized self-efficacy.

Discovery 3: There Is Always Room for Improvement in PsyCap Efficacy

Even in the domains that you thought you were very confident about, there are still tasks with which you are not really comfortable. For example, you may be a great technical person but not have great interpersonal skills; or you may have wonderful communication skills but worry that you cannot think analytically as well as you should.

Discovery 4: Your PsyCap Efficacy Is Influenced by Others

What other people tell you about yourself affects your own self-evaluation. If others believe that you can succeed, many times, they can persuade you to think the same way. At the extreme, we refer to this as a self-fulfilling prophecy or Pygmalion effect, where someone believes in you, and you come to believe in yourself. More importantly, when you watch others who may be similar to yourself in many respects accomplish certain tasks and achieve certain goals that are of interest to you, you start developing confidence that you can also do these things. This sort of vicarious learning is a very powerful form of improving your self-efficacy, oftentimes without a lot of forethought on your part. The key is your ability to identify with the model so that you can relate this individual's success to what you can do.

Discovery 5: Your PsyCap Efficacy Is Variable

Your confidence level depends on many factors. Some of those factors are within your control, such as gaining the knowledge, skills, and abilities that can help you accomplish a certain goal. Other factors may exist in the context within which you need to execute the steps necessary for a goal to be accomplished. For example, you may have a wonderful idea for an innovative product, but your organization may lack the financial resources to help you make your dream come true. Even your physical and psychological well-being can contribute to your PsyCap efficacy. For example, when you lead a healthy lifestyle and are content in your relationships, you tend to be more confident than when you have not slept very well two nights in a row or when you have just had a fight with a coworker. In fact, having the proper resources can be viewed as another form of efficacy known as "means efficacy." You can judge whether you have the means to be successful, and this can contribute to or detract from your self-efficacy.

Hopefully, you actually experienced these five discoveries about PsyCap efficacy from your reflective exercise or have at least gained insight into them. Now, as in the next three chapters, we will turn to a more in-depth discussion of the nature of and ways to develop PsyCap confidence, or self-efficacy.

WHAT IS PSYCAP EFFICACY?

Drawing from Bandura's (1986, 1997) extensive theory and research, PsyCap efficacy (or, simply, confidence) can be defined as "one's conviction (or confidence) about his or her abilities to mobilize the motivation, cognitive resources, and courses of action needed to successfully execute a specific task within a given context" (Stajkovic & Luthans, 1998b, p. 66). Although Bandura (1997) sparingly uses the term confidence and most efficacy theorists tend to treat confidence as conceptually subordinate to efficacy, especially in positive psychology the two terms are used more interchangeably (e.g., see Maddux, 2002). Moreover, when used in the more applied domain of sports or business performance, confidence is the commonly used term (e.g., see Kanter, 2004). In PsyCap, we have chosen to use the two terms interchangeably to reflect the rich theoretical and research bases of self-efficacy (e.g., Bandura, 1997) and the more applied orientation associated with confidence (e.g., Kanter, 2004). Whether we use efficacy or confidence in the definition above, it is important to emphasize the link to one's belief. Self-efficacious people are distinguished by five important characteristics.

1. They set high goals for themselves and self-select into difficult tasks.
2. They welcome and thrive on challenge.
3. They are highly self-motivated.
4. They invest the necessary effort to accomplish their goals.
5. When faced with obstacles, they persevere.

These five characteristics equip high-efficacy individuals with the capacity to develop independently and perform effectively, even with little external input for extended periods of time. People with high PsyCap efficacy do not wait for challenging goals to be set for them, which is often referred to as "discrepancy reduction." On the contrary, they create their own discrepancies by continuously challenging themselves with higher and higher self-set goals and by seeking and voluntarily opting for difficult tasks. Self-doubt, skepticism, negative feedback, social criticism, obstacles and setbacks, and even repeated failure, which can be devastating for people with low efficacy, have little impact on highly efficacious individuals (Bandura & Locke, 2003).

THE SUPPORTING COGNITIVE PROCESSES

Deeply based in Bandura's (1986, 1997, 2001) social cognitive theory, PsyCap efficacy is built on his five identified cognitive processes that are vital constituents of the efficacy equation: symbolizing, forethought, observation, self-regulation, and self-reflection. For example, Jerome is confident that he can help the firm he works for in winning an important contract. In *symbolizing*, or creating a mental image/model in his mind, he may study the potential client's decision-making process and develop a mental model of the players involved, their capacities and relative power, and the nature of their interactions. This symbolizing can then serve as a guide for future actions, such as contacting the right people at the right times, and catering to the needs of the various stakeholders involved based on their relative weight in the process.

In the process of *forethought*, Jerome plans his actions based on the level of performance that he is targeting (i.e., the performance impact point) and the consequences that he expects. For example, if Jerome's research supports that the client is looking for the cheapest possible product, he will make sure that his proposal portrays an efficient, cost-effective, no-frills solution. On the other hand, if he knows that the client emphasizes quality and professionalism, then he is likely to offer a range of competitive but upscale quality alternatives, focus on the uniqueness and sophistication of his products, return all of the client's representatives' telephone calls or e-mails very promptly, and be very prepared with information that he expects may be requested.

Jerome is also likely to utilize his *observational* (or *modeling*) *cognitive processing*, in which he would learn from relevant others, such as his manager and his more experienced colleagues. He feels that he can learn from their advice and feedback, but more importantly, he learns what tends to work and what does not by watching their performance and especially by studying the reinforcing consequences that their actions tend to accomplish. The observational component in this process highlights the importance of one's manager displaying certain behaviors and actions that will "teach" followers how to be able to achieve positive results themselves. Oftentimes, managers are not cognizant of the fact that by their actions, they are teaching followers across many domains how to be more efficacious—and, of course, ineffective managers teach their subordinates how to be less efficacious.

Jerome will need to utilize his *self-regulatory processing*, in which he acts as an agent, setting specific goals and standards for his own performance and assessing where he stands in relation to these self-set standards. This will help him better focus on the energies needed in order to develop, improve, and eventually reach his goals. For example, as Jerome prepares to win the contract (the goal), he may realize that he needs to further study his client or adapt his products in order to create a winning proposal.

Oftentimes, when we are trying to change the behavior of individuals, we are in effect trying to stimulate self-awareness to lead to a change in self-regulation. The self-regulation part is where thinking and behavior actually change, and it is probably highly impacted by the receptivity of the context to the change. For example, if the organizational values and culture encourage risk-taking and change, and if there is thus considerable social support for it, then one's self-regulated change in thinking and behavior will be reinforced and will tend to occur again in the future. In this case, we highlight that the context matters in translating self-awareness to changes in self-regulation.

Finally, and perhaps most directly relevant to Jerome's self-efficacy, he uses his *self-reflective processing*. Specifically, he reflects back on his past actions, successes, and failures. Extracting some learning from these previous experiences, Jerome reaches a specific level of self-efficacy for his current challenge: namely, winning the contract for his company. If Jerome employs and channels his cognitive processing of symbolizing, forethought, observation, self-regulation, and self-reflection in the right direction, he is likely not only to win the contract but also to build his future PsyCap self-efficacy and subsequent success. In other words, self-efficacy breeds success, and success breeds self-efficacy, but importantly, success does not equal efficacy.

Somewhat paradoxically, by looking back the individual is actually moving forward in terms of the development of self-efficacy. It is why we oftentimes argue that one needs to take the time to debrief both successes and failures in order to advance in terms of self-awareness, self-regulation, and self-development. By debriefing, we mean taking time to reflect, learn, and then to utilize that self-knowledge to improve.

OTHER FACTORS INFLUENCING PSYCAP EFFICACY

The above example provides two key points about the nature of PsyCap efficacy. First, although success has an important (in fact, the most important) input into one's confidence or efficacy, success does not equal efficacy. Instead, as demonstrated by the example of Jerome, it is not just his previous success but also his cognitive processing (i.e., symbolizing, forethought, observation, self-regulation, and self-reflection) that determines his confidence and efficacy. For example, if the success came too easily to Jerome or was not the result of his efforts and abilities, he would probably not have enhanced subsequent efficacy. The second point is that one's PsyCap efficacy tends to be specific to the domain at hand; in this example, winning a customer contract. Jerome's PsyCap efficacy does not necessarily carry over to other domains of his work or life. For example, if he is transferred to a technical job or decides to change his career, his previously built efficacy beliefs in attaining customer contracts may not be as relevant. He will need to experience success in his new domain and reinitiate his cognitive processing in order to rebuild his self-efficacy.

Another point to make about understanding PsyCap efficacy is its magnitude and strength. The magnitude dimension refers to the level of difficulty a person expects to achieve. The strength dimension, on the other hand, is one's degree of certainty about the ability to achieve each level of difficulty (Bandura, 1997; Locke, Frederick, Lee, & Bobko, 1984; Stajkovic & Luthans, 1998b). For example, in the opening reflective exercise, you were given the opportunity to assess the magnitude and strength of your own PsyCap self-efficacy. We encourage you to reflect back on these earlier responses to the rating from 0–100% of how confident you were on your selected critical tasks and to spend some time in utilizing your cognitive capacities of symbolizing, forethought, observation, self-regulation, and self-reflection in regard to what you selected for the exercise and for your various roles and life domains. This reflection can put more personal meaning and understanding of the points just discussed about the nature of self-efficacy.

PSYCAP EFFICACY AND WORK PERFORMANCE

Unlike PsyCap hope and resiliency, where workplace applications are very recent and still largely just emerging, the relationship between PsyCap efficacy and work-related performance has been well established in the research literature. For example, a meta-analytical investigation of 114 studies showed a strong positive correlation (.38) between self-efficacy and work-related performance (Stajkovic & Luthans, 1998a). Indeed, this relationship between efficacy and performance is higher than meta-analyses of other widely recognized performance impact organizational behavior concepts and techniques, such as goal-setting (Wood, Mento, & Locke, 1987); feedback (Kluger & DeNisi, 1996); job satisfaction (Judge, Thoresen, Bono, & Patton, 2001); the "big five" personality traits, including conscientiousness (Barrick & Mount, 1991); transformational leadership (Avolio, 1999); and organizational behavior modification (OB Mod; Stajkovic & Luthans, 1997, 2003).

In addition to the Stajkovic and Luthans (1998a) study, there are several other large-scale meta-analyses consistently demonstrating the strong relationship between efficacy and the level of motivation and performance (Bandura & Locke, 2003).

Although PsyCap efficacy is domain specific, there are numerous studies showing its positive impact in various workplace applications. The long list includes leadership efficacy (Chemers, Watson, & May, 2000; Hannah, 2006; Luthans, Luthans, Hodgetts, & Luthans, 2001), moral/ethical efficacy (May, Chan, Hodges, & Avolio, 2003; Youssef & Luthans, 2005), creative efficacy (Tierney & Farmer, 2002), test-taking efficacy of job applicants (Truxillo, Bauer, Campion, & Paronto, 2002), computer efficacy (Thatcher & Perrewe, 2002), job-change efficacy (Cunningham, et al., 2002), participation efficacy (Lam, Chen, & Schaubroeck, 2002), career decision-making efficacy (Nilsson, Schmidt, & Meek, 2002), learning efficacy (Ramakrishna, 2002), and entrepreneurial efficacy (Boyd & Vozikis, 1994; Chandler & Jansen, 1997; Chen, Greene, & Crick, 1998; Luthans & Ibrayeva, 2006; Neck, Neck, Manz, & Godwin, 1999).

Besides performance outcomes, self-efficacy has also been shown to relate to work attitudes across cultures (Luthans, Zhu, & Avolio, 2006) and to enhanced health and psychosocial capacities (Holden, 1991; Holden, Moncher, Schinke, & Barker, 1990). Moreover, efficacy has often been supported as a significant contributor to effective functioning under stress, fear, and challenge, primarily due to one's perceptions of personal control (Bandura & Locke, 2003). Again, this plethora of research findings supports PsyCap confidence, or efficacy, as best meeting the PsyCap criterion of having an impact on performance outcomes and, as we will see next, also being readily open to development.

As we learn more about the transfer of efficacy from one domain to another, we also may be able to accelerate the development of self-efficacy in a new, challenging domain. For example, future training efforts to develop PsyCap efficacy may focus on helping the individual to identify points of transferability from success in one domain to another. Such transferability is likely associated with the previously noted concept of generalized self-efficacy.

DEVELOPING PSYCAP EFFICACY
IN MANAGERS AND EMPLOYEES

As pointed out in chapter 1, PsyCap hope, optimism, and resiliency have theoretical and research support for being state-like. However, we will recognize in the more in-depth discussion of these constructs that they can perhaps be better presented along a conceptual continuum of being both trait-like and, as components of PsyCap, state-like and open to development. This conceptual continuum does not apply as much to self-efficacy. Following Bandura's (1997) widely recognized theory that we briefly summarized earlier, self-efficacy is clearly state-like and thus open to development.

This strong theoretical foundation and considerable research support the contention that PsyCap confidence and efficacy can be developed and enhanced in today's managers and employees. However, this efficacy development will likely vary in difficulty, depending on the challenge within the domain. In particular, Bandura (1997) and others have demonstrated that efficacy can be developed through the opportunities to experience mastery/success, vicarious learning/modeling, social persuasion and positive feedback, and psychological and physiological arousal and well-being (Bandura, 1997, 2000; Hannah, 2006; Luthans, et al., 2001; Luthans, Luthans, & Luthans, 2004; Luthans & Youssef, 2004; Maddux, 2002; Stajkovic & Luthans, 1998a, 1998b). These efficacy-building experiences can occur through highly focused workplace microinterventions (Luthans, Avey, Avolio, Norman, & Combs, 2006), as well as through simple, less formal initiatives and even through spontaneous life events (Avolio & Luthans, 2006; Luthans & Avolio, 2003). The following sections provide details of the four major identified sources of efficacy and how they can be developed.

Mastery and Successful Experiences to Develop PsyCap Efficacy

While "practice makes perfect," success builds confidence. As we noted, the most tried-and-true approach to developing PsyCap confidence, or efficacy, is repeatedly experiencing success in accomplishing the tasks in which efficacy is to be built. As we emphasized, however, success does not equate with efficacy because of the cognitive processing of the success or how it is ultimately interpreted by the individual. Yet, success definitely contributes to confidence, which in turn leads to even higher performance and success, and the spiral continues. However, this does not mean that low performers, or those who have never had any experience with a certain task, are destined to be failures.

There are many approaches that allow managers and employees to build their mastery experiences, and thus their PsyCap confidence, over time. For example, a trainer or coach can break down a complex task into sub-components and teach the trainee each of the simple subskills, one at a time. This allows the trainee to experience "small successes" more frequently, which in turn helps in building-out PsyCap efficacy. These simpler tasks and skills can then be gradually integrated into their broader, more complex whole, with opportunities for practice and mastery at each step of the way.

Another way to provide managers and employees with mastery experiences is to intentionally place them in situations where the probability of success is relatively high, where they have a good chance to experience success. This is why selection, orientation, placement, and career planning are so important. People need to be set up for success as much as possible rather than put into uncertain environments that turn out not to be a good fit for them. In order for organizational participants to build efficacy through success, they should be allowed to do what they do best every day (Buckingham & Coffman, 1999).

In the training arena, stretch goals should be established, and the training should be conducted in a risk-free and distraction-free environment.

Such training goals and conditions lead to a higher probability of correctly assimilating and applying the new knowledge, skills, and abilities. These training procedures minimize the transfer of training problems and have better chances of mastery and success, which in turn can enhance PsyCap efficacy. Simulations, case studies, what-if analyses, and other hands-on but off-the-job development techniques, which are commonly utilized in professional workshops and executive retreats, also tend to promote PsyCap efficacy in a safe, focused environment.

Vicarious Learning/Modeling to Develop PsyCap Efficacy

In many situations, opportunities for mastery and successful experiences are unavailable or just do not happen due to circumstances beyond the control of the individual, the group, or even the organization (e.g., budget constraints or the economy). Fortunately, the trial-and-error process (or, direct experience), often associated with mastery and success, is not the only way to build PsyCap confidence. Through cognitive processes, such as the vicarious learning/modeling, that were presented earlier, people can also build their own confidence by observing others' mastery experiences and successes, as well as their mistakes and failures.

Although directly experienced mastery and success are usually more effective than vicarious learning and modeling opportunities in building PsyCap efficacy, observational experiences allow individuals to process and learn from the success and mistakes of others and to selectively imitate their successful actions. This learning enhances the observer's own chances for future personal mastery experiences and success. However, in order for modeling experiences to be effective in enhancing PsyCap efficacy, there must be both model and situational similarity, and time should be allocated by the learner for some degree of reflection.

The more similar the role model is to the developing manager or employee, the more likely the observer's PsyCap efficacy will be affected by that role model's success and desired, reinforcing consequences. This implies that peer-mentors, self-managed teams, and even informally being "shown the ropes" by respected colleagues at the same level may be more effective for building PsyCap efficacy than formal training by an extremely knowledgeable but far-removed executive, professional trainer, or renowned external consultant. Peers tend to be perceived as more similar in terms of background, abilities, and career goals. Thus, observing respected peers perform and be reinforced by success can instill in the developing manager or employee the belief that "if they can do it, I can do it, too," and their efficacy is thus enhanced. By picking the right role models with whom they can identify, trainees are more likely to positively accelerate their levels of self-efficacy. Also, if one picks peers in a similar or related context, the challenges associated with transferring what was learned are minimized.

In addition to relating to the model, the more similar the situation being observed is to the real task, the more likely the observational experience will enhance PsyCap efficacy. This is in line with PsyCap efficacy being domain specific. From the analysis of traditional training experiences, it is clear that most of these interventions suffer from lack of subsequent transferability back to the real job. This is because, in the hopes of building the trainees' confidence, traditional training tends to present oversimplified, idealized versions of the job's realities and to exclude many of the complexities, interactions, and uncertainties involved. Efficacy-building interventions need to present realistically challenging expectations (e.g., a realistic job preview) rather than act as unrealistic, "incubator" training and development environments that rarely exist in today's typically turbulent workplace. The use of real cases with which the participants can identify is critical to enhancing the transferability of what was learned into efficacious practice.

Particularly in managerial decision-making, highly technical situations, and other complex cognitive endeavors, observing the final decisions and behavioral patterns of a role model may not be sufficient for efficacy-building. The developing individual also needs to be able to follow the logic of the model being observed and to understand the reasoning process, criteria, and underlying assumptions that led to the selected course of action and/or pattern of behavior. In such complex situations, the model can facilitate building the PsyCap efficacy of the observer by "thinking aloud" and encouraging the vicarious learner to do the same as they cognitively contemplate situational complexities and weigh potential alternatives.

What if relevant role models and comparable situations are not available? In today's environment, which is dominated by tumultuous change and paradigm shifts, leaders and even frontline employees are often expected to act swiftly on scarce information and uncertain probabilities. In such situations, imagining oneself succeeding in a certain situation and mentally rehearsing one's potential actions in various contingencies of the situation can also enhance PsyCap efficacy. In other words, actual mastery and vicarious learning can be substituted with "imaginal" experiences in which the imagined successful self becomes the role model in imagined challenging situations. This involves what we have referred to as bringing the future back to the present and moving from the actual self to the possible self in authentic leadership development (Avolio & Luthans, 2006). Specifically, as we emphasized in chapter 1, we are proposing that individuals should think about their possible self engaging in a new challenge. It is this imagined self that motivates a change in the current self or in what the individual feels capable of doing in a particular role or challenge.

In many developmental contexts, including leadership and efficacy-building, we are proposing that individuals need to be encouraged to see themselves in a role in which they have not served before. This can be done by providing them with successful role models to observe, by providing positive feedback, and by encouraging them to use reflection to learn from their experiences. All of these components make up what Bandura (2001) discussed as being the social learning theory process.

Social Persuasion/Positive Feedback to Develop PsyCap Efficacy

Simply hearing others urge you on (i.e., have confidence in you) and provide positive feedback on your progress can transform your self-doubting beliefs into efficacy expectancies. In other words, as you listen to others' encouraging "you can do it" and "you are doing so well in accomplishing the first step of . . . ," your internal thoughts and beliefs begin to shift to a confident "I can do it" perspective. In fact, over two decades of empirical research strongly support the impact that contingently applied positive feedback and social recognition has on enhancing employees' performance, sometimes even beyond monetary rewards and other motivational techniques (see Stajkovic & Luthans, 1997, 2003, for comprehensive meta-analyses).

The impact that these nonfinancial positive reinforcers, such as attention, recognition, and positive feedback, have on performance has only recently been interpreted in terms of cognitive processes, such as self-efficacy (Peterson & Luthans, 2006; Stajkovic & Luthans, 2001, 2003). In reality, most of today's organizations invest heavily in technical training and very costly financial reward systems. Yet, organizations and managers tend to ignore a significant resource that they possess in unlimited amounts and at no cost. This resource involves the powerful performance impact of acknowledging, appreciating, and providing feedback and recognition to employees which not only has a reinforcing effect on desired employee behaviors with performance impact but also helps to build their PsyCap efficacy.

Psychological and Physiological Arousal/Well-Being and PsyCap Efficacy

Although less directly related to efficacy beliefs than success, modeling, and persuasion/feedback, people's emotional states (or, arousal) and their psychological and physiological well-being can also contribute to their PsyCap efficacy. For instance, a positive psychological state can energize people's cognitive processes of symbolizing, inquiry, forethought, observation, self-regulation, and self-reflection. This processing will tend to invigorate their perceptions and beliefs of confidence and personal control. On the other hand, an individual with a negative psychological state and outlook (e.g., someone who is burned out or stressed to the limit) will tend to experience hopelessness, helplessness, and pessimism, leading to a downward spiral of self-doubt and deteriorating efficacy. Thus, positive psychological states can boost individuals to support and sustain changes in their perspective about what they can accomplish.

The same is true of physical health and fitness. Feeling good and being in good physical condition can have a positive impact on one's cognitive and emotional states, including efficacy beliefs and expectancies. On the other hand, being ill, fatigued, and out of shape can have a negative impact.

We know that when people are highly stressed, their physiological responses are degraded. This, in turn, can negatively impact their psychological processes, such as their confidence, information processing, and decision-making. Indeed, by boosting PsyCap, we can expect, for example, that individuals working in high reliability organizations will be more likely to sustain higher levels of veritable performance for longer periods of time.

Importantly, as we indicated, this mental and physical arousal and wellness do not have as big an impact as the other more focused sources of efficacy, but, if negative, they can be a major blow to one's level of efficacy. If one has "had it" emotionally or psychologically—or, even worse, is very physically ill—then efficacy rapidly deteriorates or goes to zero. The person really suffering psychologically or physically has little or no confidence left and may just give up, not only on a specific task, but also generally in other domains.

Although certainly more difficult to control because of its often extra-organizational nature, an employee's emotional, psychological, and physiological well-being can be managed, at least in some dimensions, by organizational intervention. From on-site exercise and wellness programs, to family-friendly benefits (such as childcare facilities), to comprehensive employee-assistance programs, and even informal social activities and gatherings, there are many ways that organizations can help today's organizational participants in managing the psychological and physical toll of an increasingly stressful work environment.

The list of so-called "Best Places to Work" (which includes the renowned software firm SAS and Southwest Airlines) is proof that organizations can manage wellness and that it can be done with not only successful outcomes, such as higher retention rates, but we would also argue, with higher levels of PsyCap confidence and efficacy leading to high performance. Key to building these organizational contexts is the nature of leadership exhibited by the top management team and CEO, which can determine the boundaries of the climate in the organization at subsequent levels. By creating a more positive, forward-seeking climate and culture that is supportive, it is likely that such leadership can reduce injury rates, stress, burnout, turnover, absenteeism, and disengagement. Positivity and authenticity from top leadership can have a contagion effect throughout the organization and not only reduce stress and conflict but also build PsyCap efficacy (Avolio & Luthans, 2006; Luthans, Norman, & Hughes, 2006).

THE CONFIDENT ORGANIZATION: COLLECTIVE EFFICACY

Today's organizations are consistently discovering that they are often at the intersection of and can experience the synergies between various technological, economic, global, and sociocultural changes. The combinatory nature of coping with and exploiting these changes can be called organizational learning. It can result in value-creation as organizational members balance the exploration of new information and mental models. The learning organization can leverage existing knowledge and approaches in new, exciting, and effective ways (e.g., Barkema & Vermeulen, 1998; Fiol, 1995; Katila & Ahuja, 2002; Vermeulen & Barkema, 2001). Such organizational learning also now plays out in the increased dependence on cross-functional teams. In addition, emphasis is being given to providing all participants, from top to bottom, as well as outside stakeholders, with exposure to the "big picture." This big picture includes the interdisciplinary nature of organizational training and developmental initiatives, as well as the importance of diversity-promotion efforts.

In this new "flat-world" environment, where everything and everybody are linked across the planet and the "playing field" is becoming more level (see Friedman, 2005), it is evident that individual mastery is necessary but no longer sufficient. Domain-specific personal efficacy can be more effectively utilized when integrated with others' PsyCap efficacy regarding their respective domains. The integrated group or team becomes the referent for such collective efficacy. Bandura (1997, p. 477) precisely defines this collective efficacy as "a group's shared belief in its conjoint capabilities to organize and execute the courses of action required to produce given levels of attainments."

The more interdependent the members' and units' roles are in an organization, the more the synergies and complementary relationships of collective efficacy can be capitalized on (Bandura, 1997). In other words, collective efficacy is a realistic admission by organizational members that no matter how efficacious they are about their own independent capabilities, their individual confidences do not mean much in the organizational context until they are tightly jigsawed side-by-side with those of others, including virtually. Put simply, shared goals and collaborative decision-making are the channels through which collective efficacy can be exercised in an organization (Maddux, 2002).

Although research on collective efficacy is not as extensive as on personal efficacy, there is still empirical evidence that collective efficacy is related to group attainment of performance outcomes (Bandura, 1993), team effectiveness and motivation (Prussia & Kinicki, 1996), transformational leadership, potency, and high unit performance (Bass, Avolio, Jung, & Berson, 2003), and problem-solving vigilance (Tasa & Whyte, 2005). Collective efficacy has also been shown to be positively related to group members' organizational commitment and job satisfaction and negatively related to job and work withdrawal (Walumbwa, Wang, Lawler, & Shi, 2004).

In a recent presentation by Professor Mohga Badran of the American University in Cairo, Egypt, collective efficacy was exhibited in a case study of organizational change at a well-known Egyptian public-sector hotel. As a developing country under heavy international debt and economic reform, Egypt is being swept by major privatization efforts. The hotel was one of the very best in the old days, but then the organizational culture became replete with apathy and disengagement. The brief facts below communicate the situation at the time the hotel was to be offered for sale to private sector investors, including well-known global chains.

- Only 25% of the rooms were occupiable, and out of those, only 10% were actually occupied.
- To avoid responsibility, managers and supervisors tended to "keep everything." This not only included accurate records and inventory controls but also broken plates, torn chairs and sofas, leaking toilets, and many other collectors' items! Of course, conference rooms were perfect for storage space (and very little beyond that).
- Many employees also worked for a private-sector hotel close by, as their wages at the public-sector hotel were dismally low. And, giving new meaning to moonlighting, they did their work at the private hotel during their working hours at the public-sector hotel! As long as they showed up at the hotel in the morning and by the end of the day, their "disappearance" during the middle of the day went unnoticed (or, probably more accurately, it was ignored by their managers, who were doing the same thing). Interestingly, and important to this discussion, these employees were seen as high performers in their alternate jobs, which is indicative of high personal efficacy.

A new managing director was hired to get the old, badly rundown hotel in shape for sale. This ambitious leader knew that he had a lot of work cut out for himself. He also knew that his primary focus had to be on changing the organizational culture. Pragmatically, he decided that he could keep no more than 20% of the existing staff. To select the managers and employees who were to stay, he interviewed every one of them, but he asked only one telling question in each of his interviews: "Do you believe that there is any hope for this hotel to go back to being the best in the country?" If they said yes, they were retained. If they said no, they were let go.

Interestingly, many of those who said yes and were kept were among those with the longest tenure. They had actually witnessed the "glory days" of this grand old hotel, so it was possible for them to imagine it at its best again. To summarize, the survivors formed an army of dedicated, motivated, hard-working staff. With an incentive program in place, the employees became very engaged and committed to making this hotel into what it once was. It was completely revamped, bought by a big international hotel chain, and, by recent accounts, returned to its glory.

The new leader in the above example realized that the hotel staff did not lack the knowledge or the skills to be high performers (they had proven that in their "other" jobs). These people also did not lack personal efficacy to perform well on the necessary tasks. However, what they were truly missing was a sense of collective belief that, as a team, they could achieve a shared goal, with their workplace being the reference point for their shared aspirations and engaged efforts. These employees may have been very individually confident about their abilities to accomplish the tasks and goals of their respective roles at the old hotel, but without collective efficacy, the outcome was a collective disaster, also fueled, of course, by the pursuit of self-interest and incentives. On the other hand, when personal efficacy was properly channeled and assimilated into a high-engagement culture of collective efficacy, with the necessary rewards/incentives in place for self-interests, positive outcomes were realized. This occurred at both the organizational and personal levels. In other words, the collective PsyCap efficacy of the personnel at the Egyptian hotel was invested in and leveraged for a successful outcome.

In a very different context, Bass, Avolio, Jung, and Berson (2003) examined the transformational leadership of U.S. Army platoon leaders in garrison prior to going off to participate in high fidelity, complex war simulations. They also measured each platoon's perception of its collective efficacy. Approximately two to three months later, these platoons went off to the Joint Readiness Training Centers (JRTC) to participate in the simulations. What the researchers found was that those platoon leaders seen by their members as more transformational had platoons that were more efficacious, and they performed significantly better in combat simulations. Where the relationship between, say, the lieutenant and the sergeant was not efficacious, the platoon was nearly broken and incapable of performing successfully in these challenging, two-week simulations. In this case, as in the Egyptian hotel example, leadership and collective efficacy mattered to the ultimate performance gains.

POTENTIAL PITFALLS OF PSYCAP EFFICACY

Mastery and success experiences, vicarious learning/modeling opportunities, social persuasion/positive feedback, and emotional, psychological, and physiological arousal/wellness can all influence PsyCap confidence or efficacy. However, in order for these factors to enhance PsyCap efficacy, it is necessary for this information to be selected, cognitively processed, and acted upon through symbolizing, forethought, observation, self-regulation, and self-reflection. In other words, an individual's perceptions and interpretations of events—not just success or failure—models, social persuasion, and wellness can boost or dull the impact on PsyCap efficacy (or, confidence).

In the military example above, instructors focus the learning on what they call After Action Reviews (AARs). In those reviews, they get the leaders and unit members to visualize what had happened, what could be improved, and how they could reengage the task more successfully. By using this AAR process, the instructors are employing a type of social learning, and specifically, they are enhancing the self-efficacy of the individuals involved and the unit's collective efficacy.

Drawing from Bandura (2000) once again, we note that he presents some key perceptual and attributional biases that can act as potential inhibitors of PsyCap efficacy development. For example, as mentioned earlier, success can lose some of its value if the developing individual perceives the task to have been too easy, attributes much of the success to others' help, focuses on how slow the rate of improvement was, or emphasizes memories of the failures that led up to the success. Again, in terms of the impact of modeling, it can be dampened by the perceived degree of dissimilarity or relevancy of the model or situation. Social persuasion/positive feedback can also be interpreted in a biased manner if the credibility, expertise, or genuineness of the source can be challenged or if there is lack of consensus across various sources of the feedback and appraisal. Even psychological and physiological states can interact with other sources of PsyCap efficacy, causing difficult-to-change but possibly inaccurate assumptions, decision-making heuristics, and inclinations.

It is also important to discuss the potential problems of PsyCap efficacy beliefs that result in unrealistic overconfidence, that is, false efficacy. Although limited in scope—and, furthermore, Bandura and Locke (2003) challenge the validity—there are some research findings which show that even when based on high past performance (mastery), unrealistic overconfidence can cause imprudence and thus may reduce subsequent performance (Vancouver, Thompson, Tischner, & Putka, 2002; Vancouver, Thompson, & Williams, 2001). Also, in a recent study, group decision-making and collective efficacy have been shown to have a curvilinear relationship with vigilant problem-solving, indicating a similar overconfidence effect at the group level as well (Tasa & Whyte, 2005).

Even though there are these few contrary study results, the vast body of extensive research supports the positive relationship between PsyCap efficacy and performance in a wide range of work (Stajkovic & Luthans, 1998a) and life domains (see Bandura & Locke, 2003, for a comprehensive review). This overwhelming positive evidence indicates that most individuals and organizations are not far enough along the confidence curve to worry about a potential overconfidence effect.

In today's workplace, where adversities and setbacks are commonplace, PsyCap efficacy is challenged on an almost daily basis. Developing PsyCap efficacy becomes critical to sustaining effective leadership and high performance over time (Avolio & Luthans, 2006). The need for and importance of PsyCap efficacy is so vital that in situations where organizations and their members may be drowning in a downward spiral of doubt and uncertainty, even minor distortions of reality that communicate a slightly inaccurate illusion of control should be encouraged. This is because this perception can result in self-fulfilling prophecies of efficacy beliefs and expectancies (Maddux, 2002). Whether frontline employees, organizational leaders, or collectively in a group, from a hotel in Egypt to a major global corporation, investment in and development of PsyCap confidence (or, efficacy) is a key contributor to competitive advantage now and certainly in the future.

Looking back over this chapter, our intent was to highlight what comprises one of the more critical components of individual development and performance, as well as to place that component in the context of social learning theory and PsyCap. We believe that if organizational leaders and human resource managers were to focus on just this single area of employee development, then they could change the performance output of their organization by at least 10% and, following the results of the large meta-analysis conducted by Stajkovic and Luthans (1998a), perhaps by considerably more. What we must now narrow in on is how to challenge managers/leaders to have the discipline to focus on enhancing each follower's level of self-efficacy and, in turn, how to be cognizant of the importance of also focusing on, developing, and nurturing collective efficacy. This PsyCap efficacy can potentially be a very powerful force for performance impact and success at the individual, group/team, and organizational levels.

FUTURE IMPLICATIONS AND DIRECTIONS FOR PSYCAP SELF-EFFICACY RESEARCH AND PRACTICE

As we indicated in the introductory comments, among the various PsyCap capacities that we have determined for best fit, self-efficacy is the most extensively studied, and its workplace implications have been established and supported with a number of years of research and practice. However, we also assert that today's environment presents researchers and practitioners alike with unprecedented opportunities to capitalize on the still-untapped potential of PsyCap self-efficacy. We end this chapter with a few of the many challenging opportunities and future directions that lie ahead.

- Although self-efficacy is domain specific, the blurring boundaries across domains, roles, and organizational levels as organizations flatten their hierarchies and increasingly utilize cross-functional teams necessitate further understanding of the mechanisms through which individuals and groups perceive themselves and their roles as concurrently unique and integrated within a larger system or network (e.g., Rouse, Cannon-Bowers, & Salas, 1992). As organizational participants experience evolving roles, the potential for flexibly defining one's domain becomes vital, as does the adaptive ability to transfer previously built efficacy to related, though different, domains.
- Also related to the above direction, both researchers and practicing managers need to be aware of the implications of levels-of-analysis issues for studying PsyCap efficacy. Bandura (1997) warns that in addition to the methodological challenges associated with the currently available tools for aggregating group beliefs and performance, there are conceptual challenges as "beliefs of personal efficacy are not detached from the larger social system in which the members function. In appraising their personal efficacies, individu-

als inevitably consider group processes that enhance or hinder their efforts. . . . [Therefore], judgments of personal efficacy are heavily infused with the unique dynamics of the group" (pp. 478–479). Future research should embrace the challenge of incorporating these cross-level synergies for better understanding of PsyCap self-efficacy. Moreover, future research needs to examine where self-efficacy among members of a group morphs into collective efficacy and how that can best be supported.

- We have also proposed that PsyCap self-efficacy can lead to an upward spiral of confidence and veritable performance (Avolio & Luthans, 2006; Luthans & Avolio, 2003; Luthans, Norman, & Hughes, 2006). The potential for upward spirals and contagion effects of PsyCap self-efficacy provides considerable development implications for both leaders and followers. In the last chapter of this book, we present various approaches for calculating the return on investment in PsyCap development and human resource management. However, if leaders' PsyCap self-efficacy can trickle down to their followers, then investments in authentic leadership development (ALD), which incorporates the development of leaders' PsyCap self-efficacy as well as the leaders' development of their own followers, are likely to yield exponential returns that far exceed our conservative estimates (Avolio & Luthans, 2006). The unwarranted assumptions of bottom-line-oriented decision-makers that human resource investments are not worth their while are being consistently challenged in today's business environment (Pfeffer, 1998), and PsyCap self-efficacy presents researchers and practitioners with yet another contribution to the increasing evidence supporting the vital role of human resources in creating sustainable competitive advantage.

- Moreover, as confidence is likely to enhance employees' ability to perform independently, various leadership-style contingencies are likely to surface. For example, it is possible that PsyCap self-efficacy may act as a leadership substitute (e.g., Kerr & Jermier, 1978), which may threaten inauthentic, power-focused leaders from developing their followers' PsyCap self-efficacy. Mediating and moderating factors (e.g., task complexity, degree of diversity) in the organizational structure and culture should also be considered in order to account more fully for the salient role of organizational leaders in nurturing versus inhibiting the development of PsyCap self-efficacy in their followers.

- In a global context, we also encourage future research to explore what constitutes PsyCap self-efficacy in working across time, distance, and cultures. What is the base point of self-efficacy for a manager leading virtually across time, distance, and culture? As yet, there is little available evidence on the level of self-efficacy of most leaders and, more importantly, on developing such self-efficacy (Avolio, Kahai, & Dodge, 2001).
- Finally, there is a tremendous potential for enhancing the external validity of PsyCap self-efficacy research through applications to new work contexts, particularly across different work environments and cross-cultural settings (e.g., Luthans, et al., 2005; Luthans & Ibrayeva, 2006; Luthans, Zhu, & Avolio, 2006).

REFERENCES

Avolio, B. J. (1999). *Full leadership development: Building the vital forces in organizations.* Thousand Oaks, CA: Sage.

Avolio, B. J., Kahai, S., & Dodge, G. E. (2001). E-leadership: Implications for theory, research, and practice. *Leadership Quarterly, 11,* 615–668.

Avolio, B. J., & Luthans, F. (2006). *The high impact leader.* New York: McGraw-Hill.

Bandura, A. (1986). *Social foundations of thought and action: A social cognitive theory.* Englewood Cliffs, NJ: Prentice-Hall.

Bandura, A. (1993). Perceived self-efficacy in cognitive development and functioning. *Educational Psychologist, 28,* 117–148.

Bandura, A. (1997). *Self-efficacy: The exercise of control.* New York: Freeman.

Bandura, A. (2000). Cultivate self-efficacy for personal and organizational effectiveness. In E. Locke (Ed.), *Handbook of principles of organizational behavior* (pp. 120–136). Oxford, UK: Blackwell.

Bandura, A. (2001). Social cognitive theory: An agentic perspective. *Annual Review of Psychology, 52,* 1–26.

Bandura, A., & Locke, E. (2003). Negative self-efficacy and goal effects revisited. *Journal of Applied Psychology, 88,* 87–99.

Barkema, H., & Vermeulen, F. (1998). International expansion through start-up or acquisition: A learning perspective. *Academy of Management Journal, 31,* 7–26.

Barrick, M. R., & Mount, M. K. (1991). The big five personality dimensions and job performance: A meta-analysis. *Personnel Psychology, 44,* 1–26.

Bass, B. M., Avolio, B. J., Jung, D. I., & Berson, Y. (2003). Predicting unit performance by transformational and transactional leadership. *Journal of Applied Psychology, 88*, 207–218.

Boyd, N. G., & Vozikis, G. S. (1994, Summer). The influence of self-efficacy on the development of entrepreneurial intentions and actions. *Entrepreneurship Theory and Practice, 18*, 63–77.

Buckingham, M., & Coffman, C. (1999). *First, break all the rules.* New York: Simon & Schuster.

Chandler, G. N., & Jansen, E. (1997). Founder self-efficacy and venture performance: A longitudinal study. *Academy of Management Proceedings*, 98–102.

Chemers, M. M., Watson, C. B., & May, S. T. (2000). Dispositional affect and leadership effectiveness: A comparison of self-esteem, optimism, and efficacy. *Personality and Social Psychology Bulletin, 26*, 267–277.

Chen, C. C., Greene, P. G., & Crick, A. (1998). Does entrepreneurial self-efficacy distinguish entrepreneurs from managers? *Journal of Business Venturing, 13*, 295–316.

Cunningham, C., Woodward, C., Shannon, H., Macintosh, J., Lendrum, B., Rosenbloom, D., & Brown, J. (2002). Readiness for organizational change: A longitudinal study of workplace, psychological and behavioral correlates. *Journal of Occupational and Organizational Psychology, 75*, 377–352.

Fiol, M. (1995). Thought worlds colliding: The role of contradiction in corporate innovation processes. *Entrepreneurship Theory and Practice, 19*(3), 71–90.

Friedman, T. L. (2005). *The world is flat.* New York: Farrar, Straus and Giroux.

Hannah, S. T. (2006). *Agentic leadership efficacy.* Unpublished doctoral dissertation. University of Nebraska–Lincoln.

Holden, G. (1991). The relationship of self-efficacy appraisals to subsequent health-related outcomes: A meta-analysis. *Social Work in Health Care, 16*, 53–93.

Holden, G., Moncher, M. Schinke, S., & Barker, K. (1990). Self-efficacy in children and adolescents. A meta-analysis. *Psychological Reports, 66*, 1044–1046.

Judge, T. A., Thoresen, C. J., Bono, J. E., & Patton, G. K. (2001). The job satisfaction–job performance relationship: A qualitative and quantitative review. *Psychological Bulletin, 127*, 376–407.

Kanter, R. M. (2004). *Confidence.* New York: Crown Business.

Katila, R., & Ahuja, G. (2002). Something old, something new: A longitudinal study of search behavior and new product introduction. *Academy of Management Journal, 45*, 1183–1194.

Kerr, S., & Jermier, J. (1978). Substitutes for leadership: Their meaning and measurement. *Organizational Behavior and Human Performance, 22*, 375–403.

Kluger, A. N., & DeNisi, A. (1996). The effects of feedback intervention on performance: A historical review, a meta-analysis, and a preliminary feedback intervention theory. *Psychological Bulletin, 119*, 254–284.

Lam, S., Chen, X., & Schaubroeck, J. (2002). Participative decision making and employee performance in different cultures: The moderating effects of allocentrism/idiocentrism and efficacy. *Academy of Management Journal, 45*, 905–914.

Locke, E., Frederick, E., Lee, C., & Bobko, P. (1984). Effects of self-efficacy, goals and task strategies on task performance. *Journal of Applied Psychology, 69,* 241–251.

Luthans, F., Avey, J. B., Avolio, B. J., Norman, S. M., & Combs, G. M. (2006). Psychological capital development: Toward a micro-intervention. *Journal of Organizational Behavior, 27,* 387–293.

Luthans, F., & Avolio, B. (2003). Authentic leadership: A positive development approach. In K. S. Cameron, J. E. Dutton, & R. E. Quinn (Eds.), *Positive organizational scholarship* (pp. 241–258). San Francisco: Berrett-Koehler.

Luthans, F., Avolio, B. J., Walumbwa, F. O., & Li, W. (2005). The psychological capital of Chinese workers: Exploring the relationship with performance. *Management and Organization Review, 1,* 249–271.

Luthans, F., & Ibrayeva, E. S. (2006). Entrepreneurial self-efficacy in central Asian transition economies: Quantitative and qualitative analyses. *Journal of International Business Studies, 37,* 92–110.

Luthans, F., Luthans, K., Hodgetts, R., & Luthans, B. (2001). Positive approach to leadership (PAL): Implications for today's organizations. *Journal of Leadership Studies, 8*(2), 3–20.

Luthans, F., Luthans, K., & Luthans, B. (2004). Positive psychological capital: Going beyond human and social capital. *Business Horizons, 47*(1), 45–50.

Luthans, F., Norman, S. M., & Hughes, L. (2006). Authentic leadership. In R. Burke & C. Cooper (Eds.), *Inspiring leaders* (pp. 84–104). London: Routledge, Taylor & Francis.

Luthans, F., & Youssef, C. M. (2004). Human, social and now positive psychological capital management: Investing in people for competitive advantage. *Organizational Dynamics, 33,* 143–160.

Luthans, F., Zhu, W., & Avolio, B. J. (2006). The impact of efficacy on work attitudes across cultures. *Journal of World Business, 41,* 121–132.

Maddux, J. E. (2002). Self-efficacy: The power of believing you can. In C. R. Snyder & S. Lopez (Eds.), *Handbook of positive psychology* (pp. 257–276). Oxford, UK: Oxford University Press.

May, D., Chan, A., Hodges, T., & Avolio, B. (2003). Developing the moral component of authentic leadership. *Organizational Dynamics, 32,* 247–260.

Neck, C. P., Neck, H. M., Manz, C. C., & Godwin, J. (1999). "I think I can; I think I can": A self leadership perspective toward enhancing entrepreneurial thought patterns, self-efficacy, and performance. *Journal of Management Psychology, 14,* 477–501.

Nilsson, J., Schmidt, C., & Meek, W. (2002). Reliability generalization: An examination of the career decision-making self-efficacy scale. *Educational and Psychological Measurement, 62,* 647–658.

Parker, S. (1998). Enhancing role-breadth self-efficacy. *Journal of Applied Psychology, 83,* 835–852.

Peterson, S. J., & Luthans, F. (2006). The impact of financial and non-financial incentives on business unit outcomes over time. *Journal of Applied Psychology, 91,* 156–165.

Pfeffer, J. (1998). *The human equation.* Boston: Harvard Business School Press.

Prussia, G., & Kinicki, A. (1996). A motivational investigation of group effectiveness using social cognitive theory. *Journal of Applied Psychology, 81,* 187–198.

Ramakrishna, H. (2002). The moderating role of updating climate perceptions in the relationship between goal orientation, self-efficacy, and job performance. *Human Performance, 15,* 275–297.

Rouse, W. B., Cannon-Bowers, J. A., & Salas, E. (1992). The role of mental models in team performance in complex systems. *IEEE Transactions on Systems, Man, and Cybernetics, 22,* 1296–1308.

Stajkovic, A. D., & Luthans, F. (1997). A meta-analysis of the effects of organizational behavior modification on task performance: 1975–95. *Academy of Management Journal, 40,* 1122–1149.

Stajkovic, A. D., & Luthans, F. (1998a). Self-efficacy and work-related performance: A meta-analysis. *Psychological Bulletin, 124,* 240–261.

Stajkovic, A. D., & Luthans, F. (1998b). Social cognitive theory and self-efficacy: Going beyond traditional motivational and behavioral approaches. *Organizational Dynamics, 26,* 62–74.

Stajkovic, A. D., & Luthans, F. (2001). Differential effects of incentive motivators on work performance. *Academy of Management Journal, 44,* 580–590.

Stajkovic, A., & Luthans, F. (2003) Behavioral management and task performance in organizations: Conceptual background, meta-analysis, and test of alternative models. *Personnel Psychology, 56,* 155–194.

Tasa, K., & Whyte, G. (2005). Collective efficacy and vigilant problem solving in group decision making: A non-linear model. *Organizational Behavior and Human Decision Processes, 96,* 119–129.

Thatcher, J., & Perrewe, P. (2002). An empirical examination of individual traits as antecedents to computer anxiety and computer self-efficacy. *MIS Quarterly, 26,* 381–396.

Tierney, P., & Farmer, S. (2002). Creative self-efficacy: Its potential antecedents and relationship to creative performance. *Academy of Management Journal, 45,* 1137–1148.

Truxillo, D., Bauer, T., Campion, M., & Paronto, M. (2002). Selection fairness information and applicant reactions: A longitudinal field study. *Journal of Applied Psychology, 87,* 1020–1031.

Vancouver, J., Thompson, C., Tischner, E., & Putka, D. (2002). Two studies examining the negative effect of self-efficacy on performance. *Journal of Applied Psychology, 87,* 506–516.

Vancouver, J., Thompson, C., & Williams, A. (2001). The changing signs in the relationship between self-efficacy, personal goals, and performance. *Journal of Applied Psychology, 86,* 605–620.

Vermeulen, F., & Barkema, H. (2001). Learning through acquisitions. *Academy of Management Journal, 44,* 457–476.

Walumbwa, F., Wang, P., Lawler, J., & Shi, K. (2004). The role of collective efficacy in the relations between transformational leadership and work outcomes. *Journal of Occupational and Organizational Psychology, 77,* 515–530.

Wood, R. E., Mento, A. J., & Locke, E. A. (1987). Task complexity as a moderator of goal effects: A meta-analysis. *Journal of Applied Psychology, 72,* 416–425.

Youssef, C. M., & Luthans, F. (2005). A positive organizational behavior approach to ethical performance. In R. A. Giacalone, C. Jurkiewicz, & C. Dunn (Eds.), *Positive psychology in business ethics and corporate social responsibility* (pp.1–22). Greenwich, CT: Information Age.

CHAPTER 3

PsyCap Hope

The Will and the Way

ARE YOU STRONG willed? Are you determined to achieve your goals? Do you feel you are in control of your own destiny? Can you go relentlessly for hours, days, even months until you have accomplished what you have set your mind to do? Is it difficult to distract you away from your targeted endeavors? When there are no set goals for you, do you tend to set your own? Are the goals you set for yourself extremely challenging? Do you enjoy engaging in such goals?

If your answers are mostly "yes" to these types of questions, then you exhibit the willpower component of hope. However, having such will is necessary, but not sufficient, for PsyCap hope. When the way is blocked, you must also know the pathway and alternative pathways to carry out your willpower. You have to have both the willpower and the pathways (i.e., the "way") to have a high level of hope to accomplish your goals successfully. To have the pathways component of a high level of PsyCap hope, you must also answer affirmatively to questions such as the following: Do you proactively determine the way to accomplish your goals? Do you tend to figure out and evaluate alternative paths to the same destination? When you are challenged, or when your efforts are frustrated with obstacles, do you have alternatives already determined that can circumvent the obstacles? Do you have strengths to draw from to manage around your areas of weakness and vulnerability?

PERSONAL REFLECTIONS EXERCISE ON PSYCAP HOPE

As an exercise to get you personally involved in hope, think about the last very difficult situation you confronted at work. What happened once you were alerted to this situation in terms of the way you thought about it and the way you addressed it? Use the questions above as your guide.

Beside the will and the way, there are many possible circumstances that may affect your level of PsyCap hope. For example, how would you react if the following types of things happened in your life? What would your immediate, short-term response be? What course(s) of action would you take over the long run?

- You work for a toxic manager.
- You manage totally disengaged employees.
- You are passed over for a promotion a second time.
- You are transferred to a less desired position, location, or both.
- You are fired after completing your most successful project.
- Your business or personal situation goes through a total financial meltdown.
- A best friend at work is laid off.
- A trusted colleague betrays you.
- A coworker gets severely injured on the job or has a serious illness.
- A major initiative you are working on gets its funding pulled.

A STORY OF HOPE

A realistic story of hope can also serve as an illustration and backdrop for this chapter as we present the theory and practice of PsyCap hope and its development in the workplace. Jeremy and Kayla are happily married. Jeremy is a claims adjuster in a small insurance company, and Kayla is a part-time customer service representative at a large retailer. Both had gone through difficulties before they met. Kayla was divorced and raising her son from the previous marriage. Jeremy came from a dysfunctional family, had dropped out of college, and had many low-paying jobs. However, they had one thing in common. They were both determined to have a successful marriage and life. They were both willing to invest the necessary time and energy and do whatever it would take to reach their goal of a good life and family.

After a few years, they thought their dreams were coming true when they had their first child together. They had both accumulated some seniority and grown in their jobs to make a decent living between them. However, their lives were suddenly shattered when Jeremy was struck by a disabling illness. He was no longer able to work at his job. Three surgeries later, Jeremy and Kayla knew that life would never be the same. They knew their troubles were there for the long haul.

How did Jeremy and Kayla handle this crisis in their lives? Definitely, despair and giving up were not options to consider. Kayla went from working part-time to full-time. She also started her own home-based business in order to bring in a little extra income. Jeremy was able to take over most of the childcare and housework duties, and he went back to community college in the evenings when medications allowed him to cope with his illness. Presently, Jeremy is scheduled to receive his associate's degree, and he plans to continue through to his bachelor's, and possibly master's, degree. His dreams are not unrealistic. So far, he has earned excellent grades throughout his coursework. He has already looked into gaining entrance into the local state university, which is willing to transfer most of his credits into their social-work program. He has also been able to establish some contacts through which he is likely to land an internship. This experience should help him find a good-paying job that he is capable of performing. In other words, drawing from their high levels of PsyCap hope (i.e., the will and the way), Kayla and Jeremy are on a new pathway to accomplishing their life goals. They defined an alternative future that was possible, not the one defined for them when Jeremy first discovered his illness.

Although this life-story is perhaps not as glamorous as those of famous historical leaders noted for their strong will and pathways, such as Winston Churchill, Franklin Roosevelt, Margaret Thatcher, Victor Frankl, or Nelson Mandela, it demonstrates the role that hope can play in accomplishing one's goals and values. Such hope is well established as having a positive impact on life in general, as in the above story, and has also been shown to be a key factor in attaining academic and athletic success. We are bringing such hope to the workplace as a key component of PsyCap. After first defining precisely what we mean by PsyCap hope, this chapter then examines in turn the relationship that hope has with performance; specific guidelines for its development; profiles of the hopeful manager, employee, and organization; and the chapter ends with some potential pitfalls that need to be avoided if one is to achieve a sustainable impact.

WHAT IS PSYCAP HOPE?

Hope is commonly used in everyday language. However, as a psychological strength, there are many misperceptions about what constitutes hope and what the characteristics of hopeful individuals, groups, and organizations are. Many confuse hope with wishful thinking, an unsubstantiated positive attitude, an emotional high, or even an illusion. C. Rick Snyder was a professor of clinical psychology at the University of Kansas until his untimely death in 2005. The most widely recognized theory-builder and researcher on hope in the positive psychology movement, he defined hope as "a positive motivational state that is based on an interactively derived sense of successful (1) agency (goal-directed energy) and (2) pathways (planning to meet goals)" (Snyder, Irving, & Anderson, 1991, p. 287).

Snyder's research supports the idea that hope is a cognitive or "thinking" state in which an individual is capable of setting realistic but challenging goals and expectations and then reaching out for those aims through self-directed determination, energy, and perception of internalized control. This is what Snyder and colleagues refer to as "agency" or "willpower." However, often overlooked in common usage of the term, but as defined by Snyder and colleagues, another equally necessary and integral component of hope is what is referred to as the "pathways" or "waypower." In this component of hope, people are capable of generating alternative paths to their desired destinations should the original ones become blocked (Snyder, 1994, 1995a, 2000; Snyder, Ilardi, Michael, & Cheavens, 2000; Snyder, Rand, & Sigmon, 2002).

The pathways component mainly separates PsyCap hope from the everyday usage of the term and from the other PsyCap states, such as resiliency, self-efficacy, and optimism (e.g., see Bryant & Cvengros, 2004; Carifio & Rhodes, 2002; Luthans & Jensen, 2002, pp. 309–312; Magaletta & Oliver, 1999; Snyder, 2002, pp. 256–258, for conceptual and empirical summaries of the distinctions, i.e., the discriminative validity of hope). Finally, there is a continuous reiteration between agency and pathways, in which one's willpower and determination motivate the search for new pathways, while the creativity, innovation, and resourcefulness involved in developing pathways in turn ignite one's energy and sense of control, which when taken together, result in an upward spiral of hope (Snyder, 1993, 2000, 2002). If one has the potential to control in terms of going down alternative pathways that "just might work," then hope remains and can even grow.

Reflecting back on the Jeremy and Kayla example at the beginning of the chapter, their embodiment of high levels of hope is clear in several ways. First, both had clear goals: to maintain and grow their marriage, children, and quality of life. Second, they were both determined to achieve their goals, as exhibited in the strength of their willpower, the amount of energy they invested, and their clear sense of agency and control over their destiny. Third, even when obstacles and setbacks were about to destroy their goals, they were able to shift to alternative, creative pathways around their problems and continue to pursue their goals. When people get stuck on the pathway (i.e., their way is blocked) and see no alternative, in the extreme, we could describe them as not only frustrated but being at an early stage of learned helplessness. In Jeremy and Kayla's case, their hope orientation was "learned helpfulness" (rather than helplessness) to help redirect them to some alternative pathways for goal attainment.

Finally, as some of this couple's new pathways proved effective, this further sparked their enthusiasm, which in turn enhanced their chances of success and had an upward spiral effect on their hope. As long as there is some possibility for forward momentum down an alternative pathway, there is the potential for a positive contagion effect, where one advance leads to another and another.

THE RELATIONSHIP BETWEEN HOPE AND PERFORMANCE

Despite the relatively recent emergence of positive psychological research in general and hope research in particular, the relationship between hope and performance in various life domains has become well established. Such domains include: academic and athletic achievement, physical and mental health, survival and coping beliefs and skills, and other desirable, positive life and well-being outcomes (Curry, Snyder, Cook, Ruby, & Rehm, 1997; Kwon, 2000; Onwuegbuzie & Snyder, 2000; Range & Pentin, 1994; Scioli, et al., 1997; Snyder, 2000).

Recent proposals and beginning research also support a positive relationship between hope and workplace performance (Adams, et al., 2003; Jensen & Luthans, 2002; Luthans, 2002a, 2002b; Luthans, Avolio, Walumbwa, & Li, 2005; Luthans & Jensen, 2002; Luthans, Van Wyk, & Walumbwa, 2004; Luthans & Youssef, 2004; Peterson & Luthans, 2003; Snyder, 1995b; Youssef & Luthans, 2003, 2006). For example, exploratory research findings support a positive relationship between employee hope and organizational profitability (Adams, et al., 2002) and between entrepreneurs' hope levels and expressed satisfaction with business ownership (Jensen & Luthans, 2002).

Peterson and Luthans (2003) found a positive relationship between organizational leaders' level of hope and the profitability of their units and the satisfaction and retention of their employees. Youssef (2004) also showed that the hope level of over 1000 managers and employees is positively related to their performance, job satisfaction, work happiness, and organizational commitment. Hope has also been applied conceptually or empirically in several cross-cultural settings such as in Egypt (Youssef & Luthans, 2006), China (Luthans et al., 2005), and South Africa (Luthans et al., 2004). All of these studies are just the beginning of showing how PsyCap hope can be both related to performance and also, importantly, how it can be developed.

DEVELOPING HOPE IN TODAY'S MANAGERS AND EMPLOYEES

Although hope has been portrayed as a dispositional trait that is thus not readily adaptable to change (Snyder, et al., 1991), consistent with our PsyCap inclusion criteria (Luthans, 2002a, 2002b), hope has also been demonstrated to be a developmental state (e.g., Snyder, 1995a, 1995b; Snyder, et al., 1996; Snyder, Tran, et al., 2000; Veninga, 2000). Several specific approaches have been successful in developing and nurturing hope. These include the following.

1. GOAL-SETTING. Substantial research support exists for the relationship between effective goal-setting and performance (e.g., Locke & Latham, 1990). In line with the theory of hope, performance gains are achieved when goals are internalized and committed to and when goal achievement is self-regulated. Moreover, consistent with the agency component of hope, goals that are self-set, participatory, or even assigned but explained using a logical rationale that one can buy into will tend to yield higher performance than dictated, unexplained goals (Latham, Erez, & Locke, 1988; Latham, Winters, & Locke, 1994). Finally, appropriate goal-setting does not only influence one's level of motivation, choices made, effort extended, and persistence but also the willingness and ability to design creative ways by which to achieve one's goals (Latham, 2000), that is, hope pathways.

2. STRETCH GOALS. Goals that are conducive to developing and nurturing hopeful thinking—and, consequently, performance enhancement—need to be specific, measurable, challenging, and yet achievable. Stretch goals are those that are difficult enough to stimulate excitement and exploration and yet are still perceived to be within reach. They warrant trial and reasonable expectations of accomplishment, given extra effort. They typically tap into the "reserve potential" that flies below the radar screen but is almost always there, ready to be tapped into to address some daunting, yet doable, challenge.

3. STEPPING. Stepping is an integral component of hopeful goal achievement. In the stepping process, difficult, long-term, and possibly even overwhelming goals are broken down into smaller, proximate, and thus more manageable milestones. As gradual progress is made toward distant goals, agency and pathways are enriched, building a more sustainable base for pursuing one's extreme challenges successfully (Latham, 2000; Luthans, 2000a, 2000b; Luthans, et al., 2004; Luthans & Jensen, 2002; Luthans & Youssef, 2004; Snyder, 1995a, 1995b; Youssef & Luthans, 2006).

4. INVOLVEMENT. Emphasis on bottom-up decision-making and communication, opportunities for participation, employee empowerment, engagement, delegation, and increased autonomy have documented, desirable workplace outcomes. For example, studies have found that such involvement works in terms of increased performance and in increasing employee satisfaction, commitment, and other desirable attitudinal outcomes, such as psychological engagement and identification (e.g., see Conger & Kanungo, 1988; Hackman & Oldham, 1980; Harter, Schmidt, & Hayes, 2002; Spreitzer, 1995; Srivastra, 1986).

In analyzing the role of involvement techniques in terms of building hope, it is clear that these approaches provide today's workforce with the power, freedom, and authority to make decisions and choices, that is, agency. They also encourage the initiation and implementation of self-designed courses of action, that is, pathways. In line with our conceptualization of PsyCap hope, the role of participation in enhancing performance is not just emotional or motivational, but it also involves cognitive processing in that it gets individuals to analyze and consider what seemed impossible to become possible (Wagner, Leana, Locke, & Schweiger, 1997).

5. REWARD SYSTEMS. The rich body of knowledge on behavioral performance management demonstrates beyond doubt that you get what you

reinforce (see meta-analyses by Stajkovic & Luthans, 1997, 2003). Reinforcing PsyCap hope thinking can be accomplished through rewarding managers and employees who contribute to the appropriate goals, take effective goal-setting initiatives, exhibit internalized control and self-regulating behaviors (agency), and creatively and relentlessly pursue multiple alternative pathways toward goal achievement. Integral to the success of such a process is the understanding that well-designed reward systems in essence align organizational goals with personal intrinsic and extrinsic rewards. In most organizational situations, reward systems typically do not make the type of connection that will result in sustainable motivation and performance. Many individuals do not see a connection between what they do and the recognition that they receive at work (Luthans, K. W., 2000). This disconnect can drain one's motivation and lower performance. Showing people how their actions are directly instrumental to specific rewards has been shown over time to be highly motivating (Peterson & Luthans, 2006; Stajkovic & Luthans, 1997, 2003).

6. RESOURCES. Becoming frustrated from blockages in trying to attain goals is inevitable in today's ever-changing, hypercompetitive environment. Thus, alternate pathways for maintaining and enhancing hope become critically important. The title found in one popular business magazine exhorted, "Change or Die." With respect to PsyCap hope, change involves alternating one's pathways to find the route that will work to achieve one's goals. However, with highly disengaged employees, situational constraints, such as the lack of access to necessary resources, can encourage an externalized, victimized perspective and quickly exhaust the available pathways, resulting in hopelessness and apathy. Needless to say, clearly set priorities and effective allocation of resources are vital to sustaining hope and attaining goals. Support from the leader and the organization to help employees explore alternative pathways also helps.

In addition to obvious material resources, managerial support and commitment are also indispensable resources. For example, without top management support, very few important goals can be attained, regardless of the amount of willpower and waypower that middle managers and employees may possess. In fact, the more hopeful organizational members are, the more frustrated they are likely to be in an environment that lacks top-down and organizational support.

In a recent interview, Jeff Immelt, the CEO of General Electric, talked about how his father would behave at the family's dinner table, depending on who was his supervisor at the time. Jeff's father also worked for G.E., and in some periods of his career, when he had a bad boss, "he came home in a bad mood, uncertain about the future. And when he had a good boss, he was pumped" (Byrne, 2005, p. 62). Notice the words he used to describe his motivation: "uncertain about the future" versus "pumped." This is what supervisor/manager support can do to provide hopelessness about the future or enthusiasm and hope for the future.

7. STRATEGIC ALIGNMENT. Contemporary strategic management perspectives tend to overlook the salience of human resources as a primary resource for competitive advantage in the current global work environment (Pfeffer, 1998). By the same token, few if any strategic leaders talk about the level of hope in their organizations. Also overlooked are the importance of matching jobs to employees' talents and strengths and the impact of a succession of "bad bosses" (Buckingham & Clifton, 2001; Buckingham & Coffman, 1999). Selection techniques still overwhelmingly look only for technical expertise, and most development strategies are oriented toward fixing weaknesses, as opposed to leveraging strengths.

In the same way that effective strategic management emphasizes the proper allocation of financial and material resources to where they yield the highest return, developing the agency and pathways ingredients of hope necessitate the careful alignment of the placement and development of human resources with each employee's talents and strengths. From hope's focus on pathways, it follows that getting people aligned provides them with a broader set of pathway choices in which to be successful at work. The opposite extreme is getting people totally mismatched with their job responsibilities to the extent that they have little chance for success. Such misalignment limits employees' pathway possibilities along with their hope.

8. TRAINING. Even organizations that act on the belief that human resources are their most important asset and that invest in their people through training still need to be careful in adopting underlying training philosophies and in implementing training programs. Why? Prescriptive training approaches can promote passiveness and limit pathways thinking. One-way, noninteractive training delivery techniques can diminish participants' sense of agency. Focus on skill-oriented programs that solely disseminate standard technical knowledge and task-specific information, though sometimes necessary, can be limiting. On the other hand, hope-promoting types of training are hands-on, interactive, and participative. They are oriented toward enhancing general competencies and developing talents into strengths,

which can subsequently be adapted to various situations. Hope-related training, coupled with learned skills, can be equipping and enabling, but it leaves room for self-awareness, self-regulation, self-evaluation, and self-development. Using this underlying perspective in highly focused microinterventions, we have been able to demonstrate positive impact on developing hope (as well as the other capacities and overall PsyCap; see chapter 8 for details). These microintervention studies have significantly developed the hope (and overall PsyCap) of management students, managers, engineers, and employees (Luthans, Avey, Avolio, Norman, & Combs, 2006).

THE HOPEFUL ORGANIZATIONAL LEADER OR MANAGER

In light of the present turmoil in today's global environment, hopeful organizational leaders and managers become crucial to the growth, if not the very survival, of any organization. Leaders and managers need to keep the organization moving ahead, and underlying such growth is hope. Hopeful managers are not just "good managers" who effectively perform the classic managerial functions of planning, organizing, and controlling. Nor are they merely individuals with just the three recognized skills that managers need: conceptual, technical, and human (Katz, 1974). Although such traditional approaches are still necessary for effective management, they are no longer sufficient in today's new paradigm, the "flat-world" competitive environment (Friedman, 2005), and neither is the classic, methodical manner of implementation. The time period we live in (and into the foreseeable future) requires that organizations take full advantage of growing the hope of their workforce in order to remain on the top end of the innovation and productivity curve. The advantage of building hope is that it is difficult to replicate by competitors without considerable effort and discipline on the part of leaders and managers, making it an enduring competitive advantage.

The hopeful manager and leader needed for today's workplace is one who possesses goal-directed willpower and waypower. Hopeful managers possess energy and determination that can trickle down to their followers, motivating them to have high performance impact. They are effective planners who can set specific, challenging goals and can align those goals to the organization's most important objectives. They stimulate and set the context for their followers to determine their own goals, establish higher standards, and stretch their limits. They accept and respect their followers as individuals, supporting their self-set goals and rewarding their creative pathways, even if these are nontraditional and unusual. Hopeful managers are mentors, coaches, and developers of their associates. They do what Jeff Immelt's father said a good boss did: get employees feeling "pumped."

Connecting this discussion with the emerging leadership literature, we see the hopeful manager as being one very critical component of being an authentic leader (Avolio & Luthans, 2006; Luthans & Avolio, 2003; Luthans, Norman, & Hughes, 2006). Hopeful managers that are self-aware and know their capabilities, identities, vulnerabilities, values, emotions, and goals are by definition more authentic. Such individuals are capable of self-regulating their cognitions, emotions, and actions in themselves and others. Their consistent desire for self-verification and self-improvement motivates them to seek their followers' feedback and involvement (Avolio, 2004; Avolio & Luthans, 2006), which over time grows both the leader and follower in what we would call a more authentic relationship.

Even when decisions are to be made quickly and with little participation, hopeful managers explain the rationale for their actions in a genuine, transparent, trust-building manner. This authentic process encourages buy-in and maintains followers' dignity, as well as their sense of agency and pathways thinking. It also helps grow them into leaders, as they are demonstrating the type of leadership one would "hope" followers would exhibit with their future followers.

THE HOPEFUL EMPLOYEE

In addition to hopeful managers and leaders, it is also beneficial and necessary to portray a snapshot of the characteristics of hopeful employees. Although hope is a malleable state and thus variable, managers who are capable of identifying hopeful tendencies (or signs of hopelessness) can be better equipped to diagnose the state of hope among their employees. Effective managers are proactively prepared to nurture and reinforce hope in their associates.

Hopeful employees tend to be independent thinkers. They possess an internal locus of control (i.e., they tend to make internal attributions such as their effort in interpreting their success on a task). Thus, they need a high degree of autonomy in order to express and utilize their agency. They may easily get offended and discouraged if micromanaged and will likely try to search for alternative pathways to regain control, which may be seen by the manager as being noncompliant. They have very strong needs for growth and achievement and are intrinsically motivated by enriched jobs, such as those described by Oldham and Hackman (1980) as having high levels of experienced meaningfulness and responsibility and providing substantial feedback. Hopeful employees tend to be creative and resourceful, even with tight budgets, but they may also portray an impression of chaos and disorganization as they pursue nontraditional, out-of-the-box pathways. In other words, on the surface, high-hopers may appear to be nonconforming troublemakers or risk-takers. Many times, however, we refer to those with such characteristics as "successful entrepreneurs."

On the other side of the coin, employees who lack hope may come off as conforming to organizational rules and being obedient to their managers. Low-hopers may be perceived by managers and coworkers as cooperative, "good soldiers." Unfortunately, most organizational reward systems are informally, if not formally, geared toward such benign attitudes and behaviors. However, if these are symptomatic of low agency and limited or no pathways, then, especially in today's environment, there are problems ahead for the manager and the organization. Such employees oftentimes become disengaged and just spend their hours at work looking busy. Worst yet, they may become disengaged and spend their time thinking of pathways to obstruct what the management and leadership are trying to accomplish.

Effective managers and leaders need to proactively deal with associates exhibiting signs of hopelessness. Low-hopers often exhibit an unwillingness or inability to assume additional responsibilities, make independent decisions, or solve challenging problems. Too many managers fall into the power trap of setting all the goals, making all the decisions, and carefully detailing every step to take for their associates. Although their intentions may be to enhance their units' performance through what they perceive to be hands-on leadership and tight controls, this micromanagement approach may breed hopelessness and complacency among their people. It certainly will not contribute to developing an adaptable employee. Fortunately, hopeful leaders and managers tend to do the opposite and develop effective, hopeful employees who not only are energized to perform their own work but also find ways to support others' work as well.

THE HOPEFUL ORGANIZATION: NURTURING A CULTURE OF HOPE AND HIGH PERFORMANCE

Hopeful leaders, managers, and employees are an important, intangible asset for today's organization. However, some of our exploratory research shows that there might be some challenges in attaining a hopeful organization. Although our research clearly shows a positive relationship between hope and performance outcomes (Luthans, Avolio, Avey, & Norman, 2006; Luthans, et al., 2005; Peterson & Luthans, 2003), a few of the organizations we have analyzed exhibit a negative relationship (Youssef, 2004). Reasons often expressed in qualitative follow-up interviews with managers and employees who scored high on hope but low on desired outcomes include frustration with dead-end jobs, vaguely defined goals and promotion criteria, petty politics and policies, micromanagement, and centralized decision-making.

Apparently, high-hope managers and employees who possess the agency and pathways for their jobs have a lot more to offer than they are allowed to give in some organizations. In a restrictive, nonsupportive work environment, hopeful managers and employees become frustrated because they have a level of energy that they are not able to allocate in positive directions. Although these high-hopers may continue to perform well in spite of their poor organizational situation, over time their deteriorating job satisfaction (e.g., Judge, Thoresen, Bono, & Patton, 2001), happiness (e.g., Fordyce, 1988), and organizational commitment (Allen & Meyer, 1990) may negatively impact their performance.

A specific example we are familiar with points to this problem. In this organization, telemarketers and telephone customer-service representatives were hired with the implied expectation of a career path in marketing or sales. It seems that the organization-wide knowledge of this expectation had a positive impact on retention of these telemarketers, which in the United States (not India) is perceived as a dead-end or at best transitional job. Informally understood promotion criteria in this firm included job tenure and pursuing and attaining a college degree. The more hopeful employees in the telemarketing jobs patiently waited for their "turn to be promoted" into sales and marketing as they put in their time and pursued their degrees. In other words, they took it upon themselves (agency) to move up (be promoted into sales or marketing) and found the means (pathways through seniority and higher education) to do so, even when the organization did not offer any tuition-reimbursement programs or even release time for attending classes.

As the "big day" came and an opening was posted in sales, those who perceived themselves to be qualified according to the "criteria" (tenure and education) applied for the sales position. However, upon interviewing these hopeful internal candidates and a few outsiders, an external candidate was selected. The chosen candidate was a fresh college graduate who had no experience in this industry and thus did not meet the perceived criteria. Internal candidates were not informed about the criteria that were used to select this outside candidate's qualifications over theirs. Disappointment and frustration caused several of these high-hope telemarketers to quit, while many others have updated their resumes and are currently job-hunting.

In terms of hope in this example, the internalized determination and motivation to move up into a better job that the hopeful employees possessed were shot down by the organization. These hopeful employees now perceived that they were faced with an unbalanced or inequitable situation. However, their strongly desired goals for growth and advancement, as well as the resourcefulness and waypower to reach these goals, stimulated them to rechannel their agency into another pathway that reduced their organizational commitment and, eventually, their job performance: they pursued alternative employment opportunities. As we noted above, if desirable alternatives are limited within the current organization and hopeful employees are forced into undesirable pathways, they may become actively disengaged and delight in derailing management's agenda. On the other hand, less-hopeful employees simply accepted the fact that their careers were determined by the organization and not through their own efforts (low agency). These low-hopers did not pursue alternative possibilities (pathways) and remained loyal but low-performing employees.

Several factors can promote the organizational culture needed for hope development and sustainability. Strategic initiatives emphasizing long-term goal-setting, coordination, integration, and contingency planning can create an organizational environment where agency and pathways thinking can thrive. Clearly, we are speaking here of organizational climate and culture that stimulate and reinforce such thinking and behavior. Organizations such as the well-known "Best Place to Work For," North Carolina software firm SAS, present their members with a well-developed "master plan" with which to align their personal and professional goals with organizational goals and thus can effectively capitalize on their participants' PsyCap hope. The organization can also provide the appropriate boundaries and open, unexplored territories for PsyCap hope to be channeled and to flourish.

Hopeful organizations are proactive in seeking and creating opportunities for members and in controlling the environment to facilitate employees in achieving their goals. When organizations explicitly verbalize their philosophies into a clear mission statement; an inspiring, value-based vision; and a practical, realistic set of objectives, they are in essence creating a realistic organizational preview for potential and existing participants. Hopeful new hires who identify with the organization's strategic direction are likely to self-select, buy into, and build on the organization's course of action. The same is true of existing hopeful managers and employees. Even those less hopeful can be socialized into the hopeful organization's culture as their agency and pathways thinking are developed and maintained.

Open and transparent flows of communication through flat, organic structures, participative decision-making, empowerment, and other flexible, high-engagement techniques can provide a culture of hope that encourages its members to take initiatives, seek responsibility, accept accountability, and expect to be treated fairly when doing so. These are ways that hopeful organizations can stimulate, maintain, and enhance the willpower and waypower of participants. In such a hopeful organizational culture, transparency and authenticity allow resources—including traditional economic, but also human, social and psychological capital—to be readily shared and swiftly allocated to their best uses (Avolio & Luthans, 2006; Luthans & Youssef, 2004; Youssef & Luthans, 2005b; Youssef & Luthans, 2006).

On the dark side, in a nontransparent or unethical organization, people figure out pathways to avoid giving up the resources they have; and in the extreme, they create what is referred to in war as an "insurgency." Moreover, organizations that thrive on policies and procedures that cover every intricate detail of their operations tend to stifle hope. The false sense of security and control that highly structured operations and heavily bureaucratic, top-down decision-making generate may appear efficient, but, because of their negative impact on hope, they can be detrimental over time. Individuals need to have the context to grow in over time, and having no options to deviate from strict rules and procedures is a recipe for stifling growth (see Youssef & Luthans, 2005a).

We recently heard a nuclear facility plant manager saying, "We are very creative in our plant to help continuously grow our employees." He then added, "now don't worry we are not being 'creative' in how we run our plant, even though in our simulations I must say we strive for absolute creativity." What this manager was saying is that even though the job had very set rules stemming from regulatory and safety reasons, there is always a way to grow one's employees, and they did so through elaborate learning simulations.

The organizational inertia caused by mechanistic structures and centralized decision-making stands in stark contrast to the agency and pathways thinking of hopeful managers and employees which is needed in today's rapidly changing, new-paradigm landscape. Indeed, in the nuclear facility (and as any high-reliability organizational context shows), you can both have creativity and pay attention to the routine, and they do not necessarily have to be in conflict. Indeed, the creativity culture of the organization may eventually unleash the power of hopeful participants to improve on that which is routine.

POTENTIAL PITFALLS

Hopeful managers, leaders, employees, and organizations are very goal-directed, *agentic*, and resourceful. They are capable of setting and accomplishing challenging goals through their determined willpower and creative waypower. The iterative nature of hope allows goal achievement to further nurture agency and pathways into even higher levels of hope. However, as with the other dimensions of PsyCap, realism is required for hope to be effective. False hope is certainly a potential threat, and it is also likely that we have an inverted, U-shaped relationship between hope and success. At some point, where hope becomes unrealistic, performance may precipitously decline along with success.

Unrealistically hopeful organizations or individuals may commit their energy and resources to goals that are beyond their reach. They may also fall into the trap of escalation of commitment and continue to enthusiastically pursue goals that may be challenging but that are no longer strategically significant or realistically attainable. Snyder (1995a) advises that along with hope development, the skill of "regoaling" is necessary to continuously redirect the energies and creativity of hopeful individuals to the right goals and away from obsolete goals or those that have proven over time to be unachievable.

Another potential pitfall for high-hope organizations and their members is to fall into "the end justifies the means" type of mentality. In their relentless pursuit of valuable organizational or personal goals, some hopeful individuals may be tempted to seek pathways that compromise their own and their organization's ethical values or social responsibility in relation to internal or external stakeholders. For example, some personal goals, agency, and pathways may be self-serving. Other goals may benefit one group of stakeholders at the expense of others, as is the case in situations such as union-management negotiations, interdepartmental competition, or shareholder wealth maximization.

On the other hand, a clearly communicated and emphasized set of organizational values, along with the proper alignment of individual, group, and organizational goals and objectives, may help guide and channel hope's willpower and waypower toward appropriate and ethically sound goals. Coupled with an equitable contingent reward system and authentic leadership, the resulting agreed-upon goals and means are likely to balance and support the needs and rights of various stakeholders. The reward system and authentic leadership can contribute to maintaining the organization's vision and enhancing its reputation and long-term, veritable, sustained performance (Avolio & Luthans, 2006; Youssef & Luthans, 2003).

Finally, as the PsyCap hope-development process takes place, let us not allow the nobleness of the cause to obscure the joy of the journey. Organizations, managers, and employees are well advised not only to admire hope's agency and pathways as terminal outcomes but also to enjoy the hope-building process, in which the components of hope are developed and maintained. Goal-setting, stretching goals, stepping, and regoaling should be perceived as invaluable to learning, growth, and self-actualization experiences. Participation, delegation, and other agency-development techniques should be designed to be perceived as opportunities for gradually increasing autonomy and responsibility rather than useless, time-wasting management fads or ways for shifting blame. Building pathways should enhance managers' and employees' creative decision-making and problem-solving repertoire and allow these hopeful organizational participants to continuously overcome frustrating obstacles and blocked routes. This PsyCap hope-building is beneficial for lifelong learning and adaptation, both personally and professionally. For those with PsyCap hope, blockages in goal achievement can be viewed as challenges and opportunities for development rather than as dead ends and excuses for disengagement, apathy, and stagnation.

FUTURE IMPLICATIONS AND DIRECTIONS
FOR PSYCAP HOPE RESEARCH AND PRACTICE

As a criteria-meeting PsyCap capacity, hope represents an invaluable but overlooked resource for human resource development and management. We conclude this chapter on PsyCap hope with some potential areas for future research and practice.

- Particularly with PsyCap hope (and optimism, as we discuss in the next chapter), the possibility for its development leading to "too much of a good thing" needs to be recognized and explored. Conceptually, Snyder (1995a) recommends, the development of hope should also constitute enhancing the skill of regoaling to avoid "false hope" or the inverted U-shaped relationship between hope and performance that we suggested in our discussion. Empirically examining such a relationship, as well as the situational contingencies that may influence its shape and threshold point(s), may be challenging but ultimately necessary for effective application. Empirical research across diverse organizational populations can contribute to such a broader spectrum of hope and performance levels. Moreover, studying and understanding "outliers," whom researchers or practicing managers may ordinarily dismiss as "too hopeful" or "too hopeless," may be of key importance.
- Relevant to the above point is the need for using more diversified tools for assessing PsyCap hope in order to triangulate findings. For example, earlier in this chapter, we mentioned how supplementing our unexpected quantitative findings on some "outliers" who exhibited high hope but low performance or satisfaction with qualitative follow-up interviews could help in better understanding some of the dysfunctional organizational factors that may have led to the frustration of some high-hopers. Embedding researchers in organizations to examine how hope is developed and how it manifests in communications, for example, would be a very useful avenue to pursue in future research.
- As more empirical research emerges, meta-analytical studies of PsyCap hope can also more accurately and comprehensively depict the breadth of these complex and possibly nonlinear relationships while also exploring potential mediating and/or moderating factors.

- In his conceptualization of hope, Snyder (1993) contends that there is a continuous reiteration between the analysis of agency and pathways related to a goal in one's cognitive activity, with hope reflecting the cumulative level of perceived agency and pathways. However, the current instruments available to assess PsyCap hope (Snyder, 2000; Snyder, et al., 1996) give hope's willpower and waypower equal additive weights. Further development in this area could account for the potential interactions between the agency and pathways components of hope, as well as any potential situational factors that may influence the relative weights that these two components bear on one's hopefulness and performance.
- We suspect that it is not only what the leader does and says but also the attributes of the leader that may give them a better starting point for building PsyCap hope. We need to learn more about how the characteristics of the leader, as well as the nature of the context, contribute to PsyCap hope development. Also, one area that needs to be examined more closely is how the impression-management strategies used by the leader contribute to PsyCap hope.
- Short interventions to boost PsyCap hope need to be explored to determine ways that both leaders' and followers' willpower and waypower can be enhanced. As with the other PsyCap components, we know relatively little about the type of interventions that will build and sustain the highest levels of PsyCap hope.
- Finally, the implications of potential cross-level issues, upward and downward spirals, contagion effects, and cross-cultural differences that we presented for PsyCap self-efficacy in the last chapter are also relevant to future PsyCap hope research and practice.

REFERENCES

Adams, V. H., Snyder, C. R., Rand, K. L., King, E. A., Sigmon, D. R., & Pulvers, K. M. (2003). Hope in the workplace. In R. Giacolone & C. Jurkiewicz (Eds.), *Handbook of workplace spirituality and organizational performance* (pp.367–377). New York: Sharpe.

Allen, N. J., & Meyer, J. P. (1990). The measurement and antecedents of affective, continuance and normative commitment to the organization. *Journal of Occupational Psychology, 63,* 1–18.

Avolio, B. J. (2004). Examining the full range model of leadership: Looking back to transform forward. In D. Day & S. Zaccarro (Eds.), *Leadership development for transforming organizations* (pp. 71–98). Mahwah, NJ: Erlbaum.

Avolio, B. J., & Luthans, F. (2006). *The high impact leader.* New York: McGraw-Hill.

Bryant, F. B., & Cvengros, J. A. (2004). Distinguishing hope and optimism. *Journal of Social and Clinical Psychology, 23,* 273–302.

Buckingham, M., & Clifton, D. (2001). *Now, discover your strengths.* New York: Free Press.

Buckingham, M., & Coffman, C. (1999). *First, break all the rules: What the world's greatest managers do differently.* New York: Free Press.

Byrne, J. (2005). The Fast Company interview: Jeff Immelt. *Fast Company, 96,* 60–65.

Carifio, J., & Rhodes, L. (2002). Construct validities and empirical relationships between optimism, hope, self-efficacy, and locus of control. *Work, 19,* 125–136.

Conger, J., & Kanungo, R. (1988). The empowerment process: Integrating theory and practice. *Academy of Management Review, 31,* 471–482.

Curry, L. A., Snyder, C. R., Cook, D. I., Ruby, B. C., & Rehm, M. (1997). The role of hope in student-athlete academic and sport achievement. *Journal of Personality and Social Psychology, 73,* 1257–1267.

Fordyce, M. W. (1988). A review of research on the happiness measures: A sixty second index of happiness and health. *Social Indicators Research, 20,* 355–381.

Friedman, T. L. (2005). *The world is flat.* New York: Farrar, Straus and Giroux.

Hackman, J., & Oldham, G. (1980). *Work redesign.* Reading, MA: Addison-Wesley.

Harter, J., Schmidt, F., & Hayes, T. (2002). Business-unit-level relationship between employee satisfaction, employee engagement, and business outcomes: A meta-analysis. *Journal of Applied Psychology, 87,* 268–279.

Jensen, S. M., & Luthans, F. (2002). The impact of hope in the entrepreneurial process: Exploratory research findings. In *Decision Sciences Institute Conference Proceedings.* San Diego, CA.

Judge, T. A., Thoresen, C. J., Bono, J. E., & Patton, G. K. (2001). The job satisfaction–job performance relationship: A qualitative and quantitative review. *Psychological Bulletin, 127,* 376–407.

Katz, R. (1974). Skills of an effective administrator. *Harvard Business Review, 52,* 90–102.

Kwon, P. (2000). Hope and dysphoria: The moderating role of defense mechanisms. *Journal of Personality, 68,* 199–223.

Latham, G. (2000). Motivate employee performance through goal-setting. In E. Locke (Ed.), *Handbook of principles of organizational behavior* (pp. 107–119). Oxford, UK: Blackwell.

Latham, G., Erez, M., & Locke, E. (1988). Resolving scientific disputes by the joint design of crucial experiments by the antagonists: Application to the Erez-Latham dispute regarding participation in goal setting. *Journal of Applied Psychology, 73,* 753–772.

Latham, G., Winters, D., & Locke, E. (1994). Cognitive and motivational effects of participation: A mediator study. *Journal of Organizational Behavior, 15,* 49–63.

Locke, E., & Latham, G. (1990). *A theory of goal setting and task performance.* Englewood Cliffs, NJ: Prentice Hall.

Luthans, F. (2002a). The need for and meaning of positive organizational behavior. *Journal of Organizational Behavior, 23,* 695–706.

Luthans, F. (2002b). Positive organizational behavior: Developing and managing psychological strengths. *Academy of Management Executive, 16,* 57–72.

Luthans, F., Avey, J. B., Avolio, B. J., Norman, S. M., & Combs, G. J. (2006). Psychological capital development: Toward a micro-intervention. *Journal of Organizational Behavior, 27,* 387–393.

Luthans, F., & Avolio, B. J. (2003). Authentic leadership: A positive development approach. In K. S. Cameron, J. E. Dutton, & R. E. Quinn (Eds.), *Positive organizational scholarship* (pp. 241–258). San Francisco: Berrett-Koehler.

Luthans, F., Avolio, B., Avey, J., & Norman, S. (2006). Psychological capital: Measurement and relationship with performance and satisfaction (Working Paper No. 2006–1). Gallup Leadership Institute, University of Nebraska–Lincoln.

Luthans, F., Avolio, B. J., Walumbwa, F. O., & Li, W. (2005). The psychological capital of Chinese workers: Exploring the relationship with performance. *Management and Organization Review, 1,* 247–269.

Luthans, F., & Jensen, S. M. (2002). Hope: A new positive strength for human resource development. *Human Resource Development Review, 1,* 304–322.

Luthans, F., Norman, S., & Hughes, L. (2006). Authentic leadership: A new approach for a new time. In R. Burke & C. Cooper (Eds.), *Inspiring leaders* (pp. 84–104). London: Routledge, Taylor & Francis.

Luthans, F., Van Wyk, R., & Walumbwa, F. O. (2004). Recognition and development of hope for South African organizational leaders. *Leadership and Organization Development Journal, 25,* 512–527.

Luthans, F., & Youssef, C. M. (2004). Human, social and now positive psychological capital management: Investing in people for competitive advantage. *Organizational Dynamics, 33,* 143–160.

Luthans, K. W. (2000). Recognition: A powerful, but often overlooked leadership tool to improve employee performance. *Journal of Leadership Studies, 7,* 31–39.

Magaletta, P. R., & Oliver, J. M. (1999). The hope construct, will and ways: Their relations with self-efficacy, optimism, and well being. *Journal of Clinical Psychology, 55,* 539–551.

Oldham, G., & Hackman, J. (1980). Work design in the organizational context. *Research in Organizational Behavior, 2,* 247–278.

Onwuegbuzie, A. J., & Snyder, C. R. (2000). Relations between hope and graduate students' coping strategies for studying and examination taking. *Psychological Reports, 86,* 803–806.

Peterson, S. J., & Luthans, F. (2003). The positive impact and development of hopeful leaders. *Leadership and Organization Development Journal, 24*(1), 26–31.

Peterson, S. J., & Luthans, F. (2006). The impact of financial and nonfinancial incentives on business-unit outcomes over time. *Journal of Applied Psychology, 91,* 156–165.

Pfeffer, J. (1998). *The human equation.* Boston: Harvard Business School Press.

Range, L., & Pentin, S. (1994). Hope, hopelessness and suicidality in college students. *Psychological Reports, 75,* 456–458.

Scioli, A., Chamberlin, C., Samor, C. M., LaPointe, A. B., Campbell, T. L., MacLeod, A. R., & McLenon, J. A. (1997). A prospective study of hope, optimism, and health. *Psychological Reports, 81,* 723–733.

Snyder, C. R. (1993). Hope for the journey. In A. P. Turnbull, J. M. Patterson, S. K. Behr, D. L. Murphy, J. G. Marquis, & M. J. Blue-Banning (Eds.), *Cognitive coping, families, and disability* (pp. 271–286). Baltimore, MD: Paul H. Brooks.

Snyder, C. R. (1994). Hope and optimism. *Encyclopedia of human behavior* (Vol. 2, pp. 535–542). San Diego: Academic Press.

Snyder, C. R. (1995a). Conceptualizing, measuring, and nurturing hope. *Journal of Counseling and Development, 73,* 355–360.

Snyder, C. R. (1995b). Managing for high hope. *R&D Innovator, 4*(6), 6–7.

Snyder, C. R. (2000). *Handbook of hope.* San Diego: Academic Press.

Snyder, C. R. (2002). Hope theory: Rainbows in the mind. *Psychological Inquiry, 13,* 249–275.

Snyder, C. R., Harris, C., Anderson, J. R., Holleran, S. A., Irving, L. M., Sigmon, S. T., Yoshinobu, L., Gibb, J., Langelle, C., & Harney, P. (1991). The will and the ways. Development and validation of an individual-differences measure of hope. *Journal of Personality and Social Psychology, 60,* 570–585.

Snyder, C. R., Ilardi, S., Michael, S. T., & Cheavens, J. (2000). Hope theory: Updating a common process for psychological change. In C. R. Snyder & R. E. Ingram (Eds.), *Handbook of psychological change: Psychotherapy processes and practices for the 21st century* (pp. 128–153). New York: John Wiley & Sons.

Snyder, C. R., Irving, L., & Anderson, J. (1991). Hope and health: Measuring the will and the ways. In C. R. Snyder & D. R. Forsyth (Eds.), *Handbook of social and clinical psychology* (pp. 285–305). Elmsford, NY: Pergamon.

Snyder, C. R., Rand, K. L., & Sigmon, D. R. (2002). Hope theory. In C. R. Snyder & S. Lopez (Eds.), *Handbook of positive psychology* (pp. 257–276). Oxford, UK: Oxford University Press.

Snyder, C. R., Sympson, S. C., Ybasco, F. C., Borders, T. F., Babyak, M. A., & Higgins, R. L. (1996). Development and validation of the state hope scale. *Journal of Personality and Social Psychology, 70,* 321–335.

Snyder, C. R., Tran, T., Schroeder, L. L., Pulvers, K. M., Adam, III, V., & Laub, L. (2000, Summer). Teaching the hope recipe: Setting goals, finding pathways to those goals, and getting motivated. *National Educational Service,* 46–50.

Spreitzer, G. (1995). Individual empowerment in the workplace: Dimensions, measurement, and validation. *Academy of Management Journal, 38,* 1442–1465.

Srivastra, S. (1986). *Executive power.* San Francisco: Jossey-Bass.

Stajkovic, A. D., & Luthans, F. (1997). A meta-analysis of the effects of organizational behavior modification on task performance: 1975–95. *Academy of Management Journal, 40,* 1122–1149.

Stajkovic, A., & Luthans F. (2003) Behavioral management and task performance in organizations: Conceptual background, meta-analysis, and test of alternative models. *Personnel Psychology, 56,* 155–194.

Veninga, R. L. (2000). Managing hope in the workplace: Five simple strategies can help transform organizations. *Health Progress, 81,* 22–24.

Wagner, III, J., Leana, C., Locke, E., & Schweiger, D. (1997). Cognitive and motivational frameworks in research on participation: A meta-analysis of effects. *Journal of Organizational Behavior, 18,* 49–65.

Youssef, C. M. (2004). *Resiliency development of organizations, leaders and employees: Multilevel theory building and individual-level, path-analytical empirical testing.* Unpublished doctoral dissertation, University of Nebraska–Lincoln.

Youssef, C. M., & Luthans, F. (2003). Immigrant psychological capital: Contribution to the war for talent and competitive advantage. *Singapore Nanyang Business Review, 2*(2), 1–14.

Youssef, C. M., & Luthans, F. (2005a). A positive organizational behavior approach to ethical performance. In R. Giacalone, C. Jurkiewicz, & C. Dunn (Eds.), *Positive psychology in business ethics and corporate social responsibility* (pp. 1–22). Greenwich, CT: Information Age.

Youssef, C. M., & Luthans, F. (2005b). Resiliency development of organizations, leaders & employees: Multi-level theory building for sustained performance. In W. Gardner, B. Avolio, & F. Walumbwa (Eds.), *Monographs in leadership and management: Volume 3. Authentic leadership theory and practice: Origins, effects and development* (pp. 303–343). Oxford, UK: Elsevier.

Youssef, C. M., & Luthans, F. (2006). Time for positivity in the Middle East: Developing hopeful Egyptian organizational leaders. In W. Mobley & E. Weldon (Eds.), *Advances in global leadership* (Vol. 4). Oxford, UK: Elsevier.

CHAPTER 4

PsyCap Optimism

Realistic and Flexible

OPTIMISM IS ONE of the most talked about but least understood psychological strengths. In everyday language, an optimist is one who expects positive and desirable events in the future, while a pessimist is one who constantly has negative thoughts and is convinced that undesirable events will happen.

As an important criteria-meeting capacity of PsyCap, optimism has this surface meaning, but it means much more. PsyCap optimism is not just about predicting that good things will happen in the future. More importantly, PsyCap optimism depends on the reasons and attributions one uses to explain why certain events occur, whether positive or negative, past, present, or future. For instance, you may spend a lot of time and energy focusing on positive events, but if you do not interpret them using an optimistic explanatory style, you may still be on the pessimistic side. As with the previous two chapters on PsyCap efficacy and hope, the following reflection exercise on optimism will help you dig deeper and go beyond what your future forecasts look like. These detailed questions can help shape the impact that various past, present, and future life events have on your own PsyCap optimism, and they will be used to help you better understand the rest of this chapter's more in-depth discussion of PsyCap optimism.

PERSONAL REFLECTIONS EXERCISE ON PSYCAP OPTIMISM

We first ask you to identify a highly memorable positive event that recently occurred in your life. It can be a work achievement, a pleasant family event, an exciting surprise, a new relationship, the revival of an old friendship, a successful purchase, or a philanthropic act. Any event that you consider favorable will qualify for this reflection exercise.

Once you can vividly recall the details of this event, answer as best you can the following questions. Remember, the more honest and thorough you are in your responses, the more insights you can gain as you delve into understanding PsyCap optimism in the rest of the chapter.

- Describe your selected positive event in detail by including your thoughts, feelings, and behaviors before, during, and after the event occurred, as well as those of anyone else involved. (Spending a little more time and attention on this should make the rest of the questions easier and faster to answer.)
- What are the possible reasons and circumstances that led to the occurrence of this favorable event?
- Which of these reasons would you give yourself credit for? In other words, which of the factors that led to the event were controlled by you?
- In what ways was this control expressed and utilized to cause the positive event to occur?
- Which of the factors would you consider to be beyond your control (e.g., luck, other people, external circumstances, and so on)?
- To what extent do you believe each of the external factors contributed to the occurrence of the positive event?
- Of the external factors you identified, are there any that you could have had control over? If so, how?
- Why do you think that you did not need to (or choose to) exhibit control over the factors that you did have power over?

Now that you have reflected on the circumstances, causes, and consequences of the selected positive event, we ask you to shift your thinking to a more future-oriented perspective and to answer the following questions.

- Do you believe that this positive event can happen again in the future?
- Of the factors that you believe to have contributed to the positive event, including both the ones that are in your control and the ones that are not, which one(s) can you safely count on to almost always exist should you need it (or them) in the future? Which one(s) do you consider to be temporary, one-time happenstances?
- Of the factors that you believe to have contributed to the positive event, both the ones that are in your control and the ones that are not, which one(s) do you believe can also be useful in other situations and events that may occur in your life in the future? Which ones do you consider to be specific to only this situation or to substantially similar ones?
- What would you do differently should you be in this same situation in the future?

Next, spend some time identifying a highly memorable negative event that you recently encountered. Again, it can be in any of your life domains, as long as you consider it unfavorable and significant enough to warrant your analysis. Once you can bring the details of this negative event to memory, we ask you to go through a similar set of questions as for the just-completed positive event analysis.

- Start off by describing in detail the negative event. Remember to address your thoughts, feelings, and behaviors before, during, and after the selected negative event.
- What are the possible causes that you believe may have led to the occurrence of this unfavorable event?
- Which of these causal factors would you consider to be beyond your control (e.g., bad luck, other people's fault, external circumstances)?
- To what extent do you believe each of the external factors contributed to the occurrence of this negative event?
- Which of the reasons that caused this unfortunate event would you blame on yourself?
- What decisions and actions did you make in trying to prevent or handle the situation?
- Which of your decisions and actions do you think were especially effective in managing the situation?

- What mistakes do you believe you personally committed, either in causing or in handing this situation?
- How could you have prevented or managed the situation in order to avoid or better deal with it?
- Overall, could you have exerted any more control than you did over any of the factors that you believe to have caused this negative event? If so, how?

Now at this point, switch your thinking to the future, and answer the following questions.

- Do you believe that this negative event can happen again in your lifetime?
- Of the factors that you believe to have contributed to the negative event, both the ones that are in your control and the ones that are not, which one(s) are you worried will continue into the future? Which one(s) do you consider to be temporary, one-time setbacks?
- Of the factors that you believe may have contributed to the negative event, both the ones that are in your control and the ones that are not, which one(s) do you feel threatened by in other future situations that you may encounter? Which one(s) do you consider to be specific only to this or to very similar situations?
- What would you do differently should you be in this situation in the future?

These questions and your answers have hopefully immersed you in thinking about the causes and your explanations of positive and negative situations and events with which you have personally encountered. This self-reflection should serve as a good point of departure for better understanding the process of PsyCap optimism.

PSYCAP OPTIMISM AS AN EXPLANATORY OR ATTRIBUTIONAL STYLE

As presented by Martin Seligman, a former president of the American Psychological Association and the recognized father of the positive psychology movement, optimism is an explanatory style that attributes positive events to personal, permanent, and pervasive causes and interprets negative events in terms of external, temporary, and situation-specific factors. On the other hand, a pessimistic explanatory style would interpret positive events with external, temporary, and situation-specific attributes and explain negative events in terms of personal, permanent, and pervasive causes (Seligman, 1998).

Based on this widely recognized definitional framework, optimists take credit for the positive happenstances in their lives. They view the causes of these desirable events as being within their power and control. Optimists would expect these causes to continue to exist into the future and to be useful in handling other situations across life domains. Thus, their optimistic explanatory style allows them to positively view and internalize the good aspects of their lives not only in the past and the present, but also into the future. For example, optimistic employees who received some positive feedback and recognition from their supervisor will attribute this positive moment to their work ethic, and they will assure themselves that they will always be able to work hard and be successful not only in this job, but in any endeavor they choose.

By the same token, when experiencing negative events or when faced with undesirable situations, optimistic people attribute the causes to be external, temporary, and specific to the situation. Thus, they continue to remain positive and confident about their future. For example, if optimistic employees receive negative feedback regarding, say, a report they presented, they will probably use rationalizations, such as they were not themselves when they worked on or presented the report, that their colleagues did not provide the necessary information to enhance the quality of the report, or that the boss was simply in a bad mood when giving the negative feedback. The report was really not that bad after all, and it certainly will not be in the future.

In contrast to this optimistic explanatory style, pessimists do not give themselves credit for the positive events that occur in their lives. For example, a pessimistic person who has just received a promotion might explain it in terms of external reasons, such as good luck, other candidates lacking the needed experience, the job being undesirable, and so forth. In addition, the attributional causes that pessimists use tend to be temporary and specific to the situation, and thus they believe that positive events hold little chance of happening again in the future.

Moreover, pessimists tend to blame themselves for the negative aspects of their lives. They internalize the causes of unfortunate situations and negative events. They assume that bad things will continue to exist for them into the future and threaten their success and well-being not only in similar situations, but across all domains of their life. For example, pessimists who just got passed over for a promotion may attribute this to, for example, their lack of intelligence. They will tend to dwell on the assumption that their intelligence deficit will continue to haunt them in the future. They assume that it will not only affect their career but may also ruin their relationships and destroy any chances they might have for higher education, training, or even an alternative career path.

So, how did you come out? Go back to your answers to the questions you reflected on in the beginning of the exercise. Review the causes you used to explain the positive event that you experienced. If most of those causes are factors that you believe to be in your control and thus are able to take the credit for them, then you are making personal attributions, which are in line with an optimistic explanatory style. Moreover, if you expect those factors to always be there over time and across situations, then you are making permanent and pervasive attributions, which are also consistent with an optimistic explanatory style. On the other hand, if most of the reasons you came up with for your identified positive event were not in your power to control, were temporary, or were situation specific, then you were using a pessimistic explanatory style. This pessimism comes through even though you were reflecting on a positive event or situation.

Next, examine the causes that you used to explain your selected negative event. If you mostly attributed causes to being external, temporary, and situation specific, one-time occurrences, then you are using an optimistic explanatory style. You are revealing an optimistic tendency when you are faced with and in how you handle negative events. On the other hand, if you mostly blamed yourself and dwelled on the permanence and pervasiveness of the causes of this negative event, then you are exhibiting more of a pessimistic explanatory style.

OTHER CONCEPTIONS OF PSYCAP OPTIMISM

In line with our chapter's opening statement, optimism is a construct that is frequently used but inadequately comprehended as a psychological strength. Several other definitions of optimism beside Seligman's explanatory or attributional style are present in various literatures. For example, optimism has been negatively viewed as emotional, shallow, irrational, unrealistic, and even as a misleading illusion (e.g., Taylor, 1989; Tiger, 1979). Moreover, a number of research studies present optimism as a dispositional personality trait, a general tendency to expect favorable events and positive outcomes to occur in the future more frequently than negative ones (e.g., Scheier & Carver, 1987).

Such traditional perspectives of optimism, of course, run counter to our state-like, open-to-development criterion of PsyCap. We will directly address and resolve these different perspectives from PsyCap optimism in the next section, which concerns realistic, flexible optimism. Suffice it to say for now that our operationalization of optimism as it relates to the workplace emphasizes the positive psychology definition of optimism as an attributional, explanatory style, but it does not preclude its emotional dimensions, its future orientation, or its motivational benefits. In fact, you have already assessed some of these aspects in your reflection exercise. For example, you were asked to assess not only your thoughts and cognitions but also your feelings and behaviors, as well as those of others. You have also given some thought to what you would do differently should those situations or similar ones occur again in the future.

There is ongoing debate regarding the frequently assumed but rarely tested unidimensionality of optimism and pessimism (see Peterson & Chang, 2002, for a comprehensive review). Although optimism and pessimism are usually negatively correlated, the way these constructs have been studied precludes definitive answers regarding their independence. Researchers often only focus on specific outcomes of interest. Some focus exclusively on positive outcomes as they relate to optimism, including physical and mental health and well-being (Peterson, 1999; Peterson & Bossio, 1991; Scheier & Carver, 1987, 1992; Seeman, 1989), effective coping with difficult life situations (Lazarus & Folkman, 1984; Scheier & Carver, 1985), recovery from illness (Scheier, Matthews, Owen, Magovern, Lefebvre, et al., 1989) and addiction (Strack, Carver, & Blaney, 1987), and life satisfaction and "authentic happiness" (Seligman, 2002). Indeed, optimism has been shown to positively relate to many desirable outcomes, including workplace performance (Luthans, Avolio, Avey, & Norman, 2006; Luthans, Avolio, Walumbwa, & Li, 2005; Seligman, 1998) and performance in various other life domains, such as education, sports, and politics (Peterson & Barrett, 1987; Peterson & Seligman, 2004; Prola & Stern, 1984; Seligman, 2002).

On the other hand, clinical psychology researchers have focused on negative outcomes, such as depression (Abrahamson, Metalsky, & Alloy, 1989; Peterson & Seligman, 1984), physical illness (Peterson, Seligman, & Vaillant, 1988), and poor performance in general. However, there is very limited research, if any, on optimism and pessimism, as well as their positive and negative outcomes, in a parallel, comprehensive manner. Studying the broad perspective of optimism and pessimism seems necessary in order to fully understand the broad spectrum of implications, possible extrapolations, and potential discontinuities.

As an example, in the reflective questions that we asked you to answer in the opening exercise, we could have only asked you to analyze a positive event. You would have then probably concluded that you have an optimistic explanatory style because most of your explanations of the positive event were personal, permanent, and pervasive (i.e., you probably would employ the well-known, self-serving bias of positive events). On the other hand, if you had used external, temporary, and situation-specific causes, the opposite conclusion of being a pessimist would have been made. By asking you to analyze both a positive and a negative event, we have increased the probability of more accurately uncovering the various explanatory styles that you use. For instance, if you used personal, permanent, and pervasive explanations in both positive and negative situations, you now have a better understanding that your explanatory style is optimistic with respect to your positive event but pessimistic with respect to your negative event. In other words, you can be both an optimist and a pessimist, depending on the nature of the event. Even further in-depth understanding can be accomplished by analyzing more than one event in each category. We will return to this important situational contingency issue of optimism and pessimism toward the end of the chapter.

THE REALISTIC AND FLEXIBLE QUALIFIERS FOR PSYCAP OPTIMISM

Optimism, like hope, has considerable intuitive appeal and is often associated with many positive and desirable outcomes. However, a nonscrutinizing optimistic explanatory style may have some undesirable side effects or even dangerous implications. In particular, nondiscriminatory, blatantly optimistic people may expose themselves to higher risks. They may underestimate the potential dangers of those risks (Davidson & Prkachin, 1997; Kok, Ho, Heng, & Ong, 1990; Peterson & Chang, 2002; Weinstein, 1989). For example, generally healthy people may decide to eat an unhealthy and imbalanced diet, exercise less, and expose themselves to tremendous amounts of stress at work. They reason that since they have had no problems to date, they optimistically assume they can handle such risk factors.

Moreover, if optimists expose themselves, their organization, units, coworkers, friends, and family to increased risks, and negative consequences result, they are less likely to learn from their mistakes. This is because they will externalize the risk factors. Unrealistic optimists fail to take charge and properly analyze the situation to understand which causes could have been personal, permanent, or pervasive and which can be safely externalized or less emphasized as temporary or situation specific. For example, it would be very irresponsible and potentially dangerous for a safety engineer to adopt an optimistic explanatory style and proceed to shift the blame to somebody or something else every time an accident takes place instead of updating and enforcing safety regulations. However, even if the safety engineer performs all the necessary responsibilities, an accident may still take place at some point in time. In this situation, once the causes have been analyzed and determined to be beyond this engineer's control, she should then be able to accept an external, temporary, and situation-specific interpretation of this unfortunate event in order to move on and overcome this setback. In other words, we would advocate that the engineer use what Peterson (2000, p. 51) refers to as "flexible optimism." In this flexible PsyCap optimism, the individual tries to correctly appraise the situation and then choose when to utilize optimistic or pessimistic explanatory styles.

Unfortunately, explanatory styles are based on one's subjective perceptions and attributions, which may not always be realistic or allow flexibility. Optimistic individuals may try to exert too much control over their lives and their destinies, thinking that if they try hard enough, they will always be successful, and that they should take credit for their success. Putting such high expectations and pressures on oneself can have undesirable consequences. For example, Peterson and Chang (2002) found that unrealistic optimism exacerbates the negative implications of repeated negative life events on physical health and psychological well-being. In other words, as the unwarranted sense of agency that optimists possess was challenged, they could not repeatedly externalize negative events (as optimists are supposed to do), and they suffered physically and emotionally. This is also in line with the research that supports the relationship between angry, aggressive personalities and susceptibility to physical problems, such as hypertension, diabetes, and heart disease (Dolnick, 1995). Seligman (1998) also supports the contention that one of the primary causes of experiencing helplessness is the increased emphasis on the self and the decreased interest in factors beyond oneself (e.g., family, religion, or national commitment). These are reasons why Schneider (2001, p. 250) advocates the need for "realistic optimism."

For PsyCap, we emphasize the need for the strength of optimism to be realistic and flexible. Effective PsyCap optimism should not take extremes, either in internalizing success and trying to take control of every aspect of one's work life, or in externalizing all types of failure and thus shirking responsibility.

Realistic, flexible PsyCap optimism should not be portrayed as just another feel-good, illusive ego boost. PsyCap optimism represents a strong lesson in self-discipline, analysis of past events, contingency planning, and preventive care. PsyCap optimism also comprehensively combines most of the earlier conceptualizations and multiple facets of optimism.

For PsyCap, we propose that realistic, flexible optimists can enjoy and learn from various life course and workplace events (or what we call trigger moments) to the fullest (Avolio & Luthans, 2006). In good times, those with high PsyCap optimism are able to enjoy both the cognitive and emotional implications of being able to take credit for their success and to be in control of their destinies without unknowingly exposing themselves to added risk or to others' disdain.

Those with high PsyCap optimism are also able to express their thanks and appreciation to relevant others and to factors that may have contributed to their success. They are able to capitalize on the opportunities that the situation may present them with, develop their skills and abilities, and thus improve their chances in the future. By the same token, in bad times, they are able to sift through the noise, find the facts, learn from their mistakes, accept what they cannot change, and move on.

DO WE NEED EMPLOYEES WITH PSYCAP OPTIMISM?

Before getting into the obvious implications that PsyCap optimism has for organizational leaders, what about employees in general? We all realize that today's employees are functioning in an environment that is very different from what used to exist not too long ago. Change and uncertainty have now become the norm. Not only is the frequency of change increasing, but the nature of today's and tomorrow's changes is fundamentally different. This change is cutting through the very core of every employee's job. The boundaries have become blurred across various jobs and professions. Not only media commentators, authors, and professors, but employees themselves are observing and experiencing how their jobs are evolving and changing as their organization transforms itself to match the turbulent environment.

To take an example of one firm that we are very familiar with, we have repeatedly witnessed how its ability to stay on top with respect to its value-based strategies and practices has been greatly facilitated by employees who are able to accept, enjoy, and capitalize on their continuously changing roles. Employees at this firm no longer define themselves using a job title but instead refer to their respective roles as "what I am paid to do." They now expect to change as frequently as necessary for their organization to stay on top in an increasingly competitive industry.

Even in professions that were traditionally considered stable and structured, enormous changes are currently taking place. For example, the plethora of accounting scandals culminated in the enactment of the Sarbanes-Oxley Act in 2002, and the face of the accounting profession as we knew it became dramatically changed (e.g., see Gullapalli, 2005). The same is true of most jobs. For example, technology workers who thought they were on the cutting edge are finding that their knowledge repeatedly faces premature obsolescence as new advances are introduced. And the list goes on.

Optimistic and pessimistic employees react very differently to these turbulent times. Optimists are more likely to embrace the changes, see the opportunities that the future holds, and focus on capitalizing on those opportunities. Optimists will react differently than pessimists to changes that cause adverse consequences. Downsizing is a classic example. A realistically optimistic employee will tend to attribute being laid off to the current economic and technological environment. Optimists interpret the layoff as being due to external, temporary, and situation-specific causal factors rather than indulging in feelings of inadequacy and self-blame. This optimistic explanatory style will help downsized employees have positive expectations about the future (e.g., the economy will improve; I can retool my technical know-how) and to act on these expectations with agency and motivation (e.g., I am going back to school to better prepare myself to ride the next wave).

Thus, an optimistic explanatory style would help employees in taking charge and being in control of their own destiny. Importantly, this optimistic processing of events is likely to cause their positive outlook to actually come true. In other words, PsyCap optimism can lead to a self-fulfilling prophecy (Peterson & Chang, 2002) and can be both motivated and motivating (Peterson, 2000) to achieving long-term success.

This value of employee PsyCap optimism can also draw from what has been identified as "career resiliency" (Waterman, Waterman, & Collard, 1994), which is discussed in the next chapter on PsyCap resiliency. As applied to optimism, today's organizations are in great need of career-resilient employees who realize that they are responsible for their own careers, for reinventing themselves to make their skills marketable (i.e., employable) and useful for their current and future employers. Career resiliency combines flexibility and adaptability with proactive, self-initiated development and continuous learning. Realistic, flexible optimism is a PsyCap capacity that can be of tremendous value for employees to build such career resiliency on more objective, self-assessments while at the same time having optimistic employees welcoming challenges with less fear, resistance, and self-doubt.

Employees' capacity to work independently is increasingly becoming necessary, not only for their career management but also for their effective performance in most jobs. Many organizations today are eliminating middle-management levels and flattening their hierarchies in hopes of enhancing their speed, responsiveness, interactive teamwork, and quality of communication. However, flattened structures also increase managers' span of control, making it impossible for them to provide close supervision. Again, optimistic and pessimistic employees will interpret this situation very differently. Optimists will welcome the challenge and enjoy being able to take credit for their accomplishments. Pessimists, on the other hand, will likely dwell on incidences of failure or poor performance and stunt their own growth opportunities as they continue to seek their lost structure and certainty in their work lives.

Seligman's (1998) work with the huge Metropolitan Life Insurance sales staff demonstrates the performance impact that optimistic employees can have. He found that optimistic sales representatives outsold pessimistic ones over time, even among those who had initially failed the traditional industry selection test. Seligman concludes that optimism is extremely important in insurance sales positions, maybe even beyond technical knowledge. We augment this argument by also proposing that an optimistic explanatory style may have promoted further technical self-development that may have corrected some of the initial knowledge deficiencies among those who failed the industry test. Pessimism, on the other hand, may have thwarted similar efforts, even among those who were initially technically competent.

In the old-paradigm environment and organizations, a slightly pessimistic workforce may have even been preferred in order to maintain responsibility, accountability, and control. Now, in the new paradigm, realistic selection for and development of employees' flexible PsyCap optimism represent a fresh opportunity for a positive, healthy, and productive workforce that is also independent, change embracing, and open to new ideas and workplace developments. Without such work forces, the chances of survival are considerably diminished.

ORGANIZATIONAL LEADERS WITH PSYCAP OPTIMISM

Would it be too risky for those in charge of today's organizations' strategic directives and decision-making to be optimistic? Would shareholders prefer that their investments be managed by conservative, and even mildly pessimistic, leaders? This "sadder-but-wiser" position has often been studied on the assumption that positivity may be associated with unrealistically favorable expectations or carelessness about the future. The heightened awareness of the needs for contingency planning and redundant systems after the dot-com bubble burst and the 9/11 tragedy exemplifies the sadder-but-wiser hypothesis (MacSweeney, 2002). However, research supports that leaders who are positive are also more authentic and effective (Avolio & Luthans, 2006; Jensen & Luthans, 2006; Luthans, Norman, & Hughes, 2006). There is also research evidence that leaders who think positively are more effective interpersonally and in terms of the quality of their decisions, including superior ability to collect and use more information and to identify and act on situational contingencies (Staw & Barsade, 1993). On the other hand, negativity has been shown to be related with various performance-inhibiting mechanisms, such as memory decay (Judge & Ilies, 2004).

As to authentic leadership, PsyCap optimism contributes to and is the result of the strong foundation of self-awareness (Avolio & Luthans, 2006; Luthans & Avolio, 2003; Luthans, Norman, & Hughes, 2006). The self-awareness of authentic leaders draws its accuracy and objectivity from multisource feedback, which is motivated by the authentic leader's genuine desire for sustainable improvement and transparent trust-building. Moreover, authentic leaders' capacity for self-regulation is conducive to adaptation, responsiveness, and continuous self-development, which are highly consistent with PsyCap optimism (Avolio & Luthans, 2006; Luthans & Avolio, 2003; Luthans, Norman, & Hughes, 2006).

Organizational leaders with a high level of PsyCap optimism are risk-takers, but because they are realistic and flexible, they tend to take only calculated and necessary risks. They know that their role is to be agents of change, not window-dressers. They dare to dream for themselves, their associates, and their organizations. They then enthusiastically pursue their dreams as they inspire, motivate, and involve their associates. In addition, however, leaders with high PsyCap optimism would have a good handle on the realities of their capacities and vulnerabilities, as well as those of their followers, and are self-aware and in control. Their PsyCap optimism motivates them to develop and improve themselves and their followers. They do not resort to blame-shifting and shallow impression-management techniques in order to take credit for more than what their efforts have warranted or to avoid responsibility or accountability. They are secure in their positive outlook and have realistic, accurate knowledge of their own and their followers' accomplishments.

Leaders with high PsyCap optimism emphasize the development of their followers. They take pride in the success of their followers rather than envying them and trying to take credit for their accomplishments as if they were their own. Most importantly, as these effective leaders develop their associates, they help them build their own realistic, flexible optimism. Rather than doing everything and making all the decisions for them, high PsyCap optimistic leaders enable, empower, delegate, and trust their followers to achieve the desired outcomes. They equip their people with the necessary knowledge, skills, abilities, and motivation not only to succeed, but also to be able to make personal, permanent, and pervasive attributions of their own.

DEVELOPING PSYCAP OPTIMISM IN TODAY'S WORKFORCE

As we noted in the introductory discussion, optimism has been depicted as both dispositional and trait-like and thus relatively fixed (e.g., Scheier, et al., 1989), but also state-like (i.e., "learned optimism," Seligman, 1998). Even though we recognize that a conceptual continuum may exist (Luthans & Avolio, 2003), in order to meet the criteria of PsyCap optimism, we emphasize its state-like, developmental properties. Specifically, PsyCap optimism can be developed by either altering a pessimistic explanatory style or enriching the dimensions of an optimistic explanatory style.

Consider Taylor, the production manager of a mid-sized electronic manufacturing plant. The plant has just failed to meet its production quota for the month. Taylor's pessimistic explanatory style would automatically drive her thought processes toward personal causes (it is my fault) that are permanent (I will never be able to meet senior management's expectations) and pervasive (I am a bad manager). Taylor is now prone to considerable stress and burnout. Moreover, if she holds on to her pessimistic explanatory style long enough, she may be a candidate for a multitude of physical and psychological problems. In addition, Taylor is likely to create negative self-fulfilling prophecies that will cause her performance to slip even further, and her attitude may result in contagious dissatisfaction, disengagement, and apathy, thereby affecting her associates.

This scenario, indicating a downward spiral of pessimism, can be avoided if this manager can be trained to adopt a more optimistic explanatory style. Schneider (2001) presents three perspectives that are particularly applicable to developing realistic optimism in the workplace:

1. leniency for the past;
2. appreciation for the present; and
3. opportunity seeking for the future.

Leniency for the past does not imply denial or an evasion of responsibility. On the contrary, in line with realistic optimism, it is a positive reframing technique that acknowledges the realities of the situation. It adopts a problem-centered coping approach toward the controllable aspects of the situation while giving oneself the benefit of the doubt and repositioning the uncontrollable aspects of the situation "in the best possible light" (Carver & Scheier, 2002). Leniency for the past can help enthusiastic managers like Taylor in managing their Type A personalities and their perfectionist tendencies. It can guide their goal-setting efforts so that they can accurately assess their resources and abilities and thus set realistic, attainable goals for themselves and their associates. This in turn can result in

Taylor creating workable plans for better utilizing the human, material, and financial resources that are within her control in order to not only meet but exceed her unit's targeted performance over time.

In the developmental process for PsyCap optimism, external attributions can be created by viewing the situation as one of high consensus, low consistency, and high distinctiveness (Kelley, 1973). If Taylor can receive some helpful feedback that (1) her plant was not the only one that did not meet this month's target (high consensus); (2) this is one of the very few times that her plant did not meet its target (low consistency); and (3) with the exception of production quantity, her plant met other performance expectations, such as quality and safety standards (high distinctiveness), then Taylor may be able to adopt a more optimistic explanatory style. Unfortunately, her regional manager may think that by sharing such positive information, Taylor may not be as motivated to work harder and meet production goals in the future. In fact, many managers fall into the trap of giving only negative feedback in such situations, thinking that this will motivate their employees to perform. Then they find out that, over time, their best associates lose their motivation and commitment to high performance.

Following Schneider's (2001) second strategy of developing realistic, flexible optimism, Taylor's explanatory style can also learn to appreciate her present. Any situation, no matter how unfavorable, has its positive aspects that can be reflected on and enjoyed. This is especially true if these aspects are also internal, permanent, and pervasive. Taylor's flexible optimism can redirect her perspective away from dwelling on the negatives and toward focusing on the positives. For example, she can learn to be thankful for the amount her plant was able to produce despite difficulties. She can still note the quality of the output, the safety of her associates, the positive relationships and teamwork that she maintains among the members of her unit, the understanding and trust of her managers and associates, and even the fact that she still has a well-paying job. Appreciation of the present can protect Taylor from a defeatist attitude, which can paralyze her planning efforts and motivation for future improvement.

Finally, if Taylor can realistically accept herself, her unit, and her organization as a "work in progress," she is more likely not only to appreciate the moment but also to look forward to the future, with all the opportunities that it presents. In fact, Taylor will be able to proactively seek and act on future opportunities for herself and her associates, based on her realistic understanding of each of their capabilities and vulnerabilities. Realistic, flexible PsyCap optimism can be a powerful tool for organizational leaders such as Taylor to inspire and motivate herself and her people to accept, and even choose, challenges to improve performance now and in the future.

THE OPTIMISTIC ORGANIZATION

Like the overall hopeful organization presented in the last chapter, can the organization also display the positive qualities associated with employees' or leaders' PsyCap optimism? We propose that in light of today's turbulence, in order for organizations even to survive, let alone thrive, they have to be optimistic. Organizations that can create sustainable competitive advantage need to emphasize an internal, permanent, and pervasive outlook that can lead to positive events now and in the future. Today's organizations cannot simply wait and react or even passively scan the environment and proactively adapt to the changes that they are facing. They have to intentionally create turbulent change themselves and break the rules of the game to their advantage, which can facilitate efficacy, as it is placing greater control in the hands of leaders. They have to create their own future, where they can be in control of their own destinies. Obviously, this is easier said than done, but successful examples speak loudly of these new realities and prove that it can be done.

Traditional sources of competitive advantage are being eroded at an accelerating rate. Organizations can no longer depend on traditional inertia-producing entry barriers along material, structural, and technological dimensions. These barriers are coming down because they are now readily available to competitors at decreasing costs; they are easily imitable, even by smaller start-ups (Luthans & Youssef, 2004). An example would be the enormous competition in the software industry from homemade (and at no cost to the user) freeware, such as Linux and Firefox.

On the other hand, organizations that capitalize on the inimitability of the human, social, and psychological capital of their valuable employees and leaders are likely to enjoy long-term competitive advantage (Pfeffer, 1998; Luthans & Youssef, 2004). For example, Southwest Airlines' long-enduring values of emphasizing people-centered practices, investing in its employees' selection and training, and not treating its employees as if they were disposable have paid off in terms of efficiency, profitability, and customer service (O'Reilly & Pfeffer, 2000). These internal, permanent, and pervasive sources of competitive advantage (i.e., Southwest's PsyCap optimism), remained viable and intact, and they helped Southwest to remain successful even in the disastrous airline industry after 9/11. Southwest refused to go with the flow of post-9/11 massive layoffs that most of its short-term-oriented competitors felt obliged to undertake.

Another case in point of the value of organizations' recognizing, investing in, and developing their PsyCap optimism can be found in their ethical decision-making and socially responsible organizational behavior. In an era where bottom-line considerations rule, organizations that have chosen to operate under morally sound values and to act in a socially responsible manner may have a hard time convincing their short-run-focused shareholders. However, over time and across situations, these organizations have been shown to prevail due to their internalized values and strong cultures (Cameron, Bright, & Caza, 2004). On the other hand, the meltdown of Enron, WorldCom, Arthur Andersen, and others stands witness to the temporary nature of a short-term profitability orientation.

Finally, in the same way that organizational leaders need to be realistic and flexible in their optimism, organizations also need to adopt realism and flexibility in optimistically interpreting the events they face, both positive and negative. Leniency for the past is necessary. Regardless of how glamorous (or infamous) an organization's history is, at some point in time, it needs to let go of the past and move on to new territories. If the past and present have been positive, a PsyCap optimistic organization would celebrate its success and extract the lessons to be learned from it. A realistic, flexible, optimistic organization would be fully cautious and aware that every success may have been temporary, situation specific, or even an external stroke of good of luck.

A PsyCap optimistic organization would not allow success to drive complacency and inertia but would continue to reinvent itself and challenge its underlying assumptions. On the other hand, even if the past and present have included failures and undesirable events, the PsyCap optimistic organization would still be able to find what is positive, to appreciate it, to learn from the controllable aspects of the situation, to give itself the benefit of the doubt about that which is truly external and uncontrollable, and to seek future opportunities accordingly.

POTENTIAL PITFALLS

Some of the traditionally discussed potential pitfalls of an optimistic explanatory style include poor physical and psychological preventive care, avoidance of responsibility and accountability, and learned helplessness as a result of overemphasized agency and individualism (see Peterson & Chang, 2002, for a comprehensive review). However, realistic, flexible optimism (i.e., PsyCap optimism) seems to overcome most of these potential pitfalls.

As we have indicated, optimistic and pessimistic explanatory styles can become self-fulfilling prophecies. Unfortunately, there has been limited discussion of the process itself or research testing the mechanisms through which one's explanatory style can lead to positive outcomes. Three general mechanisms particularly warrant our attention due to their applicability to the workplace: cognitive, social, and behavioral. People who adopt an optimistic explanatory style think, relate to others, and act in ways that actually cause more positive events to occur in their lives (i.e., become self-fulfilling). On the other hand, those with a pessimistic explanatory style do not relate well with others. Pessimists actively dwell on toxic thoughts, intentionally engage in destructive and reckless relationships and behaviors, and in a self-fulfilling manner essentially expose themselves to more and more problems (Peterson & Steen, 2002).

As a hypothetical example, Kourtney's optimistic explanatory style leads her to believe that she can perform well in her new job. This in turn facilitates Kourtney's motivation to enhance her knowledge, skills, and abilities to set challenging goals for herself and to invest more time and energy in meeting those goals. Kourtney quickly finds out that staying away from cynical, disengaged colleagues and associating with motivated high-achievers helps her learn faster, enjoy her job more, and create a more positive impression in the eyes of her manager. As she acts on these beliefs, Kourtney builds the right social relationships and utilizes the most effective impression-management techniques. She is putting herself in the right place at the right time, which gives her a better chance of being a high performer and advancing in the organization.

As another example, consider pessimistic Trevor, whose explanatory style drives him to externalize every misfortune that comes his way. Trevor fatalistically believes that nothing he can do can change what he is destined to become. Thus, he accepts the first job that he is offered, even when it is substantially below his skills and abilities. He goes through the motions of the job every day with little enthusiasm, motivation, or desire to grow. He isolates himself from sources of feedback and social support. He even does not follow the organization's safety procedures, endangering himself and others and jeopardizing his job. Ultimately, Trevor drives himself down a negative spiral of apathy and despair. He definitely increases his chances of facing more negative and undesirable events.

How can such negative spirals be reversed? It is important to capitalize on a combination of the same cognitive, social, and behavioral mechanisms to change direction upward. Schneider's (2001) previously suggested strategies of leniency for the past, appreciation for the present, and opportunity seeking for the future would be an example of such cognitive mechanisms for developing optimism. In addition, an effective social network and support (i.e., social capital) can help in breaking through the vicious cycle of pessimism. Mentoring, coaching, role-modeling, teamwork, and even simple workplace friendships and informal social events can be effective techniques to break a pessimist's isolation and catalyze the optimism-development process. Moreover, behavioral management techniques that utilize the contingent rewards, particularly positive, constructive feedback and social recognition and attention, can not only motivate positive behaviors but also challenge a pessimist's self-defeating beliefs and attitudes, triggering an upward spiral of positivity and optimism.

FUTURE IMPLICATIONS AND DIRECTIONS FOR PSYCAP OPTIMISM RESEARCH AND PRACTICE

In light of the most recent negative events and developments in the current political, economic, and social landscape in general, and in the business environment in particular, organizations may be on the verge of a downward spiral of pessimism and apathy in the near future. The need for PsyCap optimism may be greater than at any time since the Great Depression. To conclude this chapter, we offer several specific guidelines for the future development of the research and practice of PsyCap optimism.

- To fill the significant void in the optimism literature that we presented earlier (Peterson & Chang, 2002), comprehensive studies need to investigate the relationship between optimism and pessimism in order to assess their unidimensionality or independence and to examine the situational factors that may influence the existence and extent of such a relationship. In this broader perspective, a wider range of outcomes should be incorporated. Meta-analytical studies may facilitate the process of integrating current findings, thus significantly contributing to a better understanding of potential relationships, interactions, discontinuities, and moderators and/or mediators. On the other hand, integrating a broader range of findings on specific outcomes of interest may also uncover potential curvilinear relationships that are similar to those we suggested for PsyCap hope in the previous chapter.

- In line with our emphasis on flexibility as an integral component of PsyCap optimism, it becomes evident that further understanding of the specific mechanisms and processes involved in flexible optimism becomes necessary. In particular, future research should explore how people actually develop the capacity to switch back and forth between optimistic and at least "less optimistic," if not pessimistic, explanatory styles, as well as the selection criteria they employ to decide which style to use in various situations. Further theory-building in this area would enhance the ability of researchers and practicing managers to create more effective interventions for developing flexible PsyCap optimism.

- Of particular relevance to PsyCap optimism are situational factors that may influence the need for and applicability of optimism. For example, in some industries, a relatively pessimistic outlook may be predominant. Examples include accounting, finance, security management, and quality control. Others, such as marketing and sales, may benefit from a more optimistic explanatory style. Furthermore, an optimistic explanatory style may come in stark contrast to some cultural values, as some cultures strongly appreciate—and even consider as virtues—the qualities of humility, deference, and conservatism. Potential spillover effects that the specific characteristics of an industry or a national culture may have on organizational culture—and consequently, on its leaders' and employees' optimism—need to be explored.

- As with the other PsyCap components, future research needs to explore ways that we can intervene to boost realistic optimism, thus positively impacting sustainable growth and performance. It will be interesting to determine the types of developmental interventions that can be used to enhance the leader's optimism and the conditions needed to translate that optimism into a contagious optimism among followers.

REFERENCES

Abrahamson, L., Metalsky, G., & Alloy, L. (1989). Hopelessness depression: A theory-based subtype of depression. *Psychological Review, 96,* 358–372.

Avolio, B. J., & Luthans, F. (2006). *The high impact leader.* New York: McGraw-Hill.

Cameron, K., Bright, D., & Caza, A. (2004). Exploring the relationships between organizational virtuousness and performance. *American Behavioral Scientist, 47,* 766–790.

Carver, C., & Scheier, M. (2002). Optimism. In C. R. Snyder & S. Lopez (Eds.), *Handbook of positive psychology* (pp. 231–243). Oxford, UK: Oxford University Press.

Davidson, K., & Prkachin, K. (1997). Optimism and unrealistic optimism have an interacting impact on health-promoting behavior and knowledge changes. *Personality and Social Psychology Bulletin, 23,* 617–625.

Dolnick, E. (1995, July/August). Hotheads and heart attacks. *Health,* 58–64.

Gullapalli, D. (2005, May 4). Take this job and file it: Burdened by extra work created by the Sarbanes-Oxley Act, CPAs leave the big four for better life. *Wall Street Journal,* C1.

Jensen, S. M., & Luthans, F. (2006). Relationship between entrepreneurs' psychological capital and authentic leadership dimensions. *Journal of Managerial Issues, 18.*

Judge, T., & Ilies, R. (2004). Is positiveness in organizations always desirable? *Academy of Management Executive, 18,* 151–155.

Kelley, H. (1973). The process of causal attribution. *American Psychologist, 29,* 107–128.

Kok, L., Ho, M., Heng, B., & Ong, Y. (1990). A psychological study of high risk subjects for AIDS. *Singapore Medical Journal, 31,* 573–582.

Lazarus, R., & Folkman, S. (1984). *Stress, appraisal, and coping.* New York: Springer.

Luthans, F., & Avolio, B. (2003). Authentic leadership: A positive development approach. In K. S. Cameron, J. E. Dutton, & R. E. Quinn (Eds.), *Positive organizational scholarship* (pp. 241–258). San Francisco: Berrett-Koehler.

Luthans, F., Avolio, B., Avey, J., & Norman, S. (2006). Psychological capital: Measurement and relationship with performance and satisfaction (Working Paper No. 2006–1). Gallup Leadership Institute, University of Nebraska–Lincoln.

Luthans, F., Avolio, B. J., Walumbwa, F. O., & Li, W. (2005). The psychological capital of Chinese workers: Exploring the relationship with performance. *Management and Organization Review, 1,* 247–269.

Luthans, F., Norman, S., & Hughes, L. (2006). Authentic leadership: A new approach to a new time. In R. Burke & C. Cooper (Eds.), *Inspiring leaders* (pp. 84–104). London: Routledge, Taylor & Francis.

Luthans, F., & Youssef, C. M. (2004). Human, social and now positive psychological capital management: Investing in people for competitive advantage. *Organizational Dynamics, 33,* 143–160.

MacSweeney, G. (2002). Disaster recovery planning: Sadder but wiser. *Insurance and Technology, 27*(4), 20–24.

O'Reilly, III, C., & Pfeffer, J. (2000). *Hidden value: How great companies achieve extraordinary results with ordinary people.* Boston: Harvard Business School Press.

Peterson, C. (1999). Personal control and well-being. In D. Kahneman, E. Diener, & N. Schwarz (Eds.), *Well-Being: The foundations of hedonic psychology* (pp. 288–301). New York: Russell Sage.

Peterson, C. (2000). The future of optimism. *American Psychologist, 55,* 44–55.

Peterson, C., & Barrett, L. (1987). Explanatory style and academic performance among university freshmen. *Journal of Personality and Social Psychology, 53,* 603–607.

Peterson, C., & Bossio, L. (1991). *Health and optimism.* New York: Free Press.

Peterson, C., & Chang, E. (2002). Optimism and flourishing. In C. Keyes & J. Haidt (Eds.), *Flourishing: Positive psychology and the life well-lived* (pp. 55–79). Washington, DC: American Psychological Association.

Peterson, C., & Seligman, M. (1984). Causal explanations as a risk factor for depression: Theory and evidence. *Psychological Review, 91,* 347–374.

Peterson, C., & Seligman, M. (2004). *Character strengths and virtues.* Washington, DC: American Psychological Association.

Peterson, C., Seligman, M., & Vaillant, G. (1988). Pessimistic explanatory style is a risk factor for physical illness: A thirty-five year longitudinal study. *Journal of Personality and Social Psychology, 55,* 23–27.

Peterson, C., & Steen, T. (2002). Optimistic explanatory style. In C. R. Snyder & S. Lopez (Eds.), *Handbook of positive psychology* (pp. 244–256). Oxford, UK: Oxford University Press.

Pfeffer, J. (1998). *The Human Equation.* Boston: Harvard Business School Press.

Prola, M., & Stern, D. (1984). Optimism about college life and academic performance in college. *Psychological Reports, 55,* 347–350.

Scheier, M., & Carver, C. (1985). Optimism, coping, and health: Assessment and implications of generalized outcome expectancies. *Health Psychology, 4,* 219–247.

Scheier, M., & Carver, C. (1987). Dispositional optimism and physical well-being: The influence of generalized outcome expectancies on health. *Journal of Personality, 55,* 169–210.

Scheier, M., & Carver, C. (1992). Effects of optimism on psychological and physical well-being: Theoretical overview and empirical update. *Cognitive Therapy and Research, 16,* 201–228.

Scheier, M., Matthews, K., Owen, J., Magovern, G., Lefebvre, R., et al. (1989). Dispositional optimism and recovery from coronary artery bypass surgery: The beneficial effects of physical and psychological well-being. *Journal of Personality and Social Psychology, 57,* 1024–1040.

Schneider, S. L. (2001). In search of realistic optimism. *American Psychologist, 56,* 250–263.

Seeman, J. (1989). Toward a model of positive health. *American Psychologist, 44,* 1099–1109.

Seligman, M. (1998). *Learned optimism*. New York: Pocket Books.

Seligman, M. (2002). *Authentic happiness*. New York: Free Press.

Staw, B., & Barsade, S. (1993). Affect and managerial performance: A test of the sadder-but-wiser vs. happier-and-smarter hypotheses. *Administrative Science Quarterly, 38,* 304–331.

Strack, S., Carver, C., & Blaney, P. (1987). Predicting successful completion of an after-care program following treatment for alcoholism: The role of dispositional optimism. *Journal of Personality and Social Psychology, 53,* 579–584.

Taylor, S. (1989). *Positive illusions*. New York: Basic Books.

Tiger, L. (1979). *Optimism: The biology of hope*. New York: Simon and Schuster.

Waterman, R. H., Waterman, J. A., & Collard, B. A. (1994). Toward a career-resilient workforce. *Harvard Business Review, 72*(4), 87–95.

Weinstein, N. (1989). Optimistic biases about personal risks. *Science, 246,* 1232–1233.

CHAPTER 5

PsyCap Resiliency

Bouncing Back and Beyond

IT IS RARE to pick up a biography of any world-class leader and not be taken aback by the resiliency of such leaders. Failure after failure did not deter these leaders from seeking out and achieving the mission they set forth for themselves, their organization, or even entire societies. The resiliency evidenced by such leaders as Nelson Mandela, Mother Teresa, Winston Churchill, and Abraham Lincoln underscores the importance of this "bounce back" capacity in leaders who continue under the most difficult odds and, more importantly, the impact they had on their followers and broader constituencies.

Similar to the predominantly negative focus of the field of psychology prior to the positive psychology movement, for a long time, most of the resiliency research and practice has been associated with at-risk children, problem adolescents, and dysfunctional families. Those who were strong enough to lead a "normal" life after facing traumatic experiences were labeled "survivors" and admired as "exceptional" individuals. Traditionally, research focused on "who" was resilient, for example, anecdotal case studies of exceptional hardiness and the ability to bounce back despite severe problems. Resilience research then moved on to study both "who" was resilient and "what" characteristics resilient people possessed.

Now, positive psychologists such as Ann Masten (2001; Masten & Reed, 2002) through their theory-building and research recognize that resilience, as well as its ingredients, involves everyday skills and psychological strengths that can be identified, measured, maintained, and nurtured in individuals of all ages and psychological conditions. As Masten (2001, p. 235) notes, resilience comes "from the everyday magic of ordinary, normative human resources" and "has profound implications for promoting competence and human capital in individuals and society."

We have now taken this positive psychology view of resilience to the workplace (Avolio & Luthans, 2006; Luthans, 2002; Luthans, Avolio, Avey, & Norman, 2006; Luthans, Avolio, Walumbwa, & Li, 2005; Luthans, Luthans, & Luthans, 2004; Luthans & Youssef, 2004; Youssef, 2004; Youssef & Luthans, 2005b) as a criteria-meeting component of PsyCap and have defined it as "the capacity to rebound or bounce back from adversity, conflict, failure, or even positive events, progress, and increased responsibility" (Luthans, 2002, p. 702). Our goal here is to uncover the life conditions that help to facilitate such a powerful capacity in leaders, employees, and organizations.

Unfortunately, even though resiliency has generated renewed interest through positive psychology, except for our initial research with it as part of PsyCap (e.g., see Luthans, Avolio, Avey, et al., 2006; Luthans, Avolio, Walumbwa, et al., 2005; Youssef, 2004), to date the body of knowledge that applies resiliency to the workplace is rare, fragmented, and inadequate (Sutcliffe & Vogus, 2003). Even in clinical psychology, where resiliency had been studied most extensively, positively oriented perspectives and vocabulary on resiliency are just emerging (Wolin & Wolin, 2005). The purpose of this chapter is to summarize and build out from our most recent theory-building and empirical research on resiliency as an important component of PsyCap in today's highly turbulent work environment. Our intent is to solidify its place in PsyCap as an essential component that definitely helps differentiate the very successful from the unsuccessful leaders, employees, and organizations.

PERSONAL REFLECTIONS EXERCISE ON PSYCAP RESILIENCY

To better understand the more in-depth discussion of resiliency, we would like you to once again spend some time reflecting on the following questions.

- When was the last time you encountered what you would consider to be an adversity, a conflict, a failure, or even a positive event that you believe to have been overwhelming?

- What was the nature of this event or situation?
- Was it sudden and unexpected or gradual and emotionally draining?
- What were some of the coping strategies you formulated and tried to implement?
- How effective do you think these strategies were?
- Do you think you eventually bounced back and fully recovered from this event or situation? Why? Why not?
- What are some of the lessons that you learned from this experience?
- What other ways beside this situation, how you handled it, and the outcome could have taught you the lessons that you learned?
- Overall, if you were to assess yourself right now, with the event or situation behind you (or pretty much behind you), do you believe that you have grown and matured, bounced back to your "normal" condition or even beyond it, or have you deteriorated and feel somewhat diminished?

With the same questions above, you can also take a look at someone you have total respect for as a leader and/or mentor.

- How did these individuals handle the challenges of adversity and what could you learn from their resiliency that you can apply to your own development as a leader or committed follower?

We also now invite you to challenge yourself even further by trying to remember a time or times when you voluntarily went out of your way and left your comfort zone for something new and unexpected. For example, ask yourself the following questions.

When was the last time I:

- Volunteered for something new and difficult?
- Did something unusual, even though I thought it was risky and unusual for me?
- Traveled abroad?
- Tried a new food that I had never tasted before?
- Took a different route to a familiar place, just for a change?
- Chose to listen to a new type of music?
- Read about something purely out of curiosity?
- Accepted someone else's idea over my own because I actually thought it was better?

- Befriended someone despite outward appearance or obvious personality differences?
- Asked someone for help despite status differences?
- Allowed myself to go unprepared and improvise on the spot?
- Moved to a new location?
- Took a completely different direction in my career?
- Went back to school to start with a totally new focus and discipline?
- Gave people who work for me total freedom to make a critical decision?

A RESILIENCE STORY

Besides reflecting on the above questions to gain some insights into your own resiliency, consider the following story about Mary, who when she was a teenager lost her mother to cancer and had to live with her verbally abusive father, resentful stepmother, and mentally challenged, much older stepbrother. In this situation, she soon started to miss school and then had a few minor scrapes with the law. Court-ordered, traditional counseling focused on Mary's at-risk situation, which resulted in her being placed in the foster care system. She moved from one foster home to the next through no fault of her own. For example, her foster families would return her to the system in order to have a child of their own, move to a different city, or even remodel and put the room that she was occupying to a different use.

With such tremendous uncertainty and instability in her life after still another placement in a foster home, Mary had a trigger moment with a close friend at school who simply verbally challenged her to take charge of her own life. She resolutely decided after this interaction with her friend to hold on only to things that could be in her own control. She determined these to be her mind, her body, and her motivation to succeed. From that moment on, Mary immersed herself and invested her time and energy in education, sports, and worked as hard as she could at whatever she chose to do. She excelled in high school academics and athletics. This earned her a full scholarship to play soccer for one of the top universities in the state.

Besides the hard work that paid off in the classroom and on the soccer field, a less-obvious contributor to Mary's success was her ability to surround herself with caring friends and mentors. She established strong relationships not only with her peers but also with her coaches, some professors, and community leaders who were supporters of the athletic programs at the university. She would offer to assist in coaching kids in youth leagues and baby-sit for her mentors' kids. At no additional charge, she would take it upon herself to do household chores while babysitting. As her diligence and conscientiousness were observed, and she was repeatedly asked back, she became an important part of the prominent families for whom she worked. She used every opportunity to interact with not only the mentor but would also seek advice and guidance from his or her spouse and even the family's grandparents on important life decisions. She gained valuable insights and values from observing and using healthy families, a resource that she had been denied in her own life course.

Although Mary barely made the soccer team, she was able to maintain her scholarship. She sacrificed an active social life by studying hard and getting above-average grades in her marketing major. However, she also kept in constant contact with the families that she baby-sat for and was often invited to their homes for Sunday dinner or pizza after a game. This network of social contacts paid off for Mary when, after her junior year, she was offered an attractive summer internship by one of those contacts, who was president of a local bank.

Based on Mary's track record, which we have briefly revealed here, the rest of the story should be pretty predictable. However, if we go back to her early teenage years, the prediction would be very bleak. Yet, through a positive moment that mattered with a friend, her conscientious personality, human capital (good college education, playing on a team, internship experience in a bank), social capital (network of friends, mentors), and especially her psychological capital (confidence, hope, optimism, and mainly resiliency) she not only landed a good entry-level job with the bank upon graduation but in a short number of years became a vice-president in charge of the bank's marketing and retail operations. Mary chose a different pathway, which relates to our discussion of hope, but she also demonstrated her capacity to bounce back, once this was triggered by her friend's comment.

In this story, Mary, the successful bank executive, was as a young teen certainly at risk and headed for big problems. This is how many such stories would end. How she moved from at-risk teenager to successful executive can be attributed to her PsyCap resiliency. She had a moment that mattered in taking charge of her own life, and through some wise strategies, she not only bounced back but went far beyond what would be considered normal or average accomplishments. Was she set back by adverse events in her life course? Definitely. Was she resilient? Definitely. Will she continue to be resilient in her career? Hopefully, but time and understanding of PsyCap resiliency may help in finding an answer to this complex question.

What you might derive from reading this story is the idea that if people choose to bounce back, they just might be able to do so. This does not mean that one will not need support to be successful. It simply means that the support can be condolences or the support can be energizing, so one must choose pathways wisely.

THE MEANING OF PSYCAP RESILIENCY

From a clinical psychology perspective, Masten and Reed (2002, p. 75) define resiliency as "a class of phenomena characterized by patterns of positive adaptation in the context of significant adversity or risk." In our PsyCap approach, as indicated in our definition of resiliency in the introductory comments, we broadened the definition to include not only the ability to bounce back from adversity but also very positive, challenging events (e.g., record sales performance) and the will to go beyond the normal, to go beyond the equilibrium point (Avolio & Luthans, 2006; Luthans, 2002; Youssef & Luthans, 2005b).

Besides this recognition of positive as well as negative events and going beyond the normal or the return to equilibrium, there are various factors from positive psychology that have been identified and researched as contributing to or hindering the development of resiliency. These factors can be classified into assets, risk factors (Masten, 2001; Masten & Reed, 2002; Youssef & Luthans, 2005b), and values (Coutu, 2002; Kobsa, 1982; Richardson, 2002; Youssef & Luthans, 2005a). There is also recognition of adaptational processes that tie these three factors additively, interactively, and synergistically, resulting in resiliency (Cowan, Cowan, & Schulz, 1996).

Resiliency Assets

Masten and Reed (2002, p. 76) define a resiliency asset as "a measurable characteristic in a group of individuals or their situation that predicts a positive outcome in the future on a specific outcome criterion." Specifically, they identify cognitive abilities, temperament, positive self-perceptions, faith, a positive outlook on life, emotional stability, self-regulation, a sense of humor, and general appeal or attractiveness as potential assets that can contribute to higher resiliency (Masten, 2001). Wolin and Wolin (2005) offer a similar list of assets, including insight, independence, relationships, initiative, creativity, humor, and morality.

Drawing from positive psychology, as was found in the opening story about Mary, particular emphasis has been given to the importance of relationship-based assets and their contribution to resiliency, especially in the context of dealing with adverse or negative events. For example, Masten (2001) discusses the importance of care-giving adults, effective parenting, prosocial and rule-abiding peers, and collective efficacy in the community. Gorman (2005) supports the integral role of both personal- and relationship-based assets in enhancing resiliency by showing that those who can discover and hone their talents and then find effective mentors to be their "champions" have higher chances of bouncing back and becoming successful.

Resiliency Risk Factors

Masten and Reed (2002, p. 76) define resiliency risk factors as those that cause an "elevated probability of an undesirable outcome." Also referred to as "vulnerability factors" (Kirby & Fraser, 1997), risk factors may include clearly destructive and dysfunctional experiences, such as alcohol and drug abuse (e.g., Johnson, Bryant, Collins, Noe, Strader, & Berbaum, 1998; Sandau-Beckler, Devall, & de la Rosa, 2002), and exposure to trauma, such as experiencing violence (Qouta, El-Sarraj, & Punamaki, 2001). These risks can also include less obvious, gradual, but eventually detrimental factors, such as stress and burnout (e.g., Baron, Eisman, Scuello, Veyzer, & Lieberman, 1996; Smith & Carlson, 1997), poor health, undereducation, and unemployment (e.g., Collins, 2001).

Risk factors may differentially expose individuals to frequent and intense undesirable events and thus increase the probability of negative outcomes (Cowan, et al., 1996; Masten, 2001). However, the mere presence of risk factors should not be viewed as automatically conducive to failure and lack of resiliency. Risk factors are inevitable. Therefore, complete risk avoidance and sheltering oneself and others from all sources of risk is, at best, unrealistic. Moreover, the presence of challenges is actually a necessary and invaluable growth and self-actualization opportunity. If properly identified and managed, the process of using assets to overcome risks can help people overcome complacency, explore new domains, and further exploit their existing talents and strengths. In other words, as in the case of Mary, risks can stimulate growth and development and help people to reach their full potential. Just as needs are a requirement in the motivation process, risk factors are important antecedents for bouncing back and beyond in the resiliency process. Resiliency allows one to take advantage of latent potential that would go undiscovered otherwise.

Cowan and colleagues (1996, p. 9) emphasize this process-focused perspective when they state that "the active ingredients of a risk do not lie in the variable itself, but in the set of processes that flow from the variable, linking risk conditions with specific dysfunctional outcomes." They compare an individual's exposure to and dealing with risk factors to immunization, a process that exposes the person to a small dose of a disease in order to build long-term strength, endurance, and sustainability.

Similarly, Wolin and Wolin (2005) present a positive alternative to the traditional "damage model" of being at risk. The "risk paradigm" that includes the "damage model" presents a self-fulfilling prophecy. That is, those exposed to risk factors (like Mary in the opening story) are too often judged and treated as if they are going to fail. The best developmental efforts under this damage perspective are channeled toward equipping the "at-risk" individual with an inventory of adaptation and coping techniques that may result in "normal" functioning despite adversity. On the other hand, PsyCap resiliency would view adversities and setbacks as both risk factors and challenging opportunities for growth and success beyond the normal state. Such a change in perspective-taking (or meaning-making) itself could result in a more positive, self-fulfilling prophecy. Indeed, Reichard and Avolio (2005), based on a review of the last 100 years of leadership intervention research, reported that the greatest impact was attributable to Pygmalion (i.e., self-fulfilling) effects. These effects were created by getting leaders to believe that followers were more or less effective, qualified, and so forth. Such manipulated beliefs resulted in significantly different performance in followers.

When considering both assets and risk factors in the PsyCap resiliency process, it follows that the relationship is not necessarily linear. In other words, resiliency should not be assessed as the total resources and capabilities available to an individual (assets) minus the frequency and intensity of exposure to risk factors. Instead, in the PsyCap resiliency process, assets and risk factors taken together should be viewed as cumulative and interactive in nature. As Sandau-Beckler and colleagues (2002) point out, the specific order or sequence in a "risk chain" can be a fundamental predictor of one's resiliency level.

The Role of Values in Resiliency

Still another major component of PsyCap resiliency is the underlying value system that guides, shapes, and gives consistency and meaning to one's cognitions, emotions, and actions. Values and beliefs help individuals in elevating themselves over difficult and overwhelming present events, linking them to a more pleasant future in which they can look forward. For example, Avolio and Luthans (2006) note that resilient, authentic leaders can look to their future possible selves and bring them back to their present actual selves, even during periods of failure. This bringing of the future back to the present can result in leaders motivating themselves and others to higher performance. This perspective also suggests that individuals who are more motivated to develop and learn will likely sustain effort to achieve challenging goals and expectations. And motivation to learn and develop, like resiliency, is something that can be developed in individuals and/or diminished, as too often happens with poor leaders and ineffective managers.

Research supports the role of meaning-providing values and beliefs in maintaining resiliency through severe psychological (Wong & Mason, 2001) and physical (e.g., Holaday & McPhearson, 1997) challenges. For example, a positive relationship has been found between religiosity and mental health (e.g., Bergin, 1983; Larson, Pattison, Blazer, Omran, & Kaplan, 1986; Ness & Wintrob, 1980), happiness (Paul, 2005), and coping with traumatic experiences (Baron, Eisman, Scuello, Veyzer, and Lieberman, 1996; Gibbs, 1989; Tebbi, Mallon, Richards, & Bigler, 1987). Furthermore, those who act in line with their moral frameworks have been consistently found to experience increased freedom, energy, and resiliency (Richardson, 2002). Wolin and Wolin (2005) see morality as enhancing resiliency through aligning one's actions to a value system that guides judgment (distinguishing between good and bad), principles (providing a foundation for decisions and behavior), and eventually service (contributing to others' well-being). It suffices to say that a primary contribution of one's values in the process of enhancing resiliency lies in the stability of these values as a source of true meaning (Coutu, 2002; Kobsa, 1982).

It is truly amazing to see how persistent some individuals are to a cause if they have a very deep belief in that cause, purpose, or mission. We can label them insurgents, religious zealots, or patriots, but in the end, they all have a deep belief in something that extends their possible selves to a higher purpose. At the same time, this strongly held belief will likely enhance their resiliency level and the resiliency levels of those they influence. Interestingly, being materially rewarded for agreed-upon performance is not likely to contribute to the same level of resiliency.

THE PSYCAP RESILIENCY FACTORS IN ACTION

Once again reflecting back on Mary's story in the opening of the chapter, we see that she certainly possessed many significant assets, including her obvious intellectual and athletic talents, conscientious personality, and ability to formulate and execute effective life strategies. Importantly, she also had evidence of hope (the will and the way), certainly confidence/self-efficacy, and also optimism for her future. Covered in the preceding three chapters, confidence, hope, and optimism can also be considered here as assets in the resiliency process. Mary's life also contained numerous classic risk factors: the loss of her mother, her dysfunctional family, a failed foster care system, and her nonexistent material and financial resources.

Mary refused to be at the mercy of these classic risks. She challenged them versus accepting them as determining her fate and future. Capitalizing on her assets, she was able to leverage them and further them. She was able to manage her risk factors by formulating and implementing strategies (i.e., adaptational processes), such as building a reliable and diversified network of social support through friends and mentors (i.e., social capital). The strong educational and athletic records indicated that she had talent/strengths that also helped to mitigate some of her risk factors, for example, her financial limitations in obtaining a higher education. Also very evident is the role of her strong value system. Mary's strong work ethic and her being able to recognize and seize positive moments, such as her friend telling her to take control of her life, resulted in enriching her mind through education, her body through sports, and her social capital through social networking, which eventually led to her first job and eventual career success beyond normal expectations.

If Mary had been born into a wealthy and functionally healthy family (more assets, less risk factors), would she have taken the initiative, reached out, and accomplished where she is today? The answer is far from certain, but the contribution of adversity, setbacks, and risk factors in building Mary's resiliency and subsequent success cannot be ignored. Development occurs because we are challenged, not because we have obtained a level of capacity and effort that does not need to be enhanced. Thus, in extreme areas of challenge, resiliency will play a critically important role in success.

Mary's early life course is an example of how resiliency is typically portrayed in the traditional clinical and even most recent positive psychology discussions. It serves this chapter well to demonstrate the key factors of assets, risk factors, and values in the resiliency process. However, when included as a PsyCap criteria meeting psychological strength, an understanding and building of resilience do not have to be limited to life course risk factors, such as death of a loved one, a severe illness, a dysfunctional family, or failed social institutions.

For PsyCap resiliency, instead of such negative life course events, attention is given to inevitable adverse factors in today's workplace (e.g., not only the obvious ones of being fired, downsized, or passed over for promotion, but also failing to reach project goals or even more subtle ones, such as being ignored by teammates or feeling discriminated against). However, as important as the negative is, the role that PsyCap resiliency may also play in responding to positive events in the workplace can not be discounted (e.g., a significant increase in responsibility and exposure resulting from a promotion or coming off a record year with heightened expectations).

Perhaps the simplest way of expressing this reaction is that if you are positively or negatively pushed beyond some threshold capacity level, you are at the front end of tapping into resiliency. PsyCap resiliency is concerned with how it can not just propel leaders and employees back to their normal selves, but, like Mary, it can also push them to reach the capacity that is created by paying attention to their possible selves. The remainder of the chapter uses the definitions and factors discussed so far as a point of departure for examining the performance implications and development of resiliency of leaders, employees, and organizations.

RESILIENCY IN THE WORKPLACE: PERFORMANCE IMPLICATIONS

As we have discussed so far, both clinical and positive psychological research support the role of resiliency in enhancing various aspects of human functioning, especially those related to posttraumatic coping and adaptation (e.g., see Block & Kremen, 1996; Bonanno, 2004; Coutu, 2002; Cowan, et al., 1996; Egeland, Carlson, & Sroufe, 1993; Huey & Weisz, 1997; Hunter & Chandler, 1999; Johnson, et al., 1998; Kirby & Fraser, 1997; Masten, 2001; Masten & Reed, 2002; Richardson, 2002; Sandau-Beckler, et al., 2002; Smith & Carlson, 1997; Stewart, Reid, & Mangham, 1997). Our initial research as part of PsyCap has also found a positive relationship between resiliency and workplace performance outcomes (Luthans, Avolio, et al., 2006; Luthans, et al., 2005; Youssef, 2004). Other peripheral resiliency applications in the workplace are also emerging at an accelerating rate among both researchers and practitioners/consultants (e.g., see Conner, 1993, 2003; LaMarch, 1997; Vickers & Kouzmin, 2001; Waite & Richardson, 2004; Waterman, Waterman, & Collard, 1994; Zunz, 1998).

The concept of resiliency has considerable appeal in today's workplace, which is characterized as increasingly competitive, changing at a dizzying rate, and dominated by shades of gray when it comes to value systems and standards for ethical behavior. Today's organizational participants are uncertain about the underlying assumptions and values they are guided by and about their individual psychological contracts, including what they own and do not own in terms of responsibilities. For those who are only capable of passively coping and reactively adapting, this environment is unfriendly, stressful, and can be very dysfunctional for both the individual and the organization. Confining resiliency to this passive description, which just allows for reactive coping and survival from adversity, as the traditional resiliency literature emphasizes, would limit its applications to the current situation that most organizational participants now face in the "flat-world" global economy (Friedman, 2005).

Today's managers and employees realize that their organizations are looking for top performers who can thrive on chaos, proactively learn and grow through hardships, and excel no matter how many or how intense the inevitable setbacks (Hamel & Välikangas, 2003). Bouncing back to where one initially was before a problem or crisis is necessary, but it is no longer sufficient. Average performance can no longer meet today's rapidly growing expectations. The expectations and commitments have escalated to "better than OK" (Sutcliffe & Vogus, 2003). Today's organizational participants need to not only survive, cope, and recover but also to thrive and flourish through the inevitable difficulties and uncertainties that they face and to do so faster than their competition (Ryff & Singer, 2003).

PsyCap resiliency is not just a minimal coping or neutralizing agent for difficult times (Bonanno, 2004). Viewing resiliency as proactive, rather than just reactive, may lead to sustainable positive gains. Reivich and Shatte (2002) support the proactive nature of resiliency in describing it as the capacity to overcome, steer through, bounce back, and reach out to pursue new knowledge and experiences, deeper relationships with others, and finding meaning in life. Moreover, Posttraumatic Growth (PTG), as a positive alternative to Posttraumatic Stress Disorder (Tedeschi, Park, & Calhoun, 1998), emphasizes that resilient individuals use adversities as a "springboard" to reach higher ground. Ryff and Singer (2003) also assert that resilient people experience enhanced self-reliance, self-efficacy, self-awareness, self-disclosure, relationships, emotional expressiveness, and empathy.

Reflecting on adversities also helps in giving life meaning and value and in refining one's philosophy of life, goals, and priorities. Richardson's (2002) notion of "resilient reintegration" becomes particularly relevant to this perspective. He suggests that disruptions in one's life routines allow for the exploration and refinement of resilient qualities. These windows of opportunity stemming from adversities and disruptions can result in substantial growth and development, as well as valuable opportunities for reflection and self-assessment. In other words, resiliency can be expanded to include personal growth and increased strength through adversities and setbacks. This growth perspective is all-encompassing.

Pragmatically, we expect resiliency to be related to improved performance and bottom-line gains, and our preliminary research supports such a view (Luthans, Avey, et al., 2006; Luthans, Avolio, et al., 2006, Luthans, et al., 2005; Youssef, 2004). In addition, increased job satisfaction, enhanced organizational commitment, and enriched social capital are also likely to be potential positive outcomes, as well as inputs into a positive spiral of increased resiliency.

DEVELOPING RESILIENCY IN TODAY'S WORKFORCE

As we have defined it, PsyCap resiliency is a dynamic, malleable, developable psychological capacity or strength. It is not a "magical" or "mystical" capacity (Masten, 2001), a "super material" (Sutcliffe & Vogus, 2003), or a hard-wired, fixed trait. The positive psychology and business consulting fields consider resiliency open to development. For example, in positive psychology, George Vaillant (1977, 2000), the Director of the Study of Adult Development at Harvard Medical School, has clearly demonstrated that people he studied became markedly more resilient over their lifetimes, and Salvatore R. Maddi, the Director of the Hardiness Institute, has effectively used resiliency training over the years (Coutu, 2002).

As part of their Project Resilience, Wolin and Wolin (2005) offer resiliency assessment and training, which have been effective in various contexts, including education, treatment, and even prevention. In business consulting for more than 15 years, Reivich and Shatte (2002) have conducted resiliency development programs for companies. In addition, Conner (1993, 2003) offers resiliency development training interventions and solutions specifically tailored to leadership development and change-management situations. In a recent study, Waite and Richardson (2004) empirically supported the effectiveness of training interventions in enhancing resiliency in the workplace.

As a follow-up to their analysis of the factors in the resiliency process, Masten and Reed (2002) identified three sets of resiliency development strategies that can be adapted to the workplace. These can be summarized as follows.

1. ASSET-FOCUSED STRATEGIES. As the name implies, these strategies focus on enhancing the perceived and actual level of assets and resources that can increase the probability of positive outcomes. In terms of workplace applications, these assets may include human capital (education, experience, knowledge, skills, abilities), social capital (relationships, networking), and even other positive psychological capital components (self-efficacy, hope, optimism). Human capital, especially its explicit knowledge, skills and abilities, can be learned and enhanced through traditional training and development programs.

The tacit component of human capital, which is the in-depth understanding of the organization's specific values, culture, structure, strategies, and processes, can be developed through various widely recognized approaches and techniques, such as socialization, mentoring, and even job rotation. Social capital can be developed through open communication, trust-building, authenticity and transparency, feedback and recognition, teamwork, and work-life balance initiatives (Luthans & Youssef, 2004; Youssef & Luthans, 2005a, 2005b). Such approaches for developing positive psychological capital are recommended throughout the chapters of this book and support our point that we are not only building individual PsyCap but, over time, are positively contributing to collective PsyCap as well.

2. RISK-FOCUSED STRATEGIES. Under this strategy, Masten and Reed (2002) offer risk factors that can increase the probability of undesired outcomes being prevented. Although heavily emphasized in developmental psychology, in line with our positive perspective on risk factors as challenges and developmental opportunities, our developmental approach emphasizes the management rather than the avoidance of most risk factors (Luthans, Vogelgesang, & Lester, 2006). For example, based on our earlier definition of resiliency as "the developable capacity to rebound or bounce back from adversity, conflict, and failure or even positive events, progress, and increased responsibility" (Luthans, 2002, p. 702), a promotion can be viewed as a positive event and an opportunity for growth and increased responsibility, but it can also be overwhelming and might be perceived as a high-risk situation. A risk-avoidance strategy would be to turn down such a promotion. On the other hand, an alternative risk-management strategy that would fit this situation may include a developmental approach for enhancing self-efficacy in the new domain. This efficacy development would include coaching and/or mentoring and frequent constructive feedback. Through such risk-management approaches, an inventory of assets which is relevant to the new challenge is built. This asset inventory would help the individual in perceiving the new risk factors as developmental opportunities and would draw from them to bounce back and beyond. This is simply using the time-tested strategy of turning a threat into an opportunity.

Another example of a risk-focused strategy would be entrepreneurial and intrapreneurial initiatives. This would involve out-of-the-box thinking, which tends to motivate calculated but usually high risk-taking but has the potential for high returns. In the business environment, such entrepreneurial (and intrapreneurial) risk-taking is encouraged, commended, and necessary for success.

Many individuals, however, with creative capacities and high-potential ideas forgo their dreams and resort to safer risk-avoidance strategies (e.g., settle for a secure, boring job). Again, through equipping individuals with the proper assets, especially social capital (Sanders & Nee, 1996; Teixeira, 2001), even when faced with risk, potential opportunities can be realized through an entrepreneurial, out-of-the-box strategy. Nevertheless, many destructive and unnecessary risk factors still need to be avoided, even by psychologically and physically healthy adults in the context of work. For example, unhealthy eating habits and lack of physical exercise due to the long and increasingly stressful hours that Americans work (Greenhouse, 2001; Koretz, 2001) are examples of risk factors that should probably be minimized if not avoided by most organizational participants. If not avoided, they should be translated into strategies for sustaining one's performance in the face of increasing stress.

3. PROCESS-FOCUSED STRATEGIES. Masten and Reed (2002) present this third set of strategies as effective adaptational systems and processes. They are mobilized in order to identify, select, develop, employ, and maintain the proper mix of assets in managing pertinent risk factors. This allows overcoming and growing through adversities. For example, in the authentic leadership development model (Avolio & Luthans, 2006; Luthans & Avolio, 2003), the processes of self-awareness and self-regulation become integral parts of the resiliency development process. In other words, possessing all the right assets may not be conducive to effective functioning in difficult times unless the manager has the proper means to accurately assess these assets (self-awareness) and diligently employs them to overcome the risks (self-regulation). Although process-focused strategies have emphasized various coping mechanisms in the fields of child and adolescent psychology, the recent study of workplace resiliency by Harland, Harrison, Jones, and Reiter-Palmon (2005) clearly distinguishes between avoidance-coping and approach-coping. In line with our conceptualization of risk, approach-coping techniques would be more positively associated with resiliency, which takes the individual back and beyond, while avoidance-coping techniques would tend to be negatively related to the impact of resiliency.

RESILIENT LEADERS AND EMPLOYEES

The constant turmoil that is characteristic of our current environment is challenging organizational members' abilities to endure—let alone grow and develop—in any targeted, proactive manner. So far, we have emphasized that the impact of these substantial changes on resiliency is primarily dependent on the processes through which leaders' and employees' assets, risk factors, and values interact and are managed and integrated. The following examples are by no means exhaustive, but they simply serve as representative guidelines for analyzing potentially adverse changes that are likely to necessitate the need for PsyCap resiliency.

In light of the changing nature of psychological contracts (Robinson, Kraatz, & Rousseau, 1994), as we have previously discussed, organizational commitment and mutual trust among managers and their associates have declined. When organizations can no longer guarantee long-term, secure employment, managers and employees lose some valuable resiliency-enhancing assets. These lost or deteriorating assets include the human and social capital involved in caring leadership, mentoring opportunities, and long-term investments in organization-initiated development and career-planning. In addition, the increased risk associated with the loss of one's income and job insecurity can result in negative thinking and emotions, such as fear of the future, complacency, disengagement, and unwillingness to engage in organizational citizenship behaviors. It can even lead to ethically questionable behaviors out of self-interest and greed, such as embezzlement, sabotage, backstabbing, and even, in rare instances, violence.

All of the available evidence suggests that under these difficult conditions, leaders can make a profound difference in how the resulting challenges are perceived. Indeed, the very essence of what Burns (1978) and Bass (1998) describe as transformational leadership is that such leaders help followers to see looming threats as opportunities for advancement and, over time, make followers believe that they are in charge and own more of the responsibility for success. In so doing, they are able to transform followers into leaders.

EMERGING CAREER RESILIENCY

Fortunately, there may be a positive, "half-full" side to these workplace changes which may seem, on the surface, to be only dysfunctional and destructive. Today's organizational leaders and employees can learn a new type of resiliency, "career resiliency." According to Waterman, Waterman, and Collard (1994, p. 88), a career resilient workforce is "a group of employees who not only are dedicated to the idea of continuous learning but also stand ready to reinvent themselves to keep pace with change; who take responsibility for their own career management; and, last but not least, who are committed to the company's success." Leaders can help create the conditions for employees to develop such attitudes toward their future.

With this new strategy of career resiliency, the relationship between organizations and their members is shifting away from the traditional views of loyalty and commitment toward one career path within one organization and one area of specialization at all costs (elimination of uncertainty and risk). The new approach of career resiliency is toward a more volatile, flexible relationship between members and the organization that is sustained as long as it is mutually beneficial. Under the new perspective, employees become charged with continuously monitoring, benchmarking, and anticipating changes in organizational needs and then upgrading their skills and abilities (assets) accordingly.

In the meantime, this process can contribute to their organization's goals as well. What is essential to tipping the balance toward positive aspects of resiliency is having a sense of trust in the fairness of how one is treated and will be treated. Having to let people go but helping to maintain their dignity is resiliency enhancing. We propose that this approach is something that leaders can directly have an impact on in their organizations.

One manager we are aware of indicated that when he had to lay off a group of workers, he went about doing so by treating them as alumni. From both a financial and psychological perspective, he did everything he could to make them feel positive about the organization and his leadership. The net effect of his efforts was that he typically got laid-off employees to come back when the economy was better for business and to make very positive referrals to others about the company.

Under the new career-resiliency approach, organizations are no longer responsible for the traditional employment contract, but rather the "employability" of their members. This employability is accomplished through equipping rather than prescriptive training, as well as the development and support of lifelong learning that enhances employees' opportunities both within and outside the organization. In other words, career resiliency is not a violation or betrayal of the psychological contract. Instead, it is a new type of psychological contract with somewhat different but still balanced expectations (Bagshaw, 1997; Kakabadse & Kakabadse, 2000).

In the career-resiliency paradigm, risk factors that may be inherent in organizational strategic decisions, such as downsizing, reengineering, mergers and acquisitions, and outsourcing, may also trigger the development of new assets for resiliency. For example, career-resilient managers and employees are likely to invest time and energy in beefing up their resumes and in networking and building connections beyond their direct units or even their present organization. This newly developed human and social capital is a resource to draw on in times of adversity. When properly managed through well-designed organizational values, policies, and procedures (e.g., those that avoid conflict of interest), these relationships can be aligned and channeled to work for, rather than against, the interests of the organization. Moreover, adaptational mechanisms, such as self-awareness, self-regulation, and self-development, are expected to mediate the processes through which managers and employees proactively and independently develop their assets, manage their risk factors, refine their values and beliefs, and subsequently build their resiliency.

THE IMPACT OF LEADERSHIP ON FOLLOWER RESILIENCE

It is important to note that leadership is an integral contributor to enhanced employee resilience, as evidenced by some of the previous examples. We have proposed a cascading, trickle-down effect of resilience from managers to their associates (Avolio & Luthans, 2006; Youssef & Luthans, 2005b). Also, in the study by Harland, et al. (2005), it was found that the transformational leadership dimensions of attributed charisma, idealized influence, intellectual stimulation, and individualized consideration were positively related to the employees' resiliency. On the other hand, most transactional leadership dimensions were not related to employee resiliency. The researchers' assessment of resiliency was along a broader spectrum of capacities which included not only coping and bouncing back but also learning, growth, and increased strength. Clearly, a leadership approach that is consistent with follower-development, open communication, trust-building, creating more meaning and identification in one's work, and effective mentoring toward increased proactivity and independence is in tune with the recently emerging recognition of the importance of authenticity and transparency. In fact, taken in combination, the most powerful leadership approach may involve the authentic, transformational leader.

Authentic leadership is proposed to enhance follower resiliency (Avolio & Luthans, 2006; Luthans & Avolio, 2003). Seeking greater self-awareness, authentic leaders transparently open as many communication channels as possible and encourage and reinforce their followers to give them sincere feedback. Such genuine, upward feedback can help authentic leaders understand themselves and their own level of PsyCap and accurately assess their vulnerabilities. This sort of feedback could reduce the risk of unexpected challenges suddenly emerging and reducing one's level of resilience.

Self-awareness helps leaders better target their energies, actions, and resources toward further self-development, and it provides direction for areas where their followers' development, empowerment, and delegation are more likely to be effective. Such a partnership of equals encourages continuous development and improvement in a nonthreatening, trusting, transparent environment.

Leaders and followers can bounce back and beyond together while capitalizing on the resources that they can provide each other. They both can also draw from their organizational context rather than competing for resources and information through destructive power games and political maneuvering. How much energy potential is lost with the type of territorial, narrow-thinking "silo fighting" that goes on in many organizations? What are the implications of those losses for building up assets that sustains higher levels of resiliency?

THE RESILIENT ORGANIZATION: CREATING A BOUNCE BACK AND BEYOND ENVIRONMENT

Only recently has the importance of organizational resiliency been recognized. It should be clear by now that when it comes to resiliency, like overall PsyCap (see chapter 1), the whole is greater than the sum of its parts. In other words, bringing together a group of resilient managers and employees is not sufficient for the creation of a resilient organization (Coutu, 2002; Horne & Orr, 1998). Synergies occur when the organizational context in which members operate nurtures resiliency through catalyzing, augmenting, shielding, and buffering various ingredients of the resiliency development process (Youssef & Luthans, 2005b).

The positive organizational scholarship (POS) approach (e.g., Klarreich, 1998; Worline, et al., 2002) defines organizational resiliency as the structural and "processual" dynamics that equip an organization with the capacity to absorb strain, to retain coherence, to bounce back, and thus continue to effectively engage in and manage risk. Hamel and Välikangas (2003) in a recent *Harvard Business Review* article define organizational resiliency as the ability to dynamically reinvent strategies and business models in response to inevitable change.

Like individuals, we have proposed that organizations capitalize on their macrolevel assets, risk factors, values, and adaptational processes to develop and maintain their resiliency (Youssef & Luthans, 2005b). Organizational assets that can contribute to resiliency may include traditional economically oriented capital, such as financial, physical, structural, and technological resources. Organizational assets may also include the collective of human-capital ingredients discussed earlier, that is, explicit and tacit knowledge. In addition, social capital (interpersonal and interunit relationships, norms, values, trust, and community) may develop in the organization's social context (Luthans & Youssef, 2004). Most importantly, various components of PsyCap have been shown to be of particular significance even at the organizational level. An example would be collective efficacy or group potency, in which confidence results from the capacities and experiences of the group rather than the individual (Maddux, 2002).

As at the individual level, many of the prevalent occurrences and uncertainties in the current business landscape can be considered risk factors that both threaten and present unprecedented opportunities for market leadership and differentiation at the organizational level. Examples include globalization, cutthroat competition, increased consumer power, resource scarcity, litigation, ethical meltdown, shortages in qualified personnel and effective leaders, work-life balance issues, and challenges associated with strategic decisions, such as downsizing, outsourcing, and various "rightsizing" initiatives.

Our presentation of authentic leadership development (Avolio & Luthans, 2006; Luthans & Avolio, 2003) highlights the important role played by trigger events that leaders experience in their development of self-awareness, self-regulation, and, ultimately, authenticity and resiliency. Some trigger events may be unplanned and difficult to predict, thus exposing leaders to risk factors that can best be dealt with through reactive adaptation and coping mechanisms. On the other hand, in our proposed authentic-leadership development process, the organization can also proactively expose leaders to planned trigger events that can challenge them and set them on the path to an exciting journey of resiliency development (Avolio & Luthans, 2006; Luthans & Avolio, 2003). In this resiliency development process, organizational and leader strengths are effectively employed, and growth and life-long learning are monitored, managed, and experienced.

Organizational values are integral to the development of resiliency, both at the individual and organizational levels. Coutu (2002, p. 52) articulates this relationship when she states that "strong values infuse an environment with meaning because they offer ways to interpret and shape events." In other words, when well-communicated and thoroughly adopted, organizational values provide direction in times of ambiguity and turbulence. These organizational values give members stable ground to fall back on and guidelines for programmed and swift but effective ways to respond (Sutcliffe & Vogus, 2003; Weick, 1993). As organizations and their members gradually adapt, stable values allow them to regain balance, gather and organize their energies, and bounce back and beyond. Moreover, in line with the importance of values and beliefs being larger than oneself in order to provide a source of meaning (e.g., see Seligman, 1998), strong and stable organizational values that are aligned with the personal goals and aspirations of the managers and employees are likely to enhance resiliency at all levels. Such alignment can also be reinforced by the leadership of an organization, contributing further to organizational-level resiliency.

As previously noted, organizational resiliency requires effective ongoing adaptational processes, buffering mechanisms, and maintenance systems (Worline, et al., 2002; Youssef & Luthans, 2005b). These systems continuously acquire, invest in, and accumulate a wealth of structural and processual resources for the organization in times of ease and stability. They equip the organization for the proper selection, channeling, adaptation, and integration with resources to proactively forecast and effectively deal with adversities; that is, they contribute to organizational resiliency. If properly nurtured, such resources can provide the residual capability to sustain the most challenging and stressful events.

Horne and Orr (1998) propose that processes such as strategic planning, organizational alignment, organizational learning, and corporate cultural awareness can significantly enhance organizational resiliency. Specifically, strategic planning prepares the organization for difficult times through well-developed goals, objectives, and contingency plans. Alignment of organizational units with overall goals encourages unified action and effective sharing of resources and capabilities, reducing cross-silo infighting and thus allowing the collective organization to store "more energy." Organizational learning facilitates knowledge acquisition, creation, sharing, and utilization. Corporate cultural awareness allows for the accurate understanding and assessment of the organization's vision and core competencies, as well as areas of weakness—and, thus, potential risk factors.

Worline, et al. (2002) propose three buffering processes that can contribute to organizational resiliency: strengthening, replenishing, and limbering. Strengthening refers to "the dynamic combination of structures and practices that make the unit more vigorous by increasing the unit's resources of various kinds" (Worline, et al., 2002, p. 5). For example, providing quick and timely performance feedback when new members first begin working within their expected role can help them avoid wasted efforts, reinforce those behaviors that are most effective, and ultimately increase their confidence levels. On the other hand, at times when performance does decline, consistent and ongoing feedback can help identify and correct the source of the problem. In this way, the feedback is replenishing energy. This refers to "the dynamic combination of practices and structures that restore, regenerate, and renew the unit with resources of various kinds when they have been diminished or weakened in some way" (Worline, et al., 2002, p. 5).

Since feedback is an effective way to share best practices, it helps broaden the experience and knowledge base of each member. In this way, shared knowledge expands the list of known strategies and options for the entire unit, which increases its ability to adapt on its own. In this context, feedback is what Worline and colleagues (2002, p. 5) call limbering, which "pertains to the dynamic combination of structures and practices that increase the unit's ability to direct or flex resources to the need at hand, enabling the unit to switch directions or morph resources to meet unexpected needs."

Still another approach to building organizational resiliency supports the importance of employee "voice" (Vickers & Kouzmin, 2001). This view argues that an organization should create mechanisms that enhance its ability to "hear" its members. By helping followers to "find their voice," leaders are likely connecting them to the larger meaning of what gets done in the organization. At the same time, such leaders are also building a greater sense of ownership in the organization, which likely would positively impact organizational resiliency. These mechanisms include proper, transparent communication channels, openness to nonconforming ideas, and encouragement of creativity, empowerment, and engagement. Other examples of resiliency-enhancing organizational systems may include pay-for-performance, equitable and genuine recognition, goal-setting, mentoring, teamwork, and other high-performance work practices.

Organizational resiliency is an elaborate, complex, long-term process. Very few organizations, if any, can claim to have achieved their full potential in terms of their resiliency. However, drawing from the limited research that describes the characteristics of a resilient organization, Horne and Orr (1998) propose that resilient organizations enjoy what they simply label the seven "C's": community, competence, connections, commitment, communication, coordination, and consideration.

Hamel and Välikangas (2003) describe a resilient organization as one that can effectively overcome four challenges. The first is "cognitive challenge," which refers to the culture of denial and arrogance that success can breed, along with assumptions of immunity and invincibility. The second is "strategic challenge," which refers to satisfying (rather than maximizing) and which needs to be substituted with openness to a broader array of strategic possibilities. The third is "political challenge," where risky but high-potential ideas may go untried if the distribution of organizational power and politics prevents the allocation of adequate resources and support to those ideas. The fourth is "ideological challenge," in which optimization and efficiency may substitute for more-effective measures of organizational viability, such as creativity, innovation, and renewal. As an organization overcomes these four challenges, it is likely to exhibit a greater level of resiliency over time.

POTENTIAL PITFALLS OF RESILIENCY

Although resiliency can equip today's organizations and their members with tremendous capacities, energies, and protective mechanisms, many organizations and their leaders may be reluctant to intentionally let their employees experience or take part in handling their own or the organization's adversities and setbacks. In the same way that many adults hesitate to accept that allowing a child to face threats or even difficulties is an acceptable, beneficial, and morally sound decision (Wolin & Wolin, 2005), traditional, paternalistic leaders feel responsible for and obliged to handle every problem of their employees. However, such a quick-fix approach to problem-solving may not be the most effective in developing strength and endurance, nor will it help followers enrich their own repertoires of problem-solving techniques and independence from the leader. Moreover, leaders who carry an unfair burden of crisis management are likely to suffer from higher levels of stress and burnout. In addition to jeopardizing their own well-being, such leaders also hinder their organizations' and their followers' resiliency development. Instead, they may be creating dependence, vulnerability, and lack of preparedness in their followers and their units as their stress cascades down throughout the organization

Decisions made by organizations and their leaders for the "good" of the people may have significant long-term detrimental effects (Vickers & Kouzmin, 2001). When employees appear to have bounced back in the short run when leaders make decisions for them, the leaders mistakenly assume that their employees are resilient. The leaders think the employees' resiliency has protected them from the adverse impact of the leaders' unilateral decisions. However, effective short-term coping should not be equated with long-term resiliency. If employees are not provided with the proper channels to voice their own concerns, such apparent but unreal and short-lived "resiliency" comes at the high cost of future disengagement, passivity, disloyalty, and distrust of the leaders and the organization.

A case in point is an interview that we recently had with an employee who the leadership perceived to be "resilient" in an organization that had undergone a significant change with high repercussions on its employees. Four years ago, the organization automated one of its units, which resulted in a reduction in force (RIF) in this unit from over 500 employees to only five! The communication message that accompanied the RIF process conveyed to the five survivors was that they were retained because they were an "elite" group. They kept the best and the brightest. They were given pay raises, added benefits, and higher levels of responsibility and autonomy. The five elite survivors apparently learned how to cope with the situation, as evidenced by their continued employment and success in the organization. However, the very low morale of the elite five was evident not only because of the increased workload and expectations placed on them but also because each of them constantly recalled the lost work relationships, the hardships experienced by laid-off colleagues and their families, and the synergies and tacit knowledge that no longer existed in this unit. It seems that the passive coping attitudes and behaviors that these survivors exhibited were incorrectly interpreted and rewarded as a high level of resiliency. What is even worse is that such an inaccurate assumption of resiliency had led these five to expose themselves to even higher levels of risk and dysfunctional outcomes by accepting to stay with an organization that they resented (indeed, actually hated) and in which they had zero trust.

Another potential pitfall to note is that the role of values in enhancing resiliency is primarily dependent on the stability of those values rather than just their ethical soundness or their alignment with the organization's values. For example, survival-of-the-fittest mechanisms may have contributed to resiliency in many tough situations (Coutu, 2002), but when implemented in the workplace, their underlying value system may not prove to be morally acceptable. Thus, the personal beliefs and values that organizational leaders and employees may utilize in order to bounce back from adversities need to be scrutinized and continuously aligned in light of the organization's value system and standards of ethical conduct.

Still another pitfall that organizations can fall into is brought out by Rudolph and Repenning's (2002) model of disaster dynamics. The essence of this model is that over time, some organizational assets can change into risk factors that can have a negative impact on organizational resiliency. For example, many currently effective organizational systems are capable of only detecting and dealing with significant changes and discontinuities that are qualitatively different from the status quo. However, these systems may not be sensitive enough to gradually accumulate seemingly harmless events that may erode their viability. These seemingly small but frequent changes can cause the organization to reach a threshold that can lead to an unexpected "quantity-induced" disaster. In other words, an organization may have the appearance of resiliency because it is functioning smoothly and has effective self-regulating mechanisms in place, but it may actually be on the verge of collapse, even in some instances failing miserably in its success.

One example of failing miserably in its success was the now-defunct Digital Equipment Organization (DEC). The CEO and founder of this company, Ken Olsen, built the organization's success on its ability to "out-engineer" its competitors. Yet when the market shifted toward computers that were more of a commodity type, DEC kept plowing along, building over-engineered computers that were eventually totally rejected by the market. This singular focus led to catastrophic results for this venerable company.

Hamel and Välikangas (2003) also support that "business as usual" and organizational resilience are not necessarily equivalent. In the business environment of the past, organizations used to "bury their mistakes" and/ or create a momentum of entry barriers to maintain profitability. Real crises and discontinuities had to be very significant and hard to miss. They were then dealt with aggressively as one-time events. This is no longer true in the environment facing today's organizations. Dramatic, paradigmatic changes, which are the rule rather than the exception, require organizations to be constantly on the lookout for opportunities that warrant the proactive destruction of their own presently successful strategies and business models in anticipation of discontinuities and strategic shifts. PsyCap resiliency is no longer "nice to have" at the individual, leader, and organizational levels; it may be required in the new "flat-world" globalization in which we now live and compete.

FUTURE IMPLICATIONS AND DIRECTIONS FOR PSYCAP RESILIENCY RESEARCH AND PRACTICE

As can be deduced from this chapter, the current status of the body of knowledge on resiliency as it applies to the workplace can be best described as "just emerging." On the one hand, there is a rich body of established research in developmental and clinical psychology that focuses on the negative end of the continuum, with recent recognition of the need for positively oriented applications (Block & Kremen, 1996; Masten, 2001; Masten & Reed, 2002). On the other hand, there is a tremendous need for resiliency in today's uncertain workplace, but with the exception of some of our recent theory-building and empirical research (Avolio & Luthans, 2006; Luthans, 2002; Luthans & Avolio, 2003; Luthans et al., 2004; Luthans, Avolio, et al., 2006; Luthans, et al., 2005; Luthans, Vogelgesang, & Lester, 2006; Luthans & Youssef, 2004; Youssef, 2004; Youssef & Luthans, 2005a, 2005b), just limited and scattered incidences of responding to that need exist (e.g., see Sutcliffe & Vogus, 2003; also see Conner, 1993, 2003; Coutu, 2002; Hamel & Välikangas, 2003; Horne & Orr, 1998; LaMarch, 1997; Vickers & Kouzmin, 2001; Waterman, et al., 1994; Zunz, 1998, for conceptual theory-building and practitioner perspectives; Harland, et al., 2005, and Waite & Richardson, 2004, for quantitative studies; and Worline, et al., 2002, for a qualitative study). Thus, almost any direction for future

PsyCap resiliency research relevant and applicable to the workplace would seem worthwhile. However, we offer the following, which would seem to be especially important research needs for the future.

- Unlike PsyCap self-efficacy, hope, and optimism, resiliency is more reactive in nature. Organizations can accelerate the process of resiliency development through exposing their managers and employees to planned events and challenges that would trigger the process of bouncing back. However, the outcomes of resiliency development are likely to be fully realized at a later point in the future, when the developing organizational participant eventually has to exhibit the capacity to bounce "back and beyond" as un-planned setbacks take place. Thus, it is imperative that a longitudinal approach be employed in order for resiliency research to fully capture the resulting performance improvements from resiliency development, as well as the sustainability of those enhanced outcomes.
- Longitudinal resiliency research will not only facilitate the compre-hension of the full extent of resiliency outcomes but also the understanding of the processes, mechanisms, and strategies involved in the appraisal of risk factors and the employment and adaptation of various assets to mitigate risks and even capitalize on them for further growth and development. We have recently begun our theory-building in this area (Avolio & Luthans, 2006; Luthans & Avolio, 2003; Luthans, Vogelgesang, & Lester, 2006; Youssef & Luthans, 2005b), but further conceptual and empirical research is much needed.
- Although in our initial research we have found a relationship between employee resiliency and performance outcomes (Luthans, et al., 2005; Luthans, Avolio, et al., 2006) and job satisfaction (Luthans, Avolio, et al., 2006), research is also needed to examine the impact on other outcomes, such as organizational commit-ment, organizational citizenship behaviors, employee wellness, and retention.
- Most of the research on resiliency focused on the individual level, but we would advocate also looking at the group as a target for future research on resiliency. We suspect that groups that have worked very successfully together over time might develop a

unique "personality" that may better enable such groups to bounce back from difficulties and challenges.

• Finally, as with the other PsyCap capacities, although our initial studies have demonstrated that resiliency (and overall PsyCap; see chapter 8) can be developed in our short, highly focused micro-interventions (Luthans, Avey, Avolio, Norman, & Combs, 2006), experimental studies with more varied settings and levels—and even across cultures—are needed for the future.

REFERENCES

Avolio, B. J., & Luthans, F. (2006). *The high impact leader: Moments matter in accelerating authentic leadership development.* New York: McGraw-Hill.

Bagshaw, M. (1997). Employability: Creating a contract of mutual investment. *Industrial and Commercial Training, 29*(6), 187–189.

Baron, L., Eisman, H., Scuello, M., Veyzer, A., & Lieberman, M. (1996). Stress resilience, locus of control, and religion in children of Holocaust victims. *Journal of Psychology, 130,* 513–525.

Bass, B. M. (1998). *Transformational leadership.* Mahwah, NJ: Erlbaum.

Bergin, A. (1983). Religiosity and mental health: A critical re-evaluation and meta-analysis. *Professional Psychology Research and Practice, 14,* 170–184.

Block, J., & Kremen, A. M. (1996). IQ and ego-resiliency: Conceptual and empirical connections and separateness. *Journal of Personality and Social Psychology, 70,* 349–361.

Bonanno, G. A. (2004). Loss, trauma and human resilience. *American Psychologist, 59,* 20–28.

Burns, J. M. (1978). *Leadership.* New York: Free Press

Collins, M. E. (2001). Transition to adulthood for vulnerable youths: A review of research and implications for policy. *Social Service Review, 75,* 271–291.

Conner, D. (1993). *Managing at the speed of change: How resilient managers succeed and prosper where others fail.* New York: Villard Books.

Conner, D. (2003). Training & Development—Solutions at Sun Microsystems. Retrieved May 12, 2005, from http://www.odrinc.com

Coutu, D. L. (2002). How resilience works. *Harvard Business Review, 80*(5), 46–55.

Cowan, P. A., Cowan, C. P., & Schulz, M. S. (1996). Thinking about risk and resilience in families. In E. M. Hetherington & E. A. Blechman (Eds.), *Stress, coping, and resiliency in children and families* (pp. 1–38). Mahwah, NJ: Erlbaum.

Egeland, B., Carlson, E., & Sroufe, L. A. (1993). Resilience as a process. *Development and Psychopathology, 5,* 517–528.

Friedman, T. L. (2005). *The world is flat.* New York: Farrar, Strauss & Giroux.

Gibbs, M. (1989). Factors in the victim that mediate between disaster and psychotherapy: A review. *Journal of Traumatic Stress, 2*(4), 489–514.

Gorman, C. (2005, January 17). The importance of resilience. *Time, 165*(3), A52–A55.

Greenhouse, S. (2001, September 1). Report shows Americans have more labor days. *New York Times,* A6.

Hamel, G., & Välikangas (2003). The quest for resilience. *Harvard Business Review, 81*(9), 52–63.

Harland, L., Harrison, W., Jones, J., & Reiter-Palmon, R. (2005). Leadership behaviors and subordinate resilience. *Journal of Leadership and Organizational Studies, 11,* 2–14.

Holaday, M., & McPhearson, R. (1997). Resilience and severe burns. *Journal of Counseling and Development, 75,* 346–356.

Horne, J., III, & Orr, J. (1998). Assessing behaviors that create resilient organizations. *Employment Relations Today, 24*(4), 29–39.

Huey, Jr., S. J., & Weisz, J. R. (1997). Ego control, ego resiliency, and the five-factor model as predictors of behavioral and emotional problems in clinic-referred children and adolescents. *Journal of Abnormal Psychology, 106,* 404–415.

Hunter, A. J., & Chandler, G. E. (1999). Adolescent resilience. *Image: Journal of Nursing Scholarship, 31,* 243–247.

Johnson, K., Bryant, D., Collins, D., Noe, T., Strader, T., & Berbaum, M. (1998). Preventing and reducing alcohol and other drug use among high-risk youths by increasing family resilience. *Social Work, 43,* 297–308.

Kakabadse, N., & Kakabadse, A. (2000). Critical review—outsourcing: A paradigm shift. *Journal of Management Development, 19,* 670–728.

Kirby, L., & Fraser, M. (1997). Risk and resilience in childhood. In M. Fraser (Ed.), *Risk and resilience in childhood* (pp. 10–33). Washington, DC: National Association of Social Workers Press.

Klarreich, S. (1998). Resiliency: The skills needed to move forward in a changing environment. In S. Klarreich (Ed.), *Handbook of organizational health psychology: Programs to make the workplace healthier* (pp. 219–238). Madison, CT: Psychosocial Press.

Kobsa, S. C. (1982). The hardy personality. In G. S. Sanders & J. Suls (Eds.), *Social psychology of health and illness* (pp. 3–32). Hillsdale, NJ: Erlbaum.

Koretz, G. (2001, June 11). Why Americans work so hard. *Business Week, 34.*

LaMarch, J. (1997). The resilient worker: Employees who can cope with change. *Hospital Material Management Quarterly, 19*(2), 54–58.

Larson, D., Pattison, E., Blazer, D., Omran, A., & Kaplan, B. (1986). Systematic analysis of research on religious variables in four major psychiatric journals, 1978–1982. *American Journal of Psychiatry, 143,* 329–334.

Luthans, F. (2002). The need for and meaning of positive organizational behavior. *Journal of Organizational Behavior, 23,* 695–706

Luthans, F., Avey, J. B., Avolio, B. J., Norman, S. M., & Combs, G. J. (2006). Psychological capital development: Toward a micro-intervention. *Journal of Organizational Behavior, 27,* 387–393.

Luthans, F., & Avolio, B. (2003). Authentic leadership: A positive development approach.

In K. S. Cameron, J. E. Dutton, & R. E. Quinn (Eds.), *Positive organizational scholarship* (pp. 241–258). San Francisco: Berrett-Koehler.

Luthans, F., Avolio, B. J., Avey, J. B., & Norman, S. M. (2006). Psychological capital: Measurement and relationship with performance and satisfaction (Working Paper No. 2006–1). Gallup Leadership Institute, University of Nebraska–Lincoln.

Luthans, F., Avolio, B. J., Walumbwa, F. O., & Li, W. (2005). The psychological capital of Chinese workers: Exploring the relationship with performance. *Management and Organization Review, 1,* 247–269.

Luthans, F., Luthans, K., & Luthans, B. (2004). Positive psychological capital: Going beyond human and social capital. *Business Horizons, 47*(1), 45–50.

Luthans, F., Vogelgesang, G. R., & Lester, P. B. (2006). Developing the psychological capital of resilency. *Human Resource Development Review, 5,* 25–44.

Luthans, F., & Youssef, C. M. (2004). Human, social and now positive psychological capital management: Investing in people for competitive advantage. *Organizational Dynamics, 33,* 143–160.

Maddux, J. E. (2002). Self-efficacy: The power of believing you can. In C. R. Snyder & S. Lopez (Eds.), *Handbook of positive psychology* (pp. 257–276). Oxford, UK: Oxford University Press.

Masten, A. S. (2001). Ordinary magic: Resilience process in development. *American Psychologist, 56,* 227–239.

Masten, A. S., & Reed, M. J. (2002). Resilience in development. In C. R. Snyder & S. Lopez (Eds.), *Handbook of positive psychology* (pp. 74–88). Oxford, UK: Oxford University Press.

Ness, R., & Wintrob, R. (1980). The emotional impact of fundamentalist religious participation. *American Journal of Orthopsychiatry, 50,* 302–315.

Paul, P. (2005, January 17). The power to uplift. *Time, 165*(3), A46–A48.

Qouta, S., El-Sarraj, A., & Punamaki, R. (2001). Mental flexibility as resiliency factor among children exposed to political violence. *International Journal of Psychology, 36*(1), 1–7.

Reichard, R. J., & Avolio, B. J. (2005). Where are we? The status of leadership intervention research: A meta-analytic summary. In W. Gardner, B. Avolio, & F. Walumbwa (Eds.), *Monographs in leadership and management: Volume 3. Authentic leadership theory and practice: Origins, effects and development* (pp. 203–223). Oxford, UK: Elsevier.

Reivich, K., & Shatte, A. (2002). *The resilience factor: 7 essential skills for overcoming life's inevitable obstacles.* New York: Random House.

Richardson, G. (2002). The metatheory of resilience and resiliency. *Journal of Clinical Psychology, 58,* 307–321.

Robinson, S. L., Kraatz, M. S., & Rousseau, D. M. (1994). Changing obligations and the psychological contract: A longitudinal study. *Academy of Management Journal, 37,* 137–152.

Rudolph, J. W., & Repenning, N. P. (2002). Disaster dynamics: Understanding the role of quantity in organizational collapse. *Administrative Science Quarterly, 47,* 1–30.

Ryff, C., & Singer, B. (2003). Flourishing under fire: Resilience as a prototype of challenged thriving. In C. Keyes & J. Haidt (Eds.), *Flourishing: Positive psychology and the life well-lived* (pp. 15–36). Washington, DC: American Psychological Association.

Sandau-Beckler, P., Devall, E., & de la Rosa, I. (2002). Strengthening family resilience: Prevention and treatment for high-risk substance-affected families. *Journal of Individual Psychology, 58,* 305–327.

Sanders, J. M., & Nee, V. (1996). Immigrant self-employment: The family as social capital and the value of human capital. *American Sociological Review, 61,* 231–249.

Seligman, M. (1998). *Learned optimism.* New York: Pocket Books.

Smith, C., & Carlson, B. (1997). Stress, coping, and resilience in children and youth. *Social Service Review, 71,* 231–256.

Stewart, M., Reid, G., & Mangham, C. (1997). Fostering children's resilience. *Journal of Pediatric Nursing, 12,* 21–31.

Sutcliffe, K. M., & Vogus, T. (2003). Organizing for resilience. In K. S. Cameron, J. E. Dutton, & R. E. Quinn (Eds.), *Positive organizational scholarship* (pp. 94–110). San Francisco: Berrett-Koehler.

Tebbi, C., Mallon, J., Richards, M., & Bigler, L. (1987). Religiosity and locus of control of adolescent and cancer patients. *Psychological Reports, 61,* 683–696.

Tedeschi, R., Park, C., & Calhoun, L. (Eds.). (1998). *Posttraumatic growth: Positive changes in the aftermath of crisis.* Mahwah, NJ: Erlbaum.

Teixeira, C. (2001). Community resources and opportunities in ethnic economies: A case study of Portuguese and black entrepreneurs in Toronto. *Urban Studies, 38,* 2055–2078.

Vaillant, G. E. (1977). *Adaptation to life.* Boston: Little, Brown.

Vaillant, G. E. (2000). The mature defenses. *American Psychologist, 55,* 89–98.

Vickers, M. H., & Kouzmin, A. (2001). Resilience in organizational actors and rearticulating voice. *Public Management Review, 3*(1), 95–119.

Waite, P., & Richardson, G. (2004). Determining the efficacy of resiliency training in the work site. *Journal of Allied Health, 33,* 178–183.

Waterman, R. H., Waterman, J. A., & Collard, B. A. (1994). Toward a career-resilient workforce. *Harvard Business Review, 72*(4), 87–95.

Weick, K. E. (1993). The collapse of sensemaking in organizations: The Mann Gulch disaster, *Administrative Science Quarterly, 38,* 628–652.

Wolin, S., & Wolin, S. (2005). Project resilience. Retrieved June 1, 2005, from http://www.projectresilience.com

Wong, J., & Mason, G. (2001). Reviled, rejected, but resilient: Homeless people in recovery and life skills education. *Georgetown Journal on Poverty Law and Policy, 8,* 475–503.

Worline, M. C., Dutton, J. E., Frost, P. J., Kanov, J., Lilius, J. M., & Maitlis, S. (2002, August). *Creating fertile soil: The organizing dynamics of resilience.* Paper presented at the annual meeting of the Academy of Management, Denver, CO.

Youssef, C. M. (2004). Resiliency development of organizations, leaders and employees: Multi-level theory building and individual-level, path-analytical empirical testing. Unpublished doctoral dissertation, University of Nebraska–Lincoln.

Youssef, C. M., & Luthans, F. (2005a). A positive organizational behavior approach to ethical performance. In R. A. Giacalone, C. Dunn, & C. Jurkiewicz (Eds.), *Positive psychology in business ethics and corporate social responsibility* (pp. 1–22). Greenwich, CT: Information Age.

Youssef, C., & Luthans, F. (2005b). Resiliency development of organizations, leaders & employees: Multi-level theory building for sustained performance. In W. Gardner, B. Avolio, & F. Walumbwa (Eds.), *Monographs in leadership and management: Volume 3. Authentic leadership theory and practice: Origins, effects and development* (pp. 303–343). Oxford, UK: Elsevier.

Zunz, S. (1998). Resiliency and burnout: Protective factors for human service managers. *Administration in Social Work, 22*(3), 39–54.

CHAPTER 6

Selected Cognitive and Affective Strengths

Potential PsyCap?

As WE HAVE noted, the positive psychological capacities of self-efficacy, hope, optimism, and resiliency covered in the four previous chapters have been determined to best meet our PsyCap inclusion criteria laid out in chapter 1. However, these four are not meant to represent an exhaustive list. The rich emerging body of knowledge on positive psychology (e.g., Aspinwall & Straudinger, 2003; Carr, 2004; Giacalone, Jurkiewicz, & Dunn, 2005; Keyes & Haidt, 2003; Linley & Joseph, 2004; Lopez & Snyder, 2003; Peterson & Seligman, 2004; Snyder & Lopez, 2002; see www.positivepsychology.org for a continually updated website on the growing literature) and positive organizational scholarship (e.g., Cameron & Caza, 2004; Cameron, Dutton, & Quinn, 2003; see www.bus.umich.edu/Positive/) presents a wide range of unique individual, group, and organizational strengths and virtues. Many of the positive constructs found in this literature appear highly promising in terms of both their theoretical foundations and potential applicability to the workplace. Some have also been shown to be measurable and developmental. We expect over the next several years to add to the list of current psychological capital constructs that end up representing one's overall amount of psychological capital.

In this chapter and the next, we selectively introduce some of these other positive constructs, which we propose may have particular relevance and potential for inclusion in PsyCap now and in the future. We provide a concise assessment of each of these positive constructs' "fit" with PsyCap, which

TABLE 6.1. Assessment of "Fit" with PsyCap for Selected High-Potential Cognitive and Affective Strengths

Category	Positive construct	Theory-based?	Trait-like/ Relatively fixed?	State-like/ Malleable?	Measurable?	Related to work performance?	Related to other positive outcomes?
Current PsyCap	Self-efficacy	✓		✓	✓	✓	✓
	Hope	✓		✓	✓	✓	✓
	Optimism	✓	✓	✓	✓	✓	✓
	Resiliency	✓	✓	✓	✓	✓	✓
Cognitive	Creativity	✓	✓	?	✓	?	?
	Wisdom	✓	✓	✓	✓	?	?
Affective	Well-being	✓	✓	✓	✓	✓	✓
	Flow	✓	✓	✓	✓	✓	✓
	Humor	✓	✓	✓	✓	?	✓

can, hopefully, help guide future research and practice. Table 6.1 provides a very brief PsyCap criteria checklist summary of selected cognitive and affective-oriented positive capacities (i.e., creativity, wisdom, well-being, flow, and humor) covered in this chapter. Self-efficacy, hope, optimism, and resiliency are also included for benchmark comparison. In addition, beside the PsyCap inclusion criteria of the positive construct being theory-based, measurable, state-like or developmental, and related to work performance, two related assessment factors are also incorporated. These are: (1) the presence of a recognized foundation or baseline of work on the construct that directly or indirectly suggests state-like development, even though most of the work may have come from a trait-like perspective; and (2) the existence of any known relationships between the positive construct and desirable work-related outcomes other than performance. These two additional criteria provide both support and/or potential limitations of these positive constructs for potential inclusion in PsyCap.

CLASSIFICATIONS OF POTENTIAL PSYCAP CONSTRUCTS

We classify the positive psychological capacities presented in this chapter and the next into four broadly defined categories: cognitive, affective, social, and higher order. Loosely defined, cognitive and affective capacities are discussed in this chapter, while more social and higher order capacities are presented in the following chapter. Although based in social cognitive theory (Bandura, 1986, 1997, 2001) and guided by research in positive psychology, this categorization is by no means intended to be definitive.

Obviously, there is no agreed-upon, strict classification system for positive constructs in the psychological literature (e.g., see Peterson & Seligman, 2004; Snyder & Lopez, 2002). However, we believe that it may be at the intersection of the proposed alternative frameworks that a better understanding of PsyCap can result. We propose that at least one way to broadly classify the positive psychological capacities discussed in this chapter may be labeled cognitive and affective, and those in the next chapter may be labeled social and higher order.

Although our list of other potential PsyCap constructs is not meant to be exhaustive, we did make an intentional effort to exclude several types of psychological constructs that, although important and arguably somewhat related, clearly did not meet most of our PsyCap inclusion criteria. Those deliberately excluded were the following.

- Negatively oriented constructs, such as emotional labor, stress, burnout, conflict, and disengagement (e.g., see Hochschild, 1983).
- Positive, but heavily studied, traditional organizational behavior constructs (i.e., those that do not meet the uniqueness criterion), such as self-esteem, reinforcement, goal-setting, positive affectivity, prosocial/citizenship behaviors, empowerment, engagement, and participation (see Locke, 2000, and Luthans, 2005, for comprehensive reviews of these well-established organizational behavior constructs). We realize that, over time, our PsyCap constructs will also not be unique. However, at this initial stage of early development of the new core construct of PsyCap, we are simply trying to avoid the inclusion of widely studied organizational behavior constructs that also do not meet our other criteria, such as being state-like and open to development.
- Clearly hard-wired (e.g., physiological emotions) and dispositional traits that have been shown to be relatively fixed, long enduring, and thus lacking the potential for development and management, such as the Big Five personality traits (Barrick & Mount, 1991), core self-evaluations (Judge & Bono, 2001), Gallup's talent (Buckingham & Coffman, 1999) and signature strengths (Buckingham & Clifton, 2001), and mental abilities (e.g., Schmidt & Hunter, 2000).
- Psychological capacities that may neither be directly applicable nor have performance impact in today's workplace, such as appreciation of beauty, love, naturalistic tendencies, musical talent, and others (e.g., see Gardner, 1983, 1999; Peterson & Seligman, 2004).

The positive constructs that we did include as potential PsyCap strengths, as shown in table 6.1, did mostly meet the criteria we have established for inclusion in PsyCap. As shown, creativity and wisdom are placed into the cognitively oriented category because they largely have to do with thought processes.

Going as far back as Norman Vincent Peale's well-known message of the power of positive thinking, both research and practice support the idea that taking a more positive view can broaden one's perspective to different ideas and approaches. Being able to hold two very different and competing thoughts until one insight emerges requires a great deal of positive energy to maintain such a balance. Positive thoughts have become widely recognized as shaping perceptions, attributions, and interpretations of various events—and thus, our learning from the past. This positivity in turn may favorably impact behavior and performance in the present and motivation for future performance impact as well. There is an increasing likelihood for a positive spiral of desired personal and organizational outcomes to accrue from positivity over time (Frederickson, 2001, 2003). Creativity and wisdom are proposed to be two such positive cognitive processes that may have potential for becoming part of PsyCap.

CREATIVITY AS POTENTIAL PSYCAP

Although creativity is frequently associated with strikingly original and revolutionary ideas, it also incorporates the capacity to find novel approaches for day-to-day problem-solving, as well as to constructively adapt new ideas and mechanisms so that they positively contribute to oneself and others (Simonton, 2004). Traditionally, creativity has been viewed as a dispositional trait that can only be developed at early age, or it has even been seen as a genetically determined individual difference (Cassandro & Simonton, 2003; Feist, 1998). Thus, the strongest emphasis on its development has been in children (Nickerson, 1999). However, the positive psychology movement has refueled a nature-nurture debate, with genetic and environmental/developmental factors exhibiting complex multiplicative and synergistic interactions in the conceptualization of creativity (Plomin & Daniels, 1987; Simonton, 2002).

Creativity seems to represent the case for the role of nature and nurture. As Riegel (1975) noted a number of years ago, "human development can only be understood by conceiving the emergence of behavior over time as a result of an ongoing exchange between the organism and the environment" (p. 46). Going further back, Graves (1959) had similarly stated: "finally, it was assumed that just as the seed must have favorable living circumstances to flower fully so too is man's ethical potential limited by the life circumstances which the human develops" (p. 8). Finally, Plomin and Daniels (1987) concluded that "behavioral-genetics research seldom finds evidence that more than half of the variance for complex traits is due to genetic differences among individuals" (p. 1). Using such a historically established theoretic platform, various creativity-stimulating and creativity-inhibiting factors have now been identified and studied.

Particularly relevant for the workplace is the impact of intrinsic and extrinsic motivators on creativity. Intrinsic factors that have been found to spark creativity in the workplace include an interesting and challenging job, a sense of autonomy, and a satisfying work environment. Also recognized as intrinsic factors stimulating creativity would be encouraging and supportive peers, supervisors, top management, and organizational systems. On the other hand, extrinsic factors and pressures, such as contingency-based incentives, competition with peers, arbitrarily set deadlines and goals, inadequate resources, performance monitoring, rigid structures, inflexible policies and procedures, and uncaring supervisors and managers, may greatly hinder creativity.

This is not to say that a creative work environment cannot exist where monetary compensation and specific performance expectations are present. Instead, the guideline for organizations and leaders is that to stimulate creativity, they should selectively and synergistically utilize extrinsic motivators to confirm and reward, rather than control, creative behavior (Amabile, 2000). For example, research has clearly demonstrated that contingently administered financial rewards, positive feedback, and social recognition have been found to be effective incentive motivators that stimulate desired organizational behaviors and performance outcomes (Peterson & Luthans, 2006; Stajkovic & Luthans, 1997, 2001, 2003) and, by extension, creative behaviors as well.

There are many measures of creativity, with emphases given to the various dimensions of creativity: the creative person, the creative process, and the creative product or outcome (Peterson & Seligman, 2004; Simonton, 2002). For example, the Torrance Test of Creative Thinking (TTCT; Torrance, 1988) is perhaps the most supported instrument available in terms of reliability, validity, and generalizability across contexts and cultures. The TTCT is a process-oriented measure that assesses four creative abilities, which are considered to be necessary ingredients for the divergent thinking process associated with creativity: fluency, flexibility, originality, and elaboration. On the other hand, where the creative person is the referent for analysis, various personality inventories and projective tests are recommended (Kerr & Gagliardi, 2003). Finally, if the creative product or outcome is the point of emphasis, then various product-specific performance measures and/or outcomes, such as meeting customer expectations or customer engagement and loyalty, are typically employed.

As psychological capital, creative processes, persons, and products and outcomes would all seem necessary for performance impact and sustained competitiveness. Thus, to meet the measurement criterion of PsyCap, there is a need to integrate the multiple measures of creativity to include the process, personal, and outcome dimensions.

Although the theory and research criteria of PsyCap applicable to creativity are found in positive psychology (e.g., see Peterson & Seligman, 2004; Simonton, 2002), other criteria are not. For example, the criteria of being relatively unique to the field of organizational behavior and state-like (open to development) are still a challenge for creativity to become fully part of what we have defined as PsyCap. The same is true of the performance impact criterion. To date, more of the studies treat creativity as an outcome rather than an antecedent to performance or other desirable, work-related outcomes. In the future, it may be profitable to explore more contextualized versions of creativity that may better fit our PsyCap criteria. For example, if one can develop intelligence regarding the context in which one is embedded, it is certainly possible to have creative intelligence in terms of how to change the context to better suit the needs of organizational leaders and their associates.

WISDOM AS POTENTIAL PSYCAP

Another cognitively based potential candidate for PsyCap is wisdom. Traditional perspectives in philosophy and theology elevated wisdom to a status that emphasized exclusiveness, transcendence, and even aloofness (Hartman, 2004). In positive psychology, however, wisdom is defined in more pragmatic terms as "an expert knowledge system concerning the fundamental pragmatics of life, including knowledge and judgment about the conduct and meaning of life" (Baltes & Freund, 2003b, p. 252; see also Baltes & Staudinger, 2000). This definition to some degree is similar to our previously discussed notion of contextualized creativity.

This positive psychology definition of wisdom broadens its scope to incorporate both the theoretical, terminal values or ends of knowing what is right and good and the practical, instrumental values or means of applying this knowledge behaviorally toward a fulfilled life. This "optimal life" of wisdom is multidimensional and dynamic across various stages and domains (Baltes, Glück, & Kunzmann, 2002), including the workplace.

Wisdom also involves a balance between pursuing one's personal interests and pursuing those of others, that is, the common good (Sternberg, 1998). In other words, wisdom becomes very relevant and highly salient for organizational leaders in today's morally challenged environment, and it links to what Avolio, Gardner, Walumbwa, Luthans, and May (2004) have called the "balanced processing" part of their model of authentic leadership development. By balanced processing, they mean that leaders are able to take input from diverse points of view and to consider how those views may shape their interpretation and decisions regarding a particular challenge or opportunity fairly and objectively.

Theoretical Perspectives of Wisdom

Various approaches have been employed in the recent theory-building and research on wisdom. For example, implicit theories of wisdom focus on "who is wise." Commonly agreed-upon characteristics of wise individuals include cognitive (e.g., intelligence), affective/social (e.g., empathy), reflective (e.g., intuition), and motivational descriptive adjectives (Baltes, et al., 2002; Staudinger & Leipold, 2003). We selectively discuss some of these characteristics in other sections of this chapter and the next because of their potential relevance to PsyCap. On the other hand, explicit theories of wisdom emphasize the mechanisms and processes through which wisdom can be developed and practiced (Baltes & Kunzmann, 2004; Hartman, 2004). These explicit theories make wisdom more directly relevant in meeting the criteria of PsyCap in terms of development and performance management in today's workplace.

Specifically, explicit theories of wisdom offer three distinct conceptualizations. The first views wisdom as an individual difference or personality trait. The second explains wisdom in terms of transcendent maturity, dialectical thinking, and tolerance for ambiguity, uncertainty, and relativism. Third, and most relevant to positive psychology and PsyCap, is the cognitively, socially, and behaviorally integrated conceptualization of wisdom as an expert system that pragmatically deals with the practical, applied side of life, giving it meaning and value (Baltes, et al., 2002; Staudinger & Leipold, 2003).

The positive psychological perspective on wisdom (also known as the "Berlin Wisdom Paradigm") defines and measures wisdom through several important criteria (Staudinger, Smith, & Baltes, 1994).

- Factual knowledge concerning the fundamental pragmatics of life (i.e., what is important, the ends, the goals).
- Procedural knowledge of the fundamental pragmatics of life (i.e., how to reach what is important for oneself and others, the means).
- Lifespan contextualism (i.e., the integrated knowledge of various domains and contexts of life, the adaptation of focus and priorities over one's lifetime).
- Value relativism (i.e., acknowledgment, tolerance, and sensitivity to interpersonal and cross-cultural differences as individual and collective interests are pursued).
- Recognition and management of uncertainty.

Wisdom as State-Like and Open to Development

Of particular relevance to PsyCap is that wisdom seems to be not only a dispositional trait but also a developmental state or, as we have indicted throughout this book, "state-like." Contrary to conventional belief, wisdom has not necessarily been found to be a direct function of aging. In fact, similar to the research findings regarding the stability of personality variables in at least young adulthood, wisdom has also been found to have a positive relationship with age, mainly between 15 and 25, and to exhibit a more stable relationship after this age band (Baltes, Staudinger, Maercker, & Smith, 1995). Similarly, widely recognized dispositional traits, such as intelligence or personality traits, have been found to only partially account for wisdom (Staudinger, Lopez, & Baltes, 1997).

Unlike intelligence and personality traits, wisdom is now becoming recognized as being malleable and open to development. One of the non-dispositional factors which has been consistently found to contribute to wisdom is professional experience. For example, the clinical psychology profession provides educational and practice contexts that are rich in structured training, mentoring (both being mentored and mentoring others), and direct experience of issues which are of fundamental importance in developing wisdom. These developmental activities and experiences have been found to trigger and facilitate the acquisition of wisdom-related knowledge and judgment (Staudinger, Maciel, Smith, & Baltes, 1998). The same could be said for the sports coaching profession or any other profession. What will be interesting to discover is the specific nature of events that tend to trigger the learning and development of wisdom.

Parallel experiences to those found in the traditional professions can be created in many other jobs. For example, regardless of the industry or domain in which they operate, authentic leaders experience events and moments that may have been planned and structured by their organizations, targeting their development, but they are also likely to face unplanned, eye-opening life events, that is, experience "moments that matter" (Avolio & Luthans, 2006). The self-awareness and self-regulation that these events or moments trigger, along with effective mentors/coaches in a supportive organizational context, are likely to develop the leader's authenticity in terms of the capacity for developing one's self and others (Avolio & Luthans, 2006; Luthans & Avolio, 2003). This authentic leadership-development process suggested by Avolio and Luthans (2006) is also in line with Baltes and Kunzmann's (2004) wisdom-development framework. They outline the mechanisms and processes of life planning, life management, and life review. These facilitate the contribution of personal and contextual variables in the development and application of wisdom.

Other factors that have been found to contribute to the development of wisdom include resilience and adjustment (see chapter 5), creativity (see the previous discussion), motivation for learning and generativity, acceptance of life choices and outcomes, self-directed goals and tasks, relationship and career changes, and positive and negative life and career events (Hartman, 2004). Again, such factors cannot only be developed, but they can also be effectively managed in the workplace in order to enhance the wisdom of the decisions and actions of managers and employees. Moreover, interaction and collaboration with real or imaginary others has been found through research to enhance wisdom in dealing with difficult situations by as much as one standard deviation (Staudinger & Baltes, 1996). The recent emphasis in the workplace on upward communication, group decision-making, self-managed teams, and other collaborative approaches is compatible with and can be proactively used to help develop and enhance wisdom.

Wisdom as a Meta-Heuristic of Development

As defined in positive psychology, wisdom has been viewed as a meta-heuristic, a framework that coordinates and integrates the different cognitive, socioemotional, motivational, and behavioral heuristics and mental models that an individual possesses. Various heuristics have been found to be relevant in enhancing the five wisdom criteria presented earlier (factual and procedural knowledge, lifespan contextualism, value relativism, and recognition and management of uncertainty). For example, in line with our discussion of PsyCap from a resource-theory perspective in chapter 1, three resource-based life-management and behavioral-regulation heuristics from lifespan psychology lend themselves to the development of wisdom (Baltes & Freund, 2003a, 2003b; Baltes, Staudinger, & Lindenberger, 1999). These three are:

- selection (development, articulation, and choice among alternative goals, as well as commitment to selected goals and the pathways pursued);
- optimization (acquisition, investment, coordination, and refinement of resources and means to accomplish selected goals);
- compensation (acquisition, investment, and coordination of alternative means and courses of action to continue pursuing goals when original resources are lost or when original plans are hindered by obstacles).

Managers and employees are constantly bombarded with overwhelming amounts of information. Various sources and types of information compete for decision-makers' attention and for input into decisions that are likely to impact the effectiveness and sometimes the very survival of the organization. Selection mechanisms and heuristics that are founded on a clear understanding of what is truly important for balancing and furthering the interests of various stakeholders are of utmost salience for making wise decisions. Such selection mechanisms facilitate the processes of distilling accurate factual knowledge from the conflicting and distorted information at hand and of setting wise individual and organizational goals. Organizational interventions that target the decision-making, goal-setting, and problem-solving skills of managers and employees are likely to enhance the knowledge-management aspects of wisdom.

By the same token, even when accurate information is lacking, which is common in today's environment, managers and employees are still expected to make wise decisions and apply wise courses of actions. Optimization and compensation heuristics are likely to facilitate the construction, application, and flexible alteration of procedural knowledge as deemed necessary by the constant change in internal and external environmental factors. Wisely optimized and timely, updated procedural knowledge can be accomplished through the acceptance of, and even the expectation of and readiness for, uncertainty. Contingency planning, what-if analysis, and redundant systems are examples of organizational initiatives that can facilitate optimization and compensation—and, consequently, wisdom development—in an uncertain environment.

Wisdom can also be nurtured through an organizational climate where there is proactive recognition and effective management of change in priorities over time (e.g., lifespan contextualism). Such wisdom development is determined by the organization's internal strengths and weaknesses (e.g., position of various products in the product life cycle), as well as its externally determined opportunities and threats (e.g., market positioning in relation to competitors). Dynamic and consistent examination of underlying assumptions and emphasized priorities facilitates strategic planning and sustained competitiveness as the organization shifts from one set of goals, along with its relevant factual and procedural knowledge and justice, to the next set of goals and priorities. This type of climate would be expected with organizational leaders who are authentic and who constantly reinforce doing the right thing in an open and transparent manner.

Wisdom can also be enhanced in an organizational culture that acknowledges, appreciates, and even celebrates diversity (i.e., value relativism). Internal and external diversity allows for a broader set of goals and means for selection, optimization, and compensation to take place. Tolerance of individual and cultural differences does not require acceptance and conviction of every belief or idea. However, without value relativism, the pursuit of wisdom through balancing one's self-interests with those of others, who may adopt different value systems, is likely to be hindered. Intellectual and cultural diversity are likely to be key elements in developing a deep culture.

Measurement and the Performance Impact of Wisdom

Depending on the underlying theoretical tradition, several approaches have been developed for measuring wisdom. Consistent with positive psychology is the assessment of wisdom through the criteria of factual and procedural knowledge, lifespan contextualism, value relativism, and recognition and management of uncertainty. Staudinger and colleagues (1994) support the internal and external validity and reliability of asking participants to "think aloud." They are asked to contemplate carefully designed, challenging dilemmas while being rated on the five wisdom criteria by a heterogeneous panel of well-trained experts. The primary limitation of this measurement approach is the labor intensiveness of its scoring protocols (Staudinger & Leipold, 2003).

Finally, as is the case with creativity, currently, almost exclusive attention is being given to wisdom-related performance, as assessed through the five wisdom criteria. Also similar to creativity, the degree of wisdom is often being treated as an outcome in and of itself rather than as a predictor of work-related performance and desired attitudinal outcomes of organizational participants. Thus, in measuring up to the criteria that we have set for PsyCap, wisdom certainly has the theoretical foundation and seems to be open to development; but (at least to date) when applied to the workplace, the measurement and performance impact are yet to be fully demonstrated.

AFFECTIVE AND EMOTIONAL STRENGTHS

Obviously, there are many potential PsyCap strengths that have cognitive, affective, and emotional dimensions. However, as shown in table 6.1, whereas creativity and wisdom were loosely classified as more cognitively based potential PsyCap strengths, subjective well-being, flow, and humor are presented as being relatively more affective and emotionally based. As we noted, in this affective/emotional category, positive affectivity (PA) comes quickly to mind. However, PA is not considered here as potential PsyCap because it is widely recognized to be a temporally stable, cross-situationally consistent dispositional trait that provides a foundation for experiencing pleasurable emotional states (Watson, 2002). Although PA has been shown to relate to desirable workplace outcomes, such as higher managerial performance (Staw & Barsade, 1993), job satisfaction (Judge & Larsen, 2001), motivation (Erez & Isen, 2002), and team effectiveness (George, 1990), its trait-like (as opposed to state-like) nature, and its not being unique enough to the field of organizational behavior, negates the potential for being included here in PsyCap.

On the other end of the affective continuum are positive emotions, which tend to be more situation-specific, short-lived responses to specific subjectively valued occurrences. Positive emotions are found to be both ingredients and outcomes of upward spirals of positivity and optimal functioning (Fredrickson, 2002, 2003; Fredrickson & Losada, 2005). Positive emotions have also been shown to relate to various dimensions of work performance (Staw, Sutton, & Pelled, 1994). Thus, although PA and emotions fall within the domain of the value of positivity in the workplace, and we do recognize their significant impact, we do not include them here because they do not meet the specific criteria we have established for PsyCap. Affectively based strengths, such as subjective well-being, flow, and humor, seem to have relatively greater potential for being included in PsyCap as we have at least, to date, defined and supported it through theory, research, and practice.

SUBJECTIVE WELL-BEING AS POTENTIAL PSYCAP

Although often used interchangeably with happiness, subjective well-being (SWB) is generally recognized as the broader construct. SWB is also proposed to be more relevant than happiness as a psychological strength and capacity for the workplace. Philosophical perspectives and historical accounts have traditionally viewed happiness as an end in and of itself, and they have focused on the characteristics of happy individuals. On the other hand, SWB encompasses one's perceptions and feelings of emotional well-being (positive and negative affect, life satisfaction, and happiness), psychological well-being (self-acceptance, personal growth, purpose in life, environmental mastery, autonomy, and positive relations with others), and social well-being (social acceptance, actualization, contribution, coherence, and integration) (Keyes, 1998; Ryff, 1989; Ryff & Keyes, 1995; see Diener, Suh, Lucas, & Smith, 1999, and Keyes & Magyar-Moe, 2003, for comprehensive reviews). In other words, SWB as potential PsyCap incorporates emotional, psychological, and social well-being (i.e., almost everything except the currently popular and also potentially applicable to future PsyCap, physical well-being).

SWB has been shown to be directly related to various desirable workplace outcomes. Harter, Schmidt, and Hayes (2002, 2003) conceptually draw the parallels between subjective well-being in the workplace and the construct of "engagement," which has been the emphasis of the research and practice of the Gallup Organization for the last several years (Buckingham & Clifton,

2001; Buckingham & Coffman, 1999). Their meta-analytic findings provide substantial support that workplace well-being is positively related to unit-level productivity, employee retention, customer satisfaction, safety, and ultimately profitability and stock value of the company.

This "happy worker is a productive worker" hypothesis has been extensively studied and supported by considerable research over the years (e.g., see Quick & Quick, 2004; Wright & Cropanzano, 2004). Also, research by Judge and colleagues supports the contention that life satisfaction and subjective well-being are causal antecedents of job satisfaction (Judge & Watanabe, 1993), which in turn is strongly related to work performance (Judge, Thoresen, Bono, & Patton, 2001). Moreover, happiness and life satisfaction have been shown to be related to physical and psychological health (Ryff & Singer, 2003), personal striving, coping with stress (Diener & Fujita, 1995; Emmons, 1992; Folkman, 1997; Fordyce, 1988), and satisfaction with important life domains (Diener, 2000; Diener, et al., 1999).

The measurement of subjective well-being has been developed and validated (e.g., Diener, 2000; Diener, et al., 1999; Pavot & Diener, 1993). Related measures, such as Gallup's Q-12 measure of engagement, have also been clearly shown to correlate with work-related outcomes (Harter, et al., 2002, 2003). The Gallup engagement instrument includes questions about employees' perceptions concerning getting to do what they do best, knowing what is expected of them, being recognized for their value and contribution, the material and social support that they receive, and their opportunities for personal growth and development. Another comprehensive, but not workplace-specific measure of well-being, has been developed and utilized in the 1995 MacArthur Foundation national study of successful midlife. To date, this has been the only study to measure all dimensions of subjective well-being: emotional, psychological, and social (see Keyes & Magyar-Moe, 2003, for a review of this study).

Relevant to the developmental criterion of PsyCap is the recently developed "Temporal Satisfaction with Life Scale" (Pavot, Diener, & Suh, 1998). This SWB measure recognizes and distinguishes between past, present, and future life satisfaction, allowing for the assessment of well-being both as a stable trait and as a progressive state that can be developed over time.

As far as being managed for the PsyCap performance impact criterion, there is a rich tradition stemming from the "happy worker is a productive worker," satisfaction-performance, and most recently Gallup's engagement-performance body of research. Thus, in total, as shown in table 6.1, subjective well-being may best meet the PsyCap inclusion criteria beyond the four established components of efficacy, hope, optimism, and resilience.

FLOW AS POTENTIAL PSYCAP

Coming from one of the recognized founders of the positive psychology movement is Mihaly Csikszentmihalyi's concept of flow. Like SWB, flow is closely related to happiness and optimal experience. A state of flow is attained when one has both high skills and is undergoing a significant challenge (Csikszentmihalyi, 1997). Being "in flow" (a sort of euphoric zone) is a feeling that many have experienced yet that few have been able to fully define or comprehend.

Flow involves a different, even deeper perspective than intrinsic motivation. When in flow, accomplishing a task becomes rewarding as an end in itself rather than a means toward other goals (e.g., pay, promotion, impression management), causing the individual to become completely absorbed in the activity (Nakamura & Csikszentmihalyi, 2002). For a person in flow, time is distorted and may even stand still; the person is immersed in an exhilarating state that is accomplishing something difficult and worthwhile.

Flow takes place when one's subjectively experienced level of opportunity or challenge in a specific situation is entirely balanced with one's perceived abilities and skills to meet the demands of that situation. When challenges exceed perceived skills, anxiety and diminished self-efficacy preclude engagement, enjoyment, motivation, and thus flow. By the same token, when challenges are clearly below one's skill level, boredom and apathy distract attention away from the activity, causing one to lose flow (Csikszentmihalyi, 1975/2000).

Even when challenges and skills are matched but are at a low level on the challenge and skills continuum, being in flow is unlikely. Flow can only be experienced when the balanced levels of challenge and skill are both at a high level (Csikszentmihalyi, 1997). For example, the mandatory attendance of a monotonic training presentation on the new fire-alarm system will not generate feelings of being in flow. Despite the new information disseminated in such a presentation, the ability level required to grasp the information is likely to be kept by the presenter at the lowest level possible in hopes that even those who lack intelligence or attentiveness will still "get it." Moreover, the level of challenge that passive listening requires does not stretch the capabilities of the participants. Thus, in such a situation, a downward spiral of passiveness and lack of attentiveness precludes flow. On the contrary, even despite initial resistance, an interactive session or a hands-on drill may lead to more attentiveness and enjoyment, but this is still not flow, as the same messages are communicated. However, a highly skilled firefighter faced with a challenging blaze is very likely to enter into flow.

Flow as State-Like

Similar to intrinsic motivation, some studies have attempted to examine the possibility for the presence of dispositions and enduring tendencies for experiencing flow on a more frequent basis, also referred to as an "autotelic personality" (e.g., Amabile, Hill, Hennessey, & Tighe, 1994). However, the subjective and dynamic nature of flow as "emergent motivation" (Csikszentmihalyi, 1985) seems a more relevant depiction of flow as state-like. Specifically, in this view, every moment's experience is interacting with the cognitions and emotions of the individual to determine the experienced level of flow through the next moment. This is more consistent with the conceptualization of flow as a flexible state that is open to development.

Characteristics of being in a state of flow include high concentration on the activity, low self-consciousness, a strong sense of agency and control, high self-esteem, and losing track of time. There is even diminished importance of the end goal being pursued in favor of continuing with the activity for the intense enjoyment of the moment (Csikszentmihalyi, 1975/2000; Nakamura & Csikszentmihalyi, 2002). However, several exceptions to the above criteria exist. For example, challenging activities that are perceived as "work" or "school" attract more concentration and yield more satisfaction and self-esteem, especially when targeted at the right skill level—stretching yet achievable. On the other hand, activities that are perceived as "play," "relaxation" (high skill–low challenge, such as eating or socializing), or even "serious play" activities that combine work and play, such as extracurricular activities, were sometimes more enjoyed, and participants had a greater desire to be pursuing these types of activities (Csikszentmihalyi, 1997; LeFevre, 1988).

Flow in the Workplace

Several possible explanations of flow with important workplace implications can be found in the literature. For example, Csikszentmihalyi (2003) has a book devoted to applying flow to the business world. In one of the chapters, he even has a section called "The Building of Psychological Capital," which he describes as follows: "It is useful to think of enjoyment as the psychological equivalent of building capital, and of pleasure as the equivalent of consumption" (Csikszentmihalyi, 2003, p. 76). So, even though this is one of the very few times that the term psychological capital has been mentioned outside of being embedded in a couple of economics articles (found in a Google search), it is used by Csikszentmihalyi in explaining flow rather than how we are defining, conceptualizing, and applying PsyCap. Nevertheless, the mere fact that he uses the term (and also in a presentation he made at a Positive Psychology Summit) and the fact that he has a book devoted to flow in the business world suggest the potential that flow may have for inclusion in our conception and measurement of PsyCap.

In addition to Csikszentmihalyi's application of flow to business, many cultures view education and work as life domains that have to be pursued for their extrinsic rewards (e.g., finding a job, earning a living, supporting a family). Traditional organizational behavior theories, such as Maslow's hierarchy, McGregor's Theory Y, and many others through the years, have challenged these assumptions. However, in spite of these exceptions, the influence of existing cultural socialization processes reinforcing the negative connotations associated with education and work remains intact for most contemporary societies around the world.

Recent management research and practice have uncovered and attempted to deal with the serious implications of this dilemma of extrinsic versus intrinsic motivation. Most notable is the stream of research and consulting practice by Gallup, where the key to high engagement has been shown to be through the careful fitting of employees into jobs where their talents can be best utilized (i.e., employees can do what they do best every day). Concentrating on strengths is supported as a more effective approach toward engagement and resulting performance and fulfillment than attempting to "fix" weaknesses. Through such strength-based values and practices, an organization can alter its managers' and employees' perceptions of their jobs, thus potentially enhancing experiences of flow in the workplace.

The relative strength and importance of the intrinsic versus extrinsic motivation debate have not been resolved in the management and organizational behavior field (e.g., see Wiersma, 1992). However, unless organizations can find a way to enhance their managers' and employees' intrinsic motivation through or despite extrinsic motivation, organizational participants' experiencing the desirable state of flow at work will be more difficult to attain.

Potential Problems That Prevent Flow

Although intrinsic motivation and flow are likely to be facilitated by skill development and opportunities for challenges, there are also some cautions that should be noted in a positive spiral of flow. For example, research indicates that experiencing flow may require a balance between the utilization of energy and its conservation through engaging in pleasant but less demanding activities (Nakamura & Csikszentmihalyi, 2002). The stakes are extremely high in today's competitive work environment to continue to pursue growth and advancement at all costs. However, not only can such a relentless pursuit become physically, mentally, and emotionally draining, and even lead to a breakdown in ethical conduct, it can also diminish the positive experiences of flow aspired to in the first place. This is one of the core reasons why we believe that organizational leaders should be supporting and challenging their associates to enhance their flow.

Attention is a salient antecedent for experiencing and sustaining flow. Self-regulation and personal choices of fully allocating one's attentive resources to particular tasks are vital ingredients of the flow state (Csikszentmihalyi & Csikszentmihalyi, 1988). Importantly, the organizational context or culture can facilitate or hinder participants' self-regulation efforts. Although difficult to manage, cognitive distractions tend to be in abundance as organizational leaders and their associates attempt to discern and manage the overabundance of information that they receive every day. Open communication and transparency can help refocus attention and energies and thus enhance the climate needed for flow to be experienced.

Physical distractions, such as noise and uncomfortable work stations with inadequate lighting, temperature control, or ventilation problems, are potential inhibitors for experiencing flow. Even more salient, however, are the human dynamics and social distractions, such as conflict, power struggles, and lack of trust and transparency, which can be very inhibiting and cause attention to languish, drift, or become focused on being more defensive in one's behavior and processing of information. Emotional distractions, such as feelings of guilt, disengagement, or burnout from long hours resulting in inadequate work-life balance, can also preclude the attainment of flow.

Measurement of Flow

Several approaches, such as semistructured interviews and questionnaires, have been utilized for measuring flow. Some of these measures are specific to particular domains of life. However, the most recognized and supported is perhaps the Experience Sampling Method (Csikszentmihalyi & Larson, 1987). In this measurement approach to flow, through a paging device, participants can be prompted at random times to report on their level of flow by completing some questions. This method captures the cognitions and emotions of the moment. Despite its demonstrated reliability and validity (Csikszentmihalyi & Larson, 1987), one of the primary criticisms of this method is that when prompted, the participant will have to disengage from the activity to respond to the questions, which in turn may disrupt and reduce experiences of flow.

Performance Impact of Flow

There have been some empirical connections made between the positive effects of transformational leadership on group fluency and flexibility (Sosik, Avolio, & Kahai, 1998) and the role of flow and anonymity as mediators between transformational leadership and creativity (Sosik, Kahai, & Avolio, 1999). These particular studies examined how leadership mediated through technology impacted levels of creativity and flow in groups working with group-decision support systems.

In addition to the role that flow may play in organizational leadership, it has also been shown to be related to desirable outcomes in software design, computer-mediated communication, medical surgery, and, as noted above, has directly been focused on the implications for business activities of all kinds (Csikszentmihalyi, 1997, 2003). Like the other PsyCap states, flow has also been shown to relate to academic, artistic, literary, and sports performance, as well as to physical and psychological health (see Nakamura & Csikszentmihalyi, 2002, for a comprehensive review). As shown in table 6.1, like SWB, flow seems to be a good fit for the criteria of PsyCap inclusion, and especially since research has been directly conducted in the workplace, it can potentially be a promising strength for PsyCap in the future.

HUMOR AS POTENTIAL PSYCAP

Similar to the other affectively oriented positive strengths, the subjective nature of humor prevents definitional consensus. Many traditional and contemporary definitions, as well as everyday usage of the term humor, may encompass everything that is conducive to amusement and laughter. However, the humor literature distinguishes between good humor, which is associated with sympathy, tolerance, and benevolence (e.g., laughing at oneself, making fun of one's own misfortunes and mistakes, not taking oneself too seriously), versus wit, which may be rude, sarcastic, and disrespectful of others (Martin, 2003; Ruch, 2004). A comprehensive view breaks humor down into three dimensions: "(a) the playful recognition, enjoyment, and/or creation of incongruity, (b) a composed and cheerful view on adversity that allows one to see its light side and thereby sustain a good mood, and (c) the ability to make others smile or laugh" (Ruch, 2004, p. 584).

Humor generally has a positive social impact, both on the deliverer and the recipient, but it can also have a downside. For instance, a person with a good sense of humor has been shown to attract more social support, but aggressive humor has been found to repel others, causing social isolation for the deliverer, fear in observers, and reduced group cohesion.

Humor also involves complex cognitive appraisals, motivational components, and behavioral manifestations. However, humor's emotion-focused dimension seems to dominate its nature and positive outcomes. For example, emotionally based positive humor has been found to enhance one's ability to manage psychological stress and physical pain, recover from serious illness, and deal with mortality. Humor has also been associated with positive coping styles, such as approach-coping, positive reframing, and problem-focused coping, and negatively related to malfunctioning coping styles, such as avoidance and denial. The role of humor in enhancing immune-system functioning and general health is especially notable (see Lefcourt, 2002, for a comprehensive review).

Humor in the Workplace

One thing is for certain, humor has always existed in the workplace (Cooper, 2005). Every organizational participant has enjoyed being around a colleague whose sense of humor made them laugh and cheered everyone up. Yet, despite this commonly held view of the importance of humor at work, there is relatively little systematic research. Exceptions would include Avolio, Howell, and Sosik (1999), who found a positive connection between the use of humor and bottom-line performance in a Canadian financial service institution. Also, O'Hare (1992) found the use of humor as an important ingredient in organizational interactions. Leaders can use humor to deliver a difficult message to associates, as well as to reduce social distance, if the humor is viewed as self-disparaging (Geuens & De Pelsmacker, 2002). Moreover, Vinton (1989) reported that the use of humor alleviated status differentials and workplace tension between organizational members, and humor has been shown to be linked to managerial effectiveness (Rizzo, Booth-Butterfield, & Wanzer, 1999).

There are also some potential linkages between the use of humor and the creation of positive emotions that have been shown to result in "upward spirals toward optimal individual and organizational functioning" (Fredrickson, 2003, p. 163). Fredrickson's (1998) broaden-and-build theory describes the *broadening* of people's thought-action repertoires, which provides them with the ability to broaden their attention and to explore novel solutions. Fredrickson's *build* component refers to an individual's ability to develop various human-capital resources, and it has been supported by subsequent research on this model (Fredrickson & Joiner, 2002).

Positive emotions have been proposed as being able to produce patterns of thought which are both flexible and creative (Fredrickson, 2001; Fredrickson & Joiner, 2002). Such cognitive resources, which are built through broadening, have been proposed to be relatively long lasting (Fredrickson, 2002, 2003). Additional research has shown that humor was positively associated with having a more positive self-concept when dealing with positively and negatively challenging situations (Martin, Kuiper, Olinger, & Dance, 1993).

The moral, social, and even legal ramifications of aggressive—and particularly sexually and racially offensive—humor are evident in the workplace. On the other hand, the levels of work-related stress and burnout, as evidenced by the increasing levels of expenditure on employee-assistance programs, rising numbers of violent incidents in the workplace, and alcoholism and drug abuse among employed individuals, are alarming. We believe that today's business environment is in great need of more humor and laughter. Not only is a positive, humorous work environment likely to reduce medical and legal costs, it can also enhance teamwork, foster effective problem-solving, promote wider acceptance and tolerance of oneself and others, and encourage challenge-seeking and attaining results.

A humorous leader can act as a catalyst in promoting group norms that encourage and foster humor in the work environment. Playfulness, one of the most significant underlying characteristics of humor, can be enhanced or inhibited through social expectations, communicated through reinforcing humor with laughter and appreciation versus ridicule and viewing the deliverer of humor as silly or childish (Ruch, 2004). In this regard, humor can be modeled from the leader, and it is likely to be contagious.

How Humor Measures Up to the PsyCap Criteria

Humor has most often been conceptualized and measured as an individual difference, a dispositional, relatively fixed trait. However, recent interventions provide initial support for the potential of developing and managing humor through observation and imitation, specific learned skills, reinforcement, cognitive restructuring, and rediscovery of playfulness (McGhee, 1994, 1999; Nevo, Abrahamson, & Klingman, 1998). Furthermore, creativity and cheerfulness are deemed to be necessary ingredients for humor, and both have been traditionally viewed as dispositional. However, once again, recent work has shifted toward studying and applying various enabling factors toward the development and management of creativity and cheerfulness (Ruch, 2004; also see our earlier discussion in this chapter on creativity development).

In line with this fresh perspective on humor as a malleable state, Ruch, Kohler, and van Thriell (1996) developed the State-Trait Cheerfulness Inventory. This measure assesses variations in humor within months, weeks, or even days, as well as in pre-post measurement associated with humor development interventions. Although further theory, research, and developmental interventions are needed, and there need to be more direct applications to the workplace to test performance impact, as table 6.1 shows, humor may be a good candidate for future inclusion in PsyCap.

FUTURE IMPLICATIONS AND RESEARCH DIRECTIONS FOR OTHER POTENTIAL PSYCAP CAPACITIES

In this chapter, we presented five positive strengths with high potential for inclusion in PsyCap. The cognitive capacities of creativity and wisdom and the affective capacities of subjective well-being, flow, and humor do seem to meet most of the PsyCap inclusion criteria of being positive, theoretically based, measurable, developmental, and related to workplace performance. Obviously, considerable theory-building and research on all dimensions are needed on creativity, wisdom, well-being, flow, and humor before they can be fully embraced as a part of PsyCap. In the next chapter, we continue with our summary of additional potential social and higher order positive capacities that may warrant PsyCap inclusion. The intent of these two chapters is to help broaden the scope of future PsyCap and specifically to set an agenda for future theory-building, research, and practice.

REFERENCES

Amabile, T. M. (2000). Stimulate creativity by fueling passion. In E. Locke (Ed.), *The Blackwell handbook of principles of organizational behavior* (pp. 331–341). Oxford, UK: Blackwell.

Amabile, T. M., Hill, K. G., Hennessey, B. A., & Tighe, E. M. (1994). The work preference inventory: Assessing intrinsic and extrinsic motivational orientations. *Journal of Personality and Social Psychology, 66,* 950–967.

Aspinwall, L., & Staudinger, U. (Eds.). (2003). *A psychology of human strengths: Fundamental questions and future directions for a positive psychology.* Washington, DC: American Psychological Association.

Avolio, B. J., Gardner, W. L., Walumbwa, F. O., Luthans, F., & May, D. R. (2004). Unlocking the mask: A look at the process by which authentic leaders impact follower attitudes and behaviors. *Leadership Quarterly, 15,* 801–823.

Avolio, B. J., Howell, J. M., & Sosik, J. J. (1999). A funny thing happened on the way to the bottom line: Humor as a moderator of leadership style effects. *Academy of Management Journal, 42,* 219–227.

Avolio, B. J., & Luthans, F. (2006). *The high impact leader: Moments matter in accelerating authentic leadership development.* New York: McGraw-Hill.

Baltes, P., & Freund, A. (2003a). Human strengths as the orchestration of wisdom and selective optimization with compensation. In L. Aspinwall & U. Staudinger (Eds.), *A psychology of human strengths: Fundamental questions and future directions for a positive psychology* (pp. 23–35). Washington, DC: American Psychological Association.

Baltes, P., & Freund, A. (2003b). The intermarriage of wisdom and selective optimization with compensation: Two meta-heuristics guiding the conduct of life. In C. Keyes & J. Haidt (Eds.), *Flourishing: Positive psychology and the life well-lived* (pp. 249–273). Washington, DC: American Psychological Association.

Baltes, P., Glück, J., & Kunzmann, U. (2002). Wisdom: Its structure and function in regulating stressful life span development. In C. R. Snyder & S. Lopez (Eds.), *Handbook of positive psychology* (pp. 327–347). Oxford, UK: Oxford University Press.

Baltes, P., & Kunzmann, U. (2004). The two faces of wisdom: Wisdom as a general theory of knowledge and judgment about excellence in mind and virtue vs. wisdom as everyday realization in people and products. *Human Development, 47*(5), 290–299.

Baltes, P., & Staudinger, U. (2000). Wisdom: A metaheuristic to orchestrate mind and virtue toward excellence. *American Psychologist, 55,* 122–136.

Baltes, P., Staudinger, U., & Lindenberger, U. (1999). Lifespan psychology: Theory and application to intellectual functioning. *Annual Review of Psychology, 50,* 471–507.

Baltes, P., Staudinger, U., Maercker, A., & Smith, J. (1995). People nominated as wise: A comparative study of wisdom-related knowledge. *Psychology and Aging, 10,* 155–166.

Bandura, A. (1986). *Social foundations of thought and action: A social cognitive theory.* Englewood Cliffs, NJ: Prentice-Hall.

Bandura, A. (1997). *Self-efficacy: The exercise of control.* New York: Freeman.

Bandura, A. (2001). Social cognitive theory: An agentic perspective. *Annual Review of Psychology, 52,* 1–26.

Barrick, M. R., & Mount, M. K. (1991). The Big Five personality dimensions and job performance: A meta-analysis. *Personnel Psychology, 44,* 1–26.

Buckingham, M., & Clifton, D. (2001). *Now, discover your strengths.* New York: Free Press.

Buckingham, M., & Coffman, C. (1999). *First break all the rules: What the world's greatest managers do differently.* New York: Simon & Schuster.

Cameron, K. S., & Caza, A. (2004). Contributions to positive organizational scholarship. *American Behavioral Scientist, 47,* 731–866.

Cameron, K., Dutton, J., & Quinn, R. (Eds.). (2003). *Positive organizational scholarship.* San Francisco: Berrett-Koehler.

Carr, A. (2004). *Positive psychology.* New York: Brunner-Routledge.

Cassandro, V., & Simonton, K. (2003). Creativity and genius. In C. Keyes & J. Haidt (Eds.), *Flourishing: Positive psychology and the life well-lived* (pp. 163–183). Washington, DC: American Psychological Association.

Cooper, C. (2005). Just joking around: Employee humor expression as an ingratiating behavior. *Academy of Management Review, 30,* 765–776.

Csikszentmihalyi, M. (1985). Emergent motivation and the evolution of the self. *Advances in Motivation and Achievement, 4,* 93–119.

Csikszentmihalyi, M. (1997). *Finding flow.* New York: Basic.

Csikszentmihalyi, M. (2000). *Beyond boredom and anxiety.* San Francisco: Jossey-Bass. (Original work published 1975)

Csikszentmihalyi, M. (2003). *Good business.* New York: Penguin Books.

Csikszentmihalyi, M., & Csikszentmihalyi, I. (Eds.). (1988). *Optimal experience*. Cambridge: Cambridge University Press.

Csikszentmihalyi, M., & Larson, R. (1987). Validity and reliability of the experience-sampling method. *Journal of Nervous and Mental Disease, 175*, 526–536.

Diener, E. (2000). Subjective well-being: The science of happiness and a proposal for a national index. *American Psychologist, 55*, 34–43.

Diener, E., & Fujita, F. (1995). Resource, personal striving, and subjective well-being: A monothetic and idiographic approach. *Journal of Personality and Social Psychology, 68*, 926–935.

Diener, E., Suh, E., Lucas, E., & Smith, H. (1999). Subjective well-being: Three decades of progress. *Psychological Bulletin, 125*, 276–302.

Emmons, R. A. (1992). Abstract versus concrete goals: Personal striving level, physical illness, and psychological well-being. *Journal of Personality and Social Psychology, 62*, 292–300.

Erez, A., & Isen, A. (2002). The influence of positive affect on the components of expectancy motivation. *Journal of Applied Psychology, 87*, 1055–1067.

Feist, G. (1998). A meta-analysis of personality in scientific and artistic creativity. *Personality and Social Psychology Review, 2*, 290–309.

Folkman, S. (1997). Positive psychological states and coping with severe stress. *Social Science and Medicine, 45*, 1207–1221.

Fordyce, M. W. (1988). A review of research on the happiness measures: A sixty second index of happiness and health. *Social Indicators Research, 20*, 355–381.

Fredrickson, B. L. (1998). What good are positive emotions? *Review of General Psychology, 2*, 300–319.

Fredrickson, B. L. (2001). The role of positive emotions in positive psychology: The broaden-and-build theory of positive emotions. *American Psychologist, 56*, 218–226.

Fredrickson, B. (2002). Positive emotions. In C. R. Snyder & S. Lopez (Eds.), *Handbook of positive psychology* (pp. 120–134). Oxford, UK: Oxford University Press.

Fredrickson, B. (2003). Positive emotions and upward spirals in organizations. In K. S. Cameron, J. E. Dutton, & R. E. Quinn (Eds.), *Positive organizational scholarship* (pp. 163–175). San Francisco: Berrett-Koehler.

Fredrickson, B. L., & Joiner, T. (2002). Research report: Positive emotions trigger upward spirals toward emotional well-being. *Psychological Science, 13*, 172–175.

Fredrickson, B. L., & Losada, M. F. (2005). Positive affect and the complex dynamics of human flourishing. *American Psychologist, 60*, 678–686.

Gardner, H. (1983). *Frames of mind: The theory of multiple intelligences*. New York: Basic Books.

Gardner, H. (1999). *Intelligence reframed: Multiple intelligences for the 21st century*. New York: Basic Books.

George, J. M. (1990). Personality, affect, and behavior in groups. *Journal of Applied Psychology, 75*, 107–116.

Geuens, M., & De Pelsmacker, P. (2002). The role of humor in the persuasion of individuals varying in need for cognition. *Advances in Consumer Research, 29,* 50–56.

Giacalone, R. A., Jurkiewicz, C., & Dunn, C. (Eds.) (2005). *Positive Psychology in Business Ethics and Corporate Social Responsibility.* Greenwich, CT: Information Age.

Graves, C. W. (1959). *An emergent theory of ethical behavior: Based on an epigenetic model.* From the historical collection of the work of Dr. Clare W. Graves.

Harter, J., Schmidt, F., & Hayes, T. (2002). Business-unit-level relationship between employee satisfaction, employee engagement, and business outcomes: A meta-analysis. *Journal of Applied Psychology, 87,* 268–279.

Harter, J., Schmidt, F., & Hayes, T. (2003). Well-being in the workplace and its relationship to business outcomes: A review of the Gallup studies. In C. Keyes & J. Haidt (Eds.), *Flourishing: Positive psychology and the life well-lived* (pp. 205–224). Washington, DC: American Psychological Association.

Hartman, P. (2004). Perspective (wisdom). In C. Peterson & M. Seligman (Eds.), *Character strengths and virtues: A handbook and classification* (pp. 181–196). Oxford, UK: Oxford University Press.

Hochschild, A. (1983). *The managed heart: Commercialization of human feeling.* Berkeley: University of California Press.

Judge, T. A., & Bono, J. E. (2001). Relationship of core self-evaluations traits—self-esteem, generalized self-efficacy, locus of control, and emotional stability—with job satisfaction and job performance: A meta-analysis. *Journal of Applied Psychology, 86,* 80–92.

Judge, T. A., & Larsen, R. J. (2001) Dispositional affect and job satisfaction: A review and theoretical extension. *Organizational Behavior and Human Decision Processes, 86,* 67–98.

Judge, T. A., Thorensen, C. J., Bono, J. E., & Patton, G. K. (2001). The job satisfaction–job performance relationship: A qualitative and quantitative review. *Psychological Bulletin, 127,* 376–407.

Judge, T. A., & Watanabe, S. (1993). Another look at the job–life satisfaction relationship. *Journal of Applied Psychology, 78,* 939–948.

Kerr, B., & Gagliardi, C. (2003). Measuring creativity in research and practice. In S. Lopez & C. R. Snyder (Eds.), *Positive psychological assessment: A handbook of models and measures* (pp. 155–169). Washington, DC: American Psychological Association.

Keyes, C. (1998). Social well-being. *Social Psychology Quarterly, 61,* 121–140.

Keyes, C., & Haidt, J. (Eds.). (2003). *Flourishing: Positive psychology and the life well-lived.* Washington, DC: American Psychological Association.

Keyes, C., & Magyar-Moe, J. (2003). The measurement and utility of adult subjective well-being. In S. Lopez & C. R. Snyder (Eds.), *Positive psychological assessment: A handbook of models and measures* (pp. 411–425). Washington, DC: American Psychological Association.

Lefcourt, H. M. (2002). Humor. In C. R. Snyder & S. Lopez (Eds.), *Handbook of positive psychology* (pp. 619–631). Oxford, UK: Oxford University Press.

LeFevre, J. (1988). Flow and the quality of experience during work and leisure. In M. Csikszentmihalyi & I. Csikszentmihalyi (Eds.), *Optimal experience* (pp. 307–318). Cambridge: Cambridge University Press.

Linley, P. A., & Joseph, S. (Eds.). (2004). *Positive psychology in practice.* New York: Wiley.

Locke, E. (Ed.). (2000). *The Blackwell handbook of principles of organizational behavior.* Oxford, UK: Blackwell.

Lopez, S., & Snyder, C. R. (Eds.). (2003). *Positive psychological assessment: A handbook of models and measures.* Washington, DC: American Psychological Association.

Luthans, F. (2005). *Organizational behavior.* New York: McGraw-Hill/Irwin.

Luthans, F., & Avolio, B. (2003). Authentic leadership: A positive development approach. In K. S. Cameron, J. E. Dutton, & R. E. Quinn (Eds.), *Positive organizational scholarship* (pp. 241–258). San Francisco: Berrett-Koehler.

Martin, R. (2003). Sense of humor. In S. Lopez & C. R. Snyder (Eds.), *Positive psychological assessment: A handbook of models and measures* (pp. 313–326). Washington, DC: American Psychological Association.

Martin, R. A., Kuiper, N. A., Olinger, L. J., & Dance, K. A. (1993). Humor, coping with stress, self-concept, and psychological well-being. *Humor: International Journal of Humor Research, 6,* 89–104.

McGhee, P. E. (1994). *How to develop your sense of humor.* Dubuque, IA: Kendal/Hunt.

McGhee, P. E. (1999). *Humor, health and the amuse system.* Dubuque, IA: Kendal/Hunt.

Nakamura, J., & Csikszentmihalyi, M. (2002). The concept of flow. In C. R. Snyder & S. Lopez (Eds.), *Handbook of positive psychology* (pp. 89–105). Oxford, UK: Oxford University Press.

Nevo, O., Abrahamson, H., & Klingman, A. (1998). The development and evaluation of a systematic program for improving sense of humor. In W. Ruch (Ed.), *The sense of humor* (pp. 385–404). New York: Mouton de Gruyter.

Nickerson, R. S. (1999). Enhancing creativity. In R. J. Sternberg (Ed.), *Handbook of creativity* (pp. 392–430). New York: Cambridge University Press.

O'Hare, P. (1992). Work, irony and contemplative formation. *Religious Education, 87,* 28–44.

Pavot, W., & Diener, E. (1993). Review of the satisfaction with life scale. *Psychological Assessment, 5,* 164–172.

Pavot, W., Diener, E., & Suh, E. (1998). The temporal satisfaction with life scale. *Journal of Personality Assessment, 70,* 340–354.

Peterson, C., & Seligman, M. (2004). *Character strengths and virtues: A handbook and classification.* New York: Oxford University Press.

Peterson, S. J., & Luthans, F. (2006). The impact of financial and nonfinancial incentives on business-unit outcomes over time. *Journal of Applied Psychology, 91,* 156–165.

Plomin, R., & Daniels, D. (1987). Why are children in the same family so different from one another? *Behavioral and Brain Sciences, 10,* 1–16.

Quick, J. C., & Quick, J. D. (2004). Healthy, happy, productive work. *Organizational Dynamics, 23,* 329–337.

Riegel, K. F. (1975). Towards a dialectic theory of development. *Human Development, 18,* 50–64.

Rizzo, B. J., Booth-Butterfield, M., & Wanzer M. B. (1999). Individual differences in managers' use of humor: Subordinate perceptions of managers' humor. *Communication Research Reports, 16,* 360–369.

Ruch, W. (2004). Humor (playfulness). In C. Peterson & M. Seligman (Eds.), *Character strengths and virtues: A handbook and classification* (pp. 583–598). Oxford, UK: Oxford University Press.

Ruch, W., Kohler, G., & van Thriell, C. (1996). Assessing the "humorous temperament": Construction of the facet and standard trait forms of the State-Trait-Cheerfulness Inventory—STCI. *Humor, 9,* 303–340.

Ryff, C. D. (1989). Beyond Ponce de Leon and life satisfaction: New directions in quest of successful ageing. *International Journal of Behavioral Development, 12,* 35–55.

Ryff, C. D., & Keyes, C. L. M. (1995). The structure of psychological well-being revisited. *Journal of personality and social psychology, 69,* 719–727.

Ryff, C. D., & Singer, B. (2003). Ironies of the human condition: Well-being and health on the way to mortality. In L. Aspinwall & U. Staudinger (Eds.), *A psychology of human strengths: Fundamental questions and future directions for a positive psychology* (pp. 271–287). Washington, DC: American Psychological Association.

Schmidt, F., & Hunter, J. (2000). Select on intelligence. In E. Locke (Ed.), *The Blackwell handbook of principles of organizational behavior* (pp. 3–14). Oxford, UK: Blackwell.

Simonton, D. (2002). Creativity. In C. R. Snyder & S. Lopez (Eds.), *Handbook of positive psychology* (pp. 189–201). Oxford, UK: Oxford University Press.

Simonton, D. (2004). Creativity (originality, ingenuity). In C. Peterson & M. Seligman (Eds.), *Character strengths and virtues: A handbook and classification* (pp. 109–123). Oxford, UK: Oxford University Press.

Snyder, C. R., & Lopez, S. (Eds.). (2002). *Handbook of positive psychology.* Oxford, UK: Oxford University Press.

Sosik, J. J., Avolio, B. J., & Kahai, S. S. (1998). Inspiring group creativity: Comparing anonymous and identified electronic brainstorming. *Small Group Research, 29,* 3–31.

Sosik, J. J., Kahai, S. S., & Avolio, B. J. (1999). Leadership style, anonymity, and creativity in group decision support systems: The mediating role of optimal flow. *Journal of Creative Behavior, 33,* 227–257.

Stajkovic, A. D., & Luthans, F. (1997). A meta-analysis of the effects of organizational behavior modification on task performance: 1975–95. *Academy of Management Journal, 40,* 1122–1149.

Stajkovic, A., & Luthans, F. (2001). The differential effects of incentive motivators on work performance. *Academy of Management Journal, 44,* 580–590.

Stajkovic, A., & Luthans, F. (2003). Behavioral management and task performance in organizations: Conceptual background, meta-analysis, and test of alternative models. *Personnel Psychology, 56,* 155–194.

Staudinger, U., & Baltes, P. (1996). Interactive minds: A facilitative setting of wisdom-related performance? *Journal of Personality & Social Psychology, 71,* 746–762.

Staudinger, U., & Leipold, B. (2003). The assessment of wisdom-related performance. In S. Lopez & C. R. Snyder (Eds.), *Positive psychological assessment: A handbook of models and measures* (pp. 171–184). Washington, DC: American Psychological Association.

Staudinger, U., Lopez, D., & Baltes, P. (1997). The psychometric location of wisdom-related performance: Intelligence, personality, and more? *Personality and Social Psychology Bulletin, 23,* 1200–1214.

Staudinger, U., Maciel, A., Smith, J., & Baltes, P. (1998). What predicts wisdom-related performance? A first look at personality, intelligence, and facilitative experiential contexts. *European Journal of Personality, 12*(1), 1–17.

Staudinger, U., Smith, J., & Baltes, P. (1994). *Manual for the assessment of wisdom-related knowledge.* Berlin: Max-Plank-Institut für Bildungsforschung.

Staw, B., & Barsade, S. (1993). Affect and managerial performance: A test of the sadder-but-wiser vs. happier-and-smarter hypotheses. *Administrative Science Quarterly, 38,* 304–331.

Staw, B., Sutton, R., & Pelled, L. (1994). Employee positive emotion and favorable outcomes at the workplace. *Organization Science, 5,* 51–71.

Sternberg, R. (1998). A balance theory of wisdom. *Review of General Psychology, 2,* 347–365.

Torrance, E. (1988). The nature of creativity as manifest in its testing. In R. Sternberg (Ed.), *The nature of creativity* (pp. 43–75). New York: Cambridge University Press.

Vinton, K. L. (1989). Humor in the workplace: It is more than telling jokes. *Small Group Behavior, 20,* 151–166.

Watson, D. (2002). Positive affectivity: The disposition to experience pleasurable emotional states. In C. R. Snyder & S. Lopez (Eds.), *Handbook of positive psychology* (pp. 106–119). Oxford, UK: Oxford University Press.

Wiersma, U. P. (1992). The effects of extrinsic rewards in intrinsic motivation: A meta-analysis. *Journal of Occupational and Organizational Psychology, 65,* 101–114.

Wright, T. A., & Cropanzano, R. (2004). The role of psychological well-being in job performance: A fresh look at an age-old quest. *Organizational Dynamics, 33,* 338–351.

CHAPTER 7

Possible Social and Higher-Order Strengths

Future PsyCap?

IN THE PREVIOUS chapter, we introduced and assessed several high-potential cognitively and affectively oriented positive constructs for their fit with our PsyCap inclusion criteria. These PsyCap criteria once again include not only positivity, but they are also based on theory and research, valid measurement, state-like or developmental characteristics and are related to and impact work performance. In assessing other possible constructs beside the best PsyCap criteria–fitting factors of efficacy, hope, optimism, and resiliency, we also take into consideration other criteria. For example, we consider not only whether there is some minimal theoretical and research foundation or baseline for the construct but also if there are any known relationships between the construct and desirable outcomes other than performance.

Just as the last chapter drew high-potential PsyCap capacities from cognitive and affectively oriented categories, this chapter draws from two other broadly defined psychological categories. Specifically drawing from socially oriented capacities, we propose that gratitude, forgiveness, and emotional intelligence may have the potential to meet at least an expanded scope of PsyCap; and from another category of what could be termed *positive higher-order strengths or capacities*, we suggest spirituality, authenticity, and courage.

Remembering that our theory-building, research, measurement, and application of PsyCap so far in its development have focused on the factors of efficacy, hope, optimism and resiliency, we feel that the last chapter and this one become necessary for keeping PsyCap dynamic and evolving. These two chapters are simply meant to recognize the virtually unlimited potential power and impact that positive psychological capital can play in investing and leading today's, and especially the future, workforce. Just as economics and finance are continually searching for new and innovative ways to invest and develop their capital, we feel the same about psychological capital. We hope these two chapters not only send a message that PsyCap is dynamic and evolving but also provide a rough map for the continuing journey of PsyCap development. As shown in our brief checklist in table 7.1, our proposed social and higher order positive capacities do not precisely meet every one of our established PsyCap criteria; but as the following discussion indicates, they still seem worthy of recognition and consideration for future research and application.

SOCIAL POSITIVE CAPACITIES

The increasing use of teams in today's organizations has led to a surge of interest in both basic research (e.g., Beersma, et al., 2003; Hackman & Wageman, 2005) and practice (e.g., Lencioni, 2002) on social dynamics and performance impact. Basing much of our work on Bandura's (1986, 1997) social cognitive theory, we have indicated that social interactions underlie much of PsyCap development and management. Although we proposed in the first chapter that PsyCap goes beyond social capital (Luthans, Luthans, & Luthans, 2004; Luthans & Youssef, 2004), this does not deny that PsyCap capitalizes on the social embeddedness of behavior (Putnam, 1995) and extends its capacities and impact beyond the individual level through an upward and downward spiral of positive contagion in the workplace (Avolio & Luthans, 2006).

There is research evidence that relationships and social support may help explain and facilitate PsyCap (e.g., see Avolio & Luthans, 2006; Diener, 2000; Diener, Suh, Lucas, & Smith, 1999). Indeed, considerable evidence over the years has been accumulated to prove that such social processes also directly impact positive physical, mental, and psychological outcomes (see Berscheid, 2003, for a comprehensive review).

Although it is clear that social impact can facilitate PsyCap, unfortunately, it is equally true that a dysfunctional social context can also dampen or even destroy PsyCap. For example, managers who tend to run their units

TABLE 7.1. Assessment of "Fit" with PsyCap for Possible Social and Higher-Order Strengths

Category	Positive construct	Theory-based?	Trait-like/ Relatively fixed?	State-like/ Malleable?	Measurable?	Related to work performance?	Related to other positive outcomes?
Social	Gratitude	✓	✓	✓	?	?	✓
	Forgiveness	✓	✓	✓	✓	?	✓
	Emotional intelligence	✓	?	?	✓	✓	✓
	Spirituality	✓	✓	✓	✓	?	✓
Higher order	Authenticity	✓	✓	✓	✓	✓	✓
	Courage	✓	✓	✓	✓	?	✓

using frequent criticism, negative feedback, and lack of recognition will generate distrust and inauthenticity. This negativity will certainly diminish their followers' PsyCap over time, breeding disengagement, declining morale, and ultimately destructive behaviors. The same patterns can occur to the extent that coworkers act in a similar vein. Thus, discerning which relationships and interactions to approach and nurture and which to avoid or minimize becomes a necessary social and political skill in today's competitive work environments (Reis & Gable, 2003).

To add to the complexity, it should be also noted that a positive social context can foster PsyCap beyond the boundaries of the workplace. For example, organizational leaders and employees with high PsyCap will not only contribute to their own and their coworkers' positivity and performance but may also be able to proactively reach out and enrich others' PsyCap. Such positivity can influence their family, friends, and groups outside of work, including their communities as a whole. This can occur to the extent that the follower at work is a leader outside of work. This "inside-out," "outside-in" social process may result in favorable spillovers back into the workplace, as well as in the family, outside relationships and groups, and the community as a whole.

In light of the negative implications of violence, divorce, troubled kids, disengaged citizens, and other social-capital deterioration, a positive workplace can become a socially compensating and rewarding context, thus having a positive impact both in the workplace and outside. We now discuss three proposed socially oriented and potentially positively oriented capacities that, as shown in table 7.1, fairly well meet our PsyCap inclusion criteria: gratitude, forgiveness, and emotional intelligence.

THE MEANINGS AND APPLICATIONS OF GRATITUDE AND FORGIVENESS

Like the other PsyCap strengths, gratitude and forgiveness are commonly used in everyday language. However, also like the others, these two terms are carefully defined in positive psychology. For example, Emmons (2004) defines gratitude as "a sense of thankfulness and joy in response to receiving a gift, whether the gift can be a tangible benefit from a specific other or a moment of peaceful bliss evoked by natural beauty" (p. 554). Furthermore, gratitude is experienced when a motivationally relevant, congruent, and/or desirable outcome is received and attributed to the efforts of another (Emmons & Shelton, 2002). In other words, where it may not be possible for an optimistic explanatory style (personal, permanent, and pervasive; see chapter 4) to internalize a positive event, gratitude may become a substitute for a pessimistic, external appraisal.

Forgiveness, on the other hand, is defined in positive psychology as:

> the framing of a perceived transgression such that one's attachment to the transgressor, transgression, and sequel of the transgression is transformed from negative to neutral or positive. The source of a transgression, and therefore the object of forgiveness, may be oneself, another person or persons, or a situation that one views as being beyond one's control. (Yamhure-Thompson & Snyder, 2003, p. 302)

Definitions of forgiveness vary in two major ways. First, forgiveness varies to the extent that it incorporates active benevolence, prosocial change, or even love and appreciation toward the source of transgression (vs. passive tolerance, ceasing to blame, or a reduced sense of victimization). Second, is the degree to which reconciliation is considered to be an integral component of forgiveness (Enright & North, 1998; McCullough, Pargament, & Thorensen, 2000; McCullough & Witvliet, 2002).

Although positive psychology tends to treat gratitude and forgiveness as two separate constructs, for our purposes, it is more appropriate to simply introduce them as potential PsyCap and include them together. Specifically, we present gratitude and forgiveness as two sides of the same, precious coin. On one side, grateful individuals choose to focus on and appreciate the positives in their lives, including their own and others' strengths, talents, gifts, and prosocial behaviors, as well as favorable events. This gratefulness tends to promote and maintain a positive view of oneself, others, and situational factors and events. On the other side of the coin, forgiveness is a positive approach in dealing with the negatives in one's life, including faults, vulnerabilities, and negative behaviors and outcomes that are perceived in oneself, others, and situational factors and events. However, by forgiving, one is taking a positive stance with oneself or others. To forgive means to accept that the future can be more effectively optimized if one does not dwell on the negatives of the past.

A combination of gratitude and forgiveness can help shape perceptions and attributions and instill a proactive approach of *positive labeling* and *positive identity* that can enhance one's inventory (or "bank") of psychological capital. How? For instance, carrying negative thoughts about another, such as revenge, draws down the positivity of individuals and, in turn, decreases their psychological capital. In laypeople's terms, we can argue that revenge consumes the individual in negativity, taking attention away from those things that are positive.

Gratitude can be simply viewed as the extra mile willingly traveled by those with high PsyCap. In the meantime, forgiveness is facilitated and capitalized on by gratitude as transgressions are positively appraised as opportunities to learn important lessons in life. Then, from the accelerating forgiveness, one's gratitude is intensified toward other, more favorable relationships and situations, and the upward spiral of positivity continues. Forgiveness allows the victim to view the transgressor in a more positive light, resulting in enhancing the possibility for seeing through and being grateful for the positives and the lessons to be learned from that person or event.

Being able to selectively focus on and be thankful for what is positive can in turn facilitate forgiveness. For example, top management's gratitude for the organization's loyal customers and/or vendors may motivate reciprocation through socially responsible actions to and from all relevant parties (e.g., sales personnel toward customers and vendor salespeople toward the organization's purchasing agent). Promoting a culture of gratitude toward valuable customers may in turn facilitate forgiveness by employees toward occasional incidents of customer malice.

An example would be an organization we have worked with and that has referred to its customers as "guests" for over 50 years. The intent of the founder was to show his gratitude toward customers by always treating them as guests in his stores. He indeed was the first automotive distributor to focus on and offer after-sales service quality in the early 1950s, many years prior to the advent of the service quality movement.

Organizational leaders' gratitude toward employees can also be viewed as a form of positive reinforcement with performance impact (e.g., feedback and social recognition; see Stajkovic & Luthans, 2003; Peterson & Luthans, 2006). Leaders' gratitude to employees may result not only in improved performance but also in more frequent exhibition of organizational citizenship behaviors and decreased incidences of destructive behaviors, such as violence, sabotage, theft, stress, and burnout. Over time, a culture of gratitude can facilitate forgiveness in difficult times (e.g., downsizing and layoffs). This is in line with the positive psychological view of gratitude as a type of moral affect that acts as a "moral barometer" that registers received benefits, as a "moral motive" to reciprocate, and as a "moral reinforcer" for prosocial behaviors (McCullough, Kilpatrick, Emmons, & Larson, 2001).

HOW DO GRATITUDE AND FORGIVENESS MEET THE PSYCAP CRITERIA?

Among the commonalities between gratitude and forgiveness is the similar fit of both constructs with most of our PsyCap inclusion criteria (see table 7.1). For example, both gratitude and forgiveness have been conceptualized and measured not only as dispositional traits but also as developmental states, as is required to be included in PsyCap. Dispositionally, gratitude and forgiveness can be viewed as enduring tendencies, that is, the propensity to experience gratitude in higher than usual intensity, frequency, span, and/or density (Emmons, McCullough, & Tsang, 2003; McCullough, Emmons, & Tsang, 2002) or the general willingness to forgive (Hebl & Enright, 1993; Yamhure Thompson & Snyder, 2003). These both occur across time and situations.

Despite the support for being dispositional, there is also extensive theory-building and empirical research that gratitude and forgiveness can also be state-like and thus open to development. For example, Emmons and Crumpler (2000) were able to develop higher levels of gratitude through asking participants to simply keep weekly journals of things for which they could be thankful. Miller (1995) offers a more elaborate approach for developing gratitude through the identification of ungrateful attitudes, substitution of those attitudes with more grateful ones, and then transfer of those more positive attitudes into grateful behaviors. Workplace applications of gratitude development are also beginning to emerge (Emmons, 2003).

There is also evidence that forgiveness can be successfully developed through a four-step process that includes: (1) uncovering and self-awareness of underlying cognitions and emotions, such as anger and shame; (2) making a decision and commitment to forgive; (3) reframing through acceptance, empathy, and compassion toward the transgressor; and (4) overcoming and finding meaning in the forgiveness experience (Baskin & Enright, 2004). There are meta-analytical findings supporting the idea that the strongest forgiveness-development interventions are those that are individually based, process oriented, and longer in duration (Baskin & Enright, 2004; Worthington, Sandage, & Berry, 2000).

We came across a case example of forgiveness a number of years ago in an Ohio program designed to transform juvenile delinquents into productive citizens. The program was set up to show the transgressors that when they stole from small stores, they were significantly impacting the shop's very slim profit margins. Depending on how much they stole, the convicted juveniles were required to work off the amount they had stolen. Initially, the storeowners were reluctant to participate in the project; that is, they were not so willing to forgive. Over time, however, an interesting pattern emerged in both the storeowners and in the juveniles' behavior. Indeed, after the work-off period had expired, many of the shopowners, actually hired these formerly troubled juveniles permanently.

Applying the concept of forgiveness to current workplace issues, Worthington, Berry, Shivy, and Brownstein (2005) propose forgiveness as necessary and applicable in the case of downsizing. They suggest that forgiveness can be facilitated through establishing realistic expectations regarding the relative stability of the job, ensuring that the organization acts responsibly and in a transparent manner, and striving to provide help and support for displaced employees. By following guidelines for procedural justice, we expect that employees who have been downsized would be more willing to forgive their organizations.

In an earlier chapter, we briefly gave an example about an electronics organization in the Washington, DC, area that went to the extreme on this issue. The CEO indicated that when he had to downsize, he treated the displaced workers as "alumni" of the organization, staying in contact over time to make sure that they had secured new positions. Interestingly enough, not only did some of these employees come back to work with the organization when the economy rebounded, but they consistently recommended the company to friends and colleagues as a place to consider for employment.

Reliable and valid measures of state-like forgiveness, as directed toward specific persons, transgressions, or both, are available in the literature (e.g., Mauger, et al., 1992; McCullough, et al., 1998; Subkoviak, et al., 1995). Unfortunately, such measures for gratitude, on the other hand, are not found. As to developmental efforts, there is reported work on both forgiveness and gratitude by McCullough and colleagues. However, despite the recognized role of gratitude and forgiveness in promoting physical and psychological health and freedom from pathological symptoms in the clinical and positive psychology literature (see Emmons, 2004; Emmons & Shelton, 2002; McCullough, 2004; McCullough & Witvliet, 2002, for comprehensive reviews), little is still known about the potential impact of gratitude and forgiveness on work performance beyond case studies and anecdotal evidence as cited above.

In total, we suggest that both gratitude and forgiveness are highly promising candidates for being included in the future of PsyCap. They seem especially relevant for today's business environment, where questionable ethics and cutthroat competition seem to have too often promoted greed, hatred, and revenge instead of thankfulness, appreciation, sharing, empathy, and compassion. Future research to fill the void is likely to be met with a lot of gratitude and maybe forgiveness for all concerned, at the individual, group/team, organizational, and especially societal levels.

EMOTIONAL INTELLIGENCE AS POTENTIAL PSYCAP

Based on the theory-building in social and educational psychology, emotional intelligence can be defined as the ability to accurately perceive, express, understand, use, and manage emotions in oneself and others in order to facilitate cognitive, emotional, and social growth and development (Mayer & Salovey, 1997; Mayer, Salovey, & Caruso, 2000; Salovey, Mayer, & Caruso, 2002). Of all the factors of PsyCap (both the major four and all the potential ones), emotional intelligence (EI or, sometimes, EQ) has undoubtedly received the most attention in the practice of management. EI has almost become conventional wisdom with few, if any, tests of validation. By the same token, EI has also received considerable criticism in the academic field of organizational behavior (e.g., see Locke, 2005).

One of the most significant developments that triggered the academic attention given to emotional intelligence was Howard Gardner's (1983) original work on multiple intelligences. He expanded the definition of intelligence beyond cognitive mental abilities—that is, logical/mathematical and linguistic/verbal dimensions measured in traditional IQ—to include multiple and diverse domains. Gardner's recognized multiple intelligences included not only musical, spatial/visual, bodily/kinesthetic, and intrapersonal domains but also social or interpersonal intelligence.

Initially, Gardner did not specifically include the term "emotional intelligence," but following his recognition of social intelligence, Salovey and Mayer (1990) are usually given credit for the first academic work on EI. However, it was Daniel Goleman's best-selling books (1995, 1998; Goleman, Boyatzis, & McKee, 2002) that catapulted EI into its current highly popular position among management practitioners and consultants. Goleman (1998) identifies the most important dimensions of emotionally intelligent individuals as self-awareness, self-management, self-motivation, empathy, and social skills.

Unlike the still largely emerging potential PsyCap capacities presented in the last chapter and this one, applications of EI to the workplace have a considerable presence in the management and organizational behavior literature. For example, Luthans (2002b) initially included EI as part of positive organizational behavior and positive leadership (Luthans Luthans, Hodgetts, & Luthans, 2001) but soon dropped it (e.g., see Luthans, 2002a; Luthans, et al., 2004; Luthans & Youssef, 2004) because it did not measure up well enough to the PsyCap criteria (especially theoretical foundation, basic research, and valid measurement).

In terms of demonstrated impact in the workplace, Kelley and Caplan (1993) reported early on that star performers at Bell Laboratories could be predicted by emotional intelligence better than by cognitive mental abilities. Also, the failure of derailed executives studied by the Center for Creative Leadership was also said to be related to deficiencies in their emotional intelligence rather than to their lack of technical capabilities (Gibbs, 1995). In addition, Goleman and colleagues (2002) have attributed applications of emotional intelligence to effective organizational leadership and work teams. He reports that across organizational sizes, managerial levels, and even national cultures, elements of emotional intelligence account for about two thirds of the competencies sought by organizations as critical to high performance. The contribution of EI to performance became seen as even more substantial (as high as six out of seven competencies) at higher level professional and managerial positions (Goleman, 1998). However, these various findings are generally extrapolated and provide a rather shaky basis for including EI in PsyCap.

From a more academic perspective, Mayer and Salovey (2004) do review preliminary empirical evidence that relates emotional intelligence to desirable work outcomes, such as superior customer service, as well as less-direct outcomes, such as effective social functioning, coping styles, and adaptation techniques and lower incidences of drug and alcohol abuse. This type of work bolsters the potential for including EI once it is properly defined, measured, and validated.

HOW DOES EI NOW MEASURE UP TO THE PSYCAP CRITERIA?

As indicated, EI was included in the initial article on positive organizational behavior (Luthans, 2002b) but was then soon dropped for not fitting the criteria well enough (Luthans, 2002a). Now, a few years later, although there are certainly remaining problems associated with the conception and lack of research support of EI (e.g., see Locke, 2005), we are willing to recognize the advances made by Salovey's and others' theory-building, research, and measurement to once again consider EI as a potential contributing factor to PsyCap. For example, relevant to PsyCap would be guidelines for assisting EI development in the workplace (Goleman, 1998), such as the following.

- Systematic and objective assessment of the critical competencies of the job.
- Multisource assessment of the individual and using positive feedback in communicating the assessment data.
- Gauging participants' readiness for the intervention.
- Motivating self-directed and individualized planning for change.
- Focusing on clear and manageable goals.
- Prevention of potential relapses through realistic previews of trigger situations and development of contingency plans.
- Ongoing practice, support, role-modeling, reinforcement, and feedback.

Beside business contexts, there have also been a number of noteworthy applications of emotional intelligence development introduced in education, parenting, politics, and others (e.g., see Salovey, Caruso, & Mayer, 2004; Salovey, et al., 2002).

A number of measures also now exist for EI; the most established and supported are Bar-On's (1997) Emotional Quotient Inventory (EQ-i) and the Mayer-Salovey-Caruso Emotional Intelligence Test (MSCEIT)

Version 2.0 (Mayer, Salovey, & Caruso, 2001). However, Bar-On primarily defines emotional intelligence in terms of adaptive personality traits, while Mayer, Salovey, and Caruso support the developmental nature of EI as a set of learnable abilities or states (Salovey, Mayer, Caruso, & Lopes, 2003). Despite these advances, a more comprehensive theoretical framework, further empirical research, and more valid measurement remain as challenges before EI can be fully integrated into PsyCap.

HIGHER ORDER POSITIVE CAPACITIES

Our identification of other potential PsyCap constructs in the last chapter and this is not intended to be exhaustive. However, we do feel that special mention of some possible higher order capacities beyond the more traditional cognitive, emotional, and social boundaries of positive psychology is also needed. In chapter 1's theoretical framework for PsyCap and in the final chapter, which summarizes our preliminary supporting research, we propose that PsyCap itself is a higher order construct. That is, PsyCap may be synergistic, it may be greater than the sum of its four major criteria-meeting factors of hope, optimism, confidence, and resilience.

In the remainder of this chapter, we identify some representative higher order positive constructs that may also, over time, be able to contribute to the future of PsyCap. In particular, we assume that the current uniqueness of PsyCap is not limited to just expanding the inventory of positive constructs that only meet our established inclusion criteria. Like the positive psychology movement, our aspiration for the future of PsyCap is to become a far more comprehensive paradigm shift in achieving optimal positive human functioning and flourishing in the workplace.

In the spirit of our aspirational goals for PsyCap, we seek a deeper, multifaceted understanding and appreciation of what constitutes lifespan excellence and authentic leadership (see Avolio & Luthans, 2006). We are not as interested in a simple, myopic operational perspective of individual constructs. Our quest for a wide-ranging vista of positive psychological functioning in organizations must consider a higher plane—a metalevel, if you wish. Our long-range vision for PsyCap is that it can provide meaning and purpose to more pragmatic patterns coming out of cognitions, emotions, and behaviors. We propose that such higher order capacities, which may shed light at this level of functioning and also have a chance at meeting our PsyCap inclusion criteria shown in table 7.1, might include spirituality, authenticity, and courage.

SPIRITUALITY AS POTENTIAL PSYCAP

The tradition of separation between church and state in the United States, as well as other cultural values, such as freedom of religious choice, have led to very little, if any, attention given to topics such as spirituality or religiousness in research or even discussions in organizational behavior and human resources management. However, the positive psychology movement does give some recognition to the role of spirituality (e.g., see Pargament & Mahoney, 2002; Peterson & Seligman, 2004), and the Academy of Management now has a division on "Management, Spirituality, and Religion." Also, *Leadership Quarterly* (2005) has dedicated an entire special issue on the topic of spirituality. In light of these recent developments and our own quest for unique constructs that can potentially contribute to the future of PsyCap, we include at least this beginning discussion of what is meant by spirituality as it applies to the workplace and how it may measure up to the criteria of PsyCap.

The Meaning of Spirituality

Even more than the other potential constructs for PsyCap, there is considerable diversity in the conceptualization and research on spirituality and religiousness. For instance, some theorists and researchers treat spirituality and religiousness interchangeably, or at least as conceptually similar, and use the same instruments to measure both constructs. On the other hand, there is empirical research that supports spirituality and religiousness as different constructs that, although somewhat related, diverge on some of their most salient characteristics (e.g., see Zinnbauer, et al., 1997). Yet, there has also been concern that the differences between spirituality and religiousness have been overemphasized. Polarizing them as opposite constructs has been critiqued as an inaccurate perspective (Zinnbauer, Pargament, & Scott, 1999).

Hill and colleagues (2000) provide a comprehensive definition of spirituality as "the feelings, thoughts, experiences, and behaviors that arise from the search for the sacred. The term 'search' refers to attempts to identify, articulate, maintain, or transform. The term 'sacred' refers to a divine being, divine object, Ultimate Reality, or Divine Truth as perceived by the individual" (p. 66). They then go on to describe the characteristics of religiousness and how to distinguish it from spirituality. To define religiousness, they add two further dimensions to the above definition of spirituality (Hill, et al., 2000).

The first dimension contributing to religiousness is membership in, identification with, and validation and support from a group of people which provides the means and methods for the search for the sacred (e.g., organized religions). This search takes the form of specific rituals, practices, and/or behavioral expectations. The second distinguishing characteristic of religiousness is the potential for nonsacred goals to also be sought in the process. Examples of secular goals include belonging, identity, and so forth, to satisfy extrinsic motives. In other words, religiousness incorporates spirituality, as well as membership and conformance with both intrinsic sacred and extrinsic nonsacred factors.

Spirituality in Organizational Behavior and Leadership

In work drawing from these basic definitions, spirituality is recently finding its way into the organizational behavior and leadership fields. For example, integral to Fry's (2003, 2005) spiritual leadership model is membership within an empowered team where one can be understood and appreciated. Moreover, a sense of calling gives meaning and value to spiritual leadership, causing the leader and followers to be intrinsically motivated to make a difference through ethical and socially responsible values, attitudes, and behaviors.

Organizational behavior and leadership scholars who focus on spirituality have also made the connection with organizational performance. In fact, Dent, Higgins, and Wharff (2005) reviewed 87 scholarly articles written on spirituality and found that most hypothesized relationships between spirituality and organizational performance. Similarly, Reave (2005) reports from her qualitative review of the leadership literature that aspects of spirituality associated with integrity, honesty, and humility have also been found to be related to leadership success on numerous occasions. Duchon and Plowman (2005) reported a positive relationship between work-unit spirituality in hospitals and unit performance, such as patient satisfaction. They speculate that by providing meaning in work connected to the spiritual being of followers, the followers' motivation to perform will be higher than the simple transaction of pay for performance—in other words, they are more intrinsically motivated to perform (Duchon & Plowman, 2005). Similarly, many theories of leadership include constructs, such as beliefs and faith, that are part of the models of spirituality being applied to the workplace. Even the variables of gratitude and forgiveness are frequently referred to in the literature on leadership spirituality.

This more applied perspective of spirituality found in the organizational behavior and leadership fields is also consistent with research over the years on professionalism. Similar to spiritual leadership, the classic meaning of professionalism includes the attitudinal dimensions of using the professional organization as a major reference (membership and identification), a belief in service to the public (intrinsic motivation), and a sense of calling to the field (e.g., Hall, 1968; Snizek, 1972).

Relevancy of Spirituality to PsyCap

For our purposes of potential PsyCap, we integrate the above views on spirituality to include a search for the sacred, as well as a sense of team membership, meaning and sense making, calling, and intrinsic and extrinsic motivation. Such dimensions seem most relevant to the role spirituality may play in PsyCap. Those with spiritual PsyCap may perceive their jobs as a calling rather than just the traditional transactional employment contract. They may still be extrinsically motivated, but more important to them may be their intrinsic motivation to meet or exceed expectations. Put in other terms, those with spiritual PsyCap may exhibit organizational citizenship behaviors that are above and beyond the call of duty, even when they are not directly recognized by the organization's extrinsic reward system (see Organ, 1988, for a discussion of such organizational citizenship).

This view of spirituality relevant to PsyCap is also similar to the effects of transformational over transactional leadership articulated by Bass (1985). Specifically, transformational leaders connect followers through their identification with a higher cause to something more significant and meaningful than a simple transactional exchange. In other words, leaders with spiritual PsyCap may raise their followers' level of identification with the work to be accomplished and, in turn, their motivation and commitment.

Supported, understood and appreciated by other members of their empowered teams, organizational members with spiritual PsyCap may yield highly desirable performance and attitudinal outcomes. Similar to other types of PsyCap, and PsyCap as a whole, a contagion effect of spirituality may also occur among "go to's," peers, and followers. For example, spiritual leadership may result in organizational vision and values being transformed toward more ethical and socially responsible goals and strategies that may be permeated throughout the organization (Fry, 2005).

Drawing from the literature, we should also note that dimensions of spirituality may deliberately lead to conformance and extrinsic motivation toward nonsacred goals (e.g., Hill, et al., 2000). This provides support to negative reactions to organized religions. Moreover, conformance has been associated with dysfunctional group dynamics, such as "groupthink" (Janis, 1982) and rigidity (Barker, 1993), and extrinsic motivation has been debated as a possible diminishing factor for intrinsic motivation (Wiersma, 1992). In other words, spirituality has been associated with both positive and negative outcomes. For example, if spirituality includes extrinsic motivation to nonsacred goals, then this has led to negative reactions, such as charges of hypocrisy. To counter such negativity and support the relevancy to positive PsyCap, spirituality scholars, such as positive psychologist Kenneth Pargament (2002), point out the need to understand and clarify the perceived nature of the "sacred" being searched for, the search process itself, and the underlying motives (i.e., extrinsic vs. intrinsic).

HOW DOES SPIRITUALITY MEASURE UP TO THE PSYCAP CRITERIA?

In terms of positive impact, one of the most significantly supported contributions of spirituality is in relation to effective coping with hardships (Pargament, 1997). Other positive outcomes associated with spirituality include enhanced relationships, prosocial (e.g., organizational citizenship) behaviors, physical and psychological well-being, and avoidance of antisocial behaviors, such as drug abuse and aggression (see Mattis, 2004, for a comprehensive review). As reviewed above, the work coming out of the organizational behavior and leadership fields is providing some support that the outcomes of spirituality are transferable to the workplace in terms of individual-level performance, commitment, and well-being, as well as organizational-level profitability and social responsibility (e.g., Fry 2003, 2005; Marques, Dhiman, & King, 2005).

Positive psychology suggests that spirituality in general, and religiousness in particular, is based on some enduring traits acquired through heredity and socialization (e.g., see Mattis, 2004). Yet it is also recognized that the lack of longitudinal and life-span research precludes any conclusive findings.

Fry (2005) provides a multilevel model of the spiritual leadership-development process. Specifically, he proposes that spirituality can be enhanced through vision, strategies, systems, and goals at the organizational level; empowerment, communication, and power-sharing at the team level; and values such as trust, forgiveness, integrity, honesty, courage, and excellence at the individual level. In addition, research on perceptions of sanctification (Mahoney, et al., 2005) and desecration (Pargament, Magyar, Benore, and Mahoney, 2005), as well as spiritual conversion (Mahoney & Pargament, 2004) and purification and reframing (Pargament & Mahoney, 2002), supports the contention that spirituality and religiousness may be developmental states. As challenging moments that represent crossroads in one's life are encountered, important perceptions, attributions, and attitudes about life may be altered, as well as one's view of his or her spiritual self (Avolio & Luthans, 2006). Such moments may enhance or diminish the dimensions of spirituality and religiousness.

In line with spirituality and religiousness being both dispositional traits and developmental states, Tsang and McCullough (2003) provide a hierarchical model for conceptualizing and measuring these constructs. They utilize measures that assess operational-level, practical, day-to-day spirituality, while controlling for any potential individual differences. Self-report, single-item measures of religiousness (e.g., how often do you pray/meditate/attend religious services?) may be effective in measuring dispositions toward spirituality. However, more elaborate and diversified measures and approaches are necessary to assess the various dimensions of spirituality as a state, such as preliminary ones emerging in the leadership literature (Fry, Vitucci, & Cedillo, 2005).

Although there are a number of existing measures of spirituality, they have been found to have limitations. For example, Tsang and McCullough (2003) suggest that researchers should stop developing new spirituality and religiousness instruments until the current scales are revised and integrated to reflect at least four components: disposition (trait), motivation (intrinsic/sacred vs. extrinsic/nonsacred), coping style (process), and practices (e.g., meditation). Similarly, Fry and colleagues' (2005) spiritual-leadership measure mixes behavioral and attribution items, as well as levels of analysis in the same scales, leaving open to question what exactly is being measured with such survey instruments.

Obviously, like other potential PsyCap factors, much more theory-building, research, and valid measurement is needed on spirituality in order to reach the threshold level of the criteria to make a significant contribution to PsyCap. Table 7.1 does recognize that it may meet at least minimal levels of the criteria but certainly not to the depth of the four key factors of PsyCap nor, in its present state of development, most of the other potential PsyCap variables. However, like the other possibilities for future PsyCap, the potential power of spirituality in the workplace must be acknowledged in discussions of the future of PsyCap.

AUTHENTICITY AS POTENTIAL PSYCAP

Since the dawning of civilization, authenticity has been of interest to philosophers, politicians, theologians, and now positive psychologists (e.g., see Harter, 2002; Seligman, 2002). Being true to one's self is considered in this literature to be the essence of genuine authentic behavior. Authenticity is viewed as both a terminal value and as instrumental to many other desirable outcomes, such as morality, peace, happiness, and contentment. In the destructive aftermath of the recent wave of corporate ethical scandals and downsizing, where society in general and employees in particular have questioned the morality of and have lost trust in their organizational leaders, organizational behavior and leadership scholars and practitioners alike have taken an increased interest in authenticity as it applies to both leadership and human resource development (Avolio & Luthans, 2006; Avolio, Gardner, Walumbwa, Luthans, and May, 2004; Cashman, 1998; Gardner, Avolio, Luthans, May, Walumbwa, 2005; George, 2003).

In positive psychology, Harter (2002) defines authenticity as "owning one's own personal experiences, be they thoughts, emotions, needs, wants, preferences, or beliefs . . . [so] that one acts in accord with the true self, expressing oneself in ways that are consistent with inner thoughts and feelings" (p. 382). Others also define authenticity in terms of one's ownership, acceptance, responsibility, and accurate public and private representation of internal states, commitments, feelings, intentions, and behaviors (Sheldon, Davidson, & Pollard, 2004).

Beside positive psychology, substantial conceptual work has been published on what Avolio and colleagues call authentic leadership development (e.g., see the June 2005 special issue of *Leadership Quarterly*). Avolio and Luthans (2006) define authentic leadership development, or what they simply call ALD, as "the process that draws upon a leader's life course, psychological capital, moral perspective, and a highly developed supporting organizational climate to produce greater self-awareness and self-regulated positive behaviors, which in turn foster continuous, positive self-development resulting in veritable, sustained performance" (p. 2). Various stages of research on ALD are currently underway (see briefing reports and links to this research at the University of Nebraska's Gallup Leadership Institute website at www.gli.unl.edu and www.e-leading.com).

Although PsyCap is already depicted as an important input and outcome of authentic leadership (Avolio & Luthans, 2006; Luthans & Avolio, 2003; Luthans, Norman, & Hughes, 2006), as a potential PsyCap capacity per se, authenticity is not limited to just the role that it may play in leadership. For example, research on self-determination has shown that when leaders facilitate autonomy, provide noncontrolling positive feedback, and acknowledge others' perspectives, this can be conducive to their followers' authenticity (Sheldon, et al., 2004). Building authentic followers can result in perceptions of affect toward, and satisfaction with, their work teams and the organization. Such authenticity may manifest itself in terms of increased trust, quality of supervision and of the organizational environment, good feelings, and satisfaction with job characteristics (Deci, Connell, & Ryan, 1989). Authenticity has also been found to be associated with self-esteem, positive affect, and hope (Harter, 2002), as well as sustained efforts and an upward spiral of goal attainment (Sheldon, et al., 2004).

In addition to the cognitive perspective on authenticity provided by, for example, self-determination theory (Deci, et al., 1989), the negative consequences of affective inauthenticity have also been extensively studied in the context of business ethics and specific areas such as emotional labor (Hochschild, 1979, 1983; Martin, Knopoff, & Beckman, 1998; Morris & Feldman, 1996; Sutton, 1991). At the group or organizational level, authenticity may also enhance trust, which in turn can increase communication, creativity, innovation, initiative, and ultimately employee performance, commitment, and retention (Salam, 2000). In other words, authenticity has been shown to be associated with positive psychological functioning and desirable performance and attitudinal work outcomes. By the same token, inauthenticity has also been associated with negative outcomes, such as unethical behaviors and stress from emotional labor. In other words, authenticity may have convergent and discriminant validity with other PsyCap constructs.

HOW DOES AUTHENTICITY MEASURE UP TO THE PSYCAP CRITERIA?

There are multiple measures for assessing authenticity. However, due to the nature of the construct, "faking good" (i.e., social desirability effects) is a potential threat to validity, particularly with existing self-report instruments. Thus, multisource input becomes desirable in measuring authenticity. For example, Henderson and Hoy's (1983) measure is an observation-based instrument that allows followers to assess their leader's authenticity.

As with the other potential PsyCap constructs, there could be several pitfalls associated with conceptualizing and measuring authenticity, as well as with its potential outcomes. For example, in the pursuit of extreme authenticity and honesty, some people may lack the social tact of exhibiting empathy while telling the truth. This may cause others to be hurt, get discouraged, feel resentful, or perceptually distort the authentic person's input and feedback. Moreover, as people fill multiple and sometimes conflicting roles, they may adopt several mutually exclusive selves in various contexts, causing estrangement of one's true self (Harter, 2002).

Each of the above pitfalls of authenticity implicitly assumes that people possess one, static, true self. We believe that this is not the case. We take the position that people possess multiple selves, some actual and some possible, as noted in the cognitive psychology and leadership literature (Lord & Brown, 2004; Avolio & Luthans, 2006). In order to enhance their authenticity, people do not just need to "discover" a true, actual self that is hidden somewhere. They need to employ their self-awareness, self-regulation, and self-development energies in order to realistically understand the strengths and limitations of their actual selves. They then need to explore and attempt to balance these actual selves with their possible selves so that they can actualize their full potential (Avolio & Luthans, 2006; Gardner, et al., 2005; Luthans & Avolio, 2003).

As one gradually strives toward a desirable, challenging, but attainable possible self (or set of possible selves), the actual self tends to adapt, grow, and develop. Hence, over time, the possible self becomes actualized into one's true self. Authenticity has thus been developed (Avolio & Luthans, 2006).

This perspective on being able to develop authenticity is particularly relevant to today's challenging work environment. Similar to our discussions on developing the other PsyCap capacities, we offer a developmental perspective that allows organizational members to internally gain control over, and to more authentically act on, their true, possible selves rather than becoming complacent and satisfied with a suboptimal, actual self that has been imposed on them through socialization or cultural barriers (Avolio & Luthans, 2006).

It is also important to note the significant role that others play in authenticity development. Parents, spouses, friends, leaders, mentors, peers, and associates (i.e., significant others) can all contribute to or hinder one's authenticity. Reinforcement of self-expression, support for autonomy and creativity, acceptance of one's own and others' strengths and limitations, and tolerance to unorthodox, out-of-the-box thinking can all contribute to an environment where authenticity can be enhanced, both through internal comprehension and external expression of one's actual, true self (see Harter, 2002). However, others can also contribute to the process of visualizing and shaping one's possible selves through challenging counterproductive or complacent views of the self, pushing us outside our comfort zones and acting as role models with similar applicable life experiences that can guide the authenticity development process (Avolio & Luthans, 2006).

In total, authenticity development is a dynamic process. It involves multiple selves that are discovered, explored, and tested within multiple social contexts and diversified interpersonal relationships. Authenticity may result in a wide range of capacities (leader, follower, peer, spouse, friend, parent, and so on), all acting as catalysts for changes and effective outcomes. As table 7.1 shows, although mostly associated with leadership so far, such authenticity may have considerable potential for meeting the criteria and contributing to PsyCap development and impact.

COURAGE AS POTENTIAL PSYCAP

Contrary to widely held views, and like the other PsyCap constructs often used in everyday language, courage should not just be equated with some common term such as fearlessness. It is also not just a virtue that presents itself in extraordinary situations characterized by extremely high risks. In positive psychology, courageous individuals are generally defined as those who are able to accomplish worthwhile goals despite fear or opposition (Peterson & Seligman, 2004). In addition, positive psychology posits that courage can be exhibited in both ordinary and extraordinary occasions (Lopez, O'Byrne, & Peterson, 2003). In the context of organizations, although perceived or actual risk is usually considered a prerequisite for the manifestation of courage, prudent assessment of potential risks and acceptance of the possibility of undesirable consequences also represent integral components of courage (Worline & Steen, 2004). Indeed, Worline (2003) describes courage as the linkage between "making up" and "making real," or the impossible made possible, in an organization.

Despite its intuitive and emotional appeal, courage may not always be welcomed in the workplace. Various constraints may exist in an organizational culture that hinder courageous action or render courageous individuals in a negative light as rule-breakers, troublemakers, or norm-violators. For example, Worline and Quinn (2003) show that organizational form (market, bureaucracy, clan, or organized anarchy) may enable some values and activities while constraining others. Courageous, principled action occurs when individuals capitalize on their cognitive, affective, and social resources in order to challenge the status quo in support of constrained values that may be in the organization's best interest to explore.

The dominant values of organizations in market economies emphasize ambition, competition, efficiency, and initiative. Courageous, principled action by participants may become necessary in order to promote values that might receive less weight in typical organizations, for example, loyalty, trust, honesty, and integrity (Worline & Quinn, 2003). As a specific example, ethical decision-makers need courage to face shareholders' demands for stock value as they attempt to balance the interests of a broader set of stakeholders through socially responsible decisions and actions. In another example, team members may courageously decide to set aside their differences, self-interests, and personal power and control in order to seek what is best for their team's/unit's effectiveness and performance. Open communication, transparency, trust, and resource sharing may be vital values for any individual, team, or organization. However, such values may not be facilitated by the competitiveness of the situation in the drive for growth and stock value. Only through courage can such competitive failures be corrected and the more intrinsic values become guidelines for action.

Similarly, bureaucracies and autocratic leaders tend to value accountability, discipline, obedience, and predictability. However, these values may not serve the organization very well in times of turmoil and revolutionary change. Adaptability and innovation may be stifled in such a regimented environment, threatening the very survival of the organization. Innovators and change agents in such an organizational climate need courage to effectively communicate their ideas and perspectives (Worline & Quinn, 2003).

Whistle-blowing is one of the most frequently cited examples of courageous action in today's organizations. Although controversial, most would agree that whistle-blowing tends to be in the best interest of the organization, at least in the long run. Whistle-blowing can protect the organization's reputation and save considerable financial resources that could otherwise be wasted in litigation costs and damaged reputations and public relations fallout. However, whistle-blowers take substantial risks, as they might challenge some of their organizations' established rules and regulations, as well as negatively affect at least short-term profitability and competitiveness. From a personal perspective, risks associated with whistle-blowing may include loss of one's job, retaliation, loss of trust, or social disapproval. Whistle-blowers likely appraise the returns on their risky actions, in terms of justice, greater good, and possibly personal and psychological gains, in order to feel adequate and worthwhile (Miceli & Near, 2005).

In line with these definitions and relevant examples, although courage is viewed as a virtue in positive psychology (Peterson & Seligman, 2004) and thus a highly desirable terminal value, at least in the organizational domain, it may still render both positive and negative outcomes. The courageous organizational participant may reap material, physical, social, and psychological gains, but the potential risks associated with a courageous act may also cause parallel losses. For example, a courageous idea that challenges the status quo may be met with praise and recognition, or it may be rejected. Courageously telling the truth (blowing the whistle) regarding a colleague's wrongdoing may save the organization substantial financial resources and reinforce its ethical values and culture, but it may also weaken interpersonal trust within the work team or reduce the propensity for future open communication.

HOW DOES COURAGE MEASURE UP
TO THE PSYCAP CRITERIA?

Table 7.1 indicates that except for having a demonstrated impact on work performance outcomes, courage as potential PsyCap seems to at least minimally meet the criteria. In one of the few studies with performance implications, Worline (2003) reported qualitatively gathered courageous stories from the workplace. She found four consistent elements appearing in these stories. The dimensions of courage included individuation, duress, involvement, and constructive opposition. Absent these elements, individuals coding these stories did not view them as representing courage.

Individuation was based on viewing the actor as thinking for oneself, being reflective, and able to act outside of daily expectations, that is, standing apart from others. Duress represented susceptibility to outside forces. Involvement represented having a sense of the organization as a whole and an awareness of common direction. Finally, constructive opposition was a felt opposition to one's social group that triggers the person to take individuated action against the flow of what is transpiring in order to reduce duress. Taken together, Worline (2003) reported that individuation, duress, and involvement in combination contributed to individuals described in workplace stories of courage as taking constructive opposition. Thus, constructive opposition is viewed as the outcome of the other three factors making up courage. Although conducted in the workplace, this study does not directly test for performance impact.

To date, very diverse approaches have been utilized for measuring courage. Existing measurement approaches include monitoring of physiological responses associated with courage, qualitative techniques such as structured and unstructured interviews, content analysis, and observation. Adequate self-report survey measures also exist (Lopez, et al., 2003). Overall, the use of multiple measures and the utilization of various methodologies have enhanced the understanding and assessment of courage. Furthermore, there seems to be a high level of agreement emerging in the literature, summarized above, on the definition of courage. This general agreement can facilitate the triangulation of the conceptual and empirical study of courage.

Traditionally, courage has been portrayed as a disposition. For example, Shelp (1984) defined courage as "the disposition to voluntarily act, perhaps fearfully, in dangerous circumstance, where the risks are reasonably appraised, in an effort to obtain or preserve some perceived good for oneself or others, recognizing that the desired good may not be realized" (p. 354).

There are also recent inferences of dispositional courage associated with negative affectivity and proactive personality (Miceli & Near, 2005). However, there are also several approaches that have been proposed for developing and facilitating courageous action. For example, Worline (2003) describes courage not as a disposition but as a property of social life in which it occurs—or, in our terms, being more state-like. Courage is seen by Worline as a part of social life produced by moments that matter. Thus, enactment of courage depends on the relationship between individuals and the social life/moments in which they find themselves embedded. Worline's (2003) specific definition of courage is a "form of social life in which individuation is in its constructive opposition to involvement to remedy duress to social life" (p. 99). In other words, courage can change what others view is possible as part of one's social life, whether inside or outside of work in organizations.

Similar to self-efficacy (see chapter 2), courage can be enhanced through successful mastery experiences and practice, modeling of brave actions by relevant others, social persuasion and "en-courage-ment" by others, and psychological and physical arousal and wellness. Fostering group cohesion and mutual responsibility may also create a culture where courageous actions are enabled (Worline & Steen, 2004). Specific developmental attitudes and coping mechanisms have also been found to contribute to the development of courage (Haase, 1987). For example, whistle-blowing, as discussed above, can be encouraged through proactively making internal reporting channels available and open, making the organization's stance regarding unethical activity clear, and establishing measures for the protection of whistle-blowers. As whistle-blowing occurs, the organization can react by conducting high-quality investigations of reported violations, promptly correcting wrongdoing, communicating (to the extent possible within privacy limitations) the organization's intolerance to similar offenses, and reinforcing the positive actions taken to deal with the situation (Miceli & Near, 2005).

While enhancing courage through building self-efficacy may result in proactive, courageous actions despite risk, reducing the risk factors associated with courageous action may at the same time eliminate the need for courage. As generally defined, the presence of risk seems a necessary antecedent for courage. Although further theory development and research studies of the issues raised with regard to courage are necessary, and there is especially a need for better understanding of the role of courage in enhancing work performance, like the other constructs in the last chapter and this one, the future looks very promising for courage to be included in PsyCap.

FUTURE IMPLICATIONS AND DIRECTIONS FOR RESEARCH AND PRACTICE

In this chapter and the previous one, we have presented several positive capacities for potential inclusion in PsyCap. The cognitive capacities of creativity and wisdom, the affective capacities of subjective well-being, flow, and humor, which were discussed in the previous chapter, as well as the higher order capacity of authenticity discussed in this chapter seem to meet most of the PsyCap inclusion criteria of being positive, theory and researched based, measurable, developmental, and related to workplace performance. On the other hand, it is probably fair to say that the jury is still out on whether the social capacities of gratitude, forgiveness, and emotional intelligence or the higher order capacities of spirituality and courage will fully meet the PsyCap criteria for inclusion. Nevertheless, exploring how all these other positive constructs relate to those already included in PsyCap not only enriches our understanding of PsyCap but also enriches our understanding of these other seemingly relevant positive constructs.

As noted throughout these two chapters, this overview is not meant to provide a comprehensive list of all potential PsyCap capacities, nor is our current assessment of these potential capacities conclusive. Our purpose has been to present some directions for future research and practice that would help expand the realm of PsyCap and keep it dynamic. This can be done through further investigation of the existing and potential PsyCap capacities that we present in this book as additional research emerges, as well as through exploring still others using our inclusion criteria as guidelines for assessment and applicability.

REFERENCES

Avolio, B. J., Gardner, W. L., Walumbwa, F. O., Luthans, F., & May, D. R. (2004). Unlocking the mask: A look at the process by which authentic leaders impact follower attitudes and behaviors. *Leadership Quarterly, 15,* 801–823.

Avolio, B. J., & Luthans, F. (2006). *The high impact leader: Moments matter in accelerating authentic leadership development.* New York: McGraw-Hill.

Bandura, A. (1986). *Social foundations of thought and action.* Englewood Cliffs, NJ: Prentice-Hall.

Bandura, A. (1997). *Self-efficacy: The exercise of control.* New York: Freeman.

Bar-On, R. (1997). *BarOn Emotional Quotient Inventory (EQ-i): Technical manual.* Toronto: Multi-Health Systems.

Barker, J. R. (1993). Tightening the iron cage: Concertive control in self-managing teams. *Administrative Science Quarterly, 38,* 408–437.

Baskin, T., & Enright, R. (2004). Intervention studies on forgiveness: A meta-analysis. *Journal of Counseling & Development, 82,* 79–90.

Bass, B. M. (1985). *Leadership and performance beyond expectations.* New York: Free Press.

Beersma, B., Hollenbeck, J., Humphrey, S., Moon, H., Conlon, D., & Ilgen, D. (2003). Cooperation, competition, and team performance: Toward a contingency approach. *Academy of Management Journal, 46,* 572–590.

Berscheid, E. (2003). The human's greatest strength: Other humans. In L. Aspinwall & U. Staudinger (Eds.), *A psychology of human strengths: Fundamental questions and future directions for a positive psychology* (pp. 37–47). Washington, DC: American Psychological Association.

Cashman, K. (1998). *Leadership from the inside out: Becoming a leader for life.* Provo, UT: Executive Excellence Publishing.

Deci, E. L., Connell, J. P., & Ryan, R. M. (1989). Self-determination in a work organization. *Journal of Applied Psychology, 74,* 580–590.

Dent, E. B., Higgins, M. E., & Wharff, D. M. (2005). Spirituality and leadership: An empirical review of definitions, distinctions, and embedded assumptions. *Leadership Quarterly, 16,* 625–654.

Diener, E. (2000). Subjective well-being: The science of happiness and a proposal for a national index. *American Psychologist, 55,* 34–43.

Diener, E., Suh, E., Lucas, E., & Smith, H. (1999). Subjective well-being: Three decades of progress. *Psychological Bulletin, 125,* 276–302.

Duchon, D., & Plowman, D. A. (2005). Nurturing the spirit at work: Impact on work unit peformance. *Leadership Quarterly, 16,* 807–834.

Emmons, R. A. (2003). Acts of gratitude in organizations. In K. S. Cameron, J. E. Dutton, & R. E. Quinn (Eds.), *Positive organizational scholarship* (pp. 81–93). San Francisco: Berrett-Koehler.

Emmons, R. A. (2004). Gratitude. In C. Peterson & M. Seligman (Eds.), *Character strengths and virtues: A handbook and classification* (pp. 553–568). Oxford, UK: Oxford University Press.

Emmons, R. A., & Crumpler, C. A. (2000). Gratitude as a human strength: Appraising the evidence. *Journal of Social and Clinical Psychology, 19,* 56–69.

Emmons, R., McCullough, M., & Tsang, J. (2003). The assessment of gratitude. In

S. Lopez & C. R. Snyder (Eds.), *Positive psychological assessment: A handbook of models and measures* (pp. 327–341). Washington, DC: American Psychological Association.

Emmons, R. A., & Shelton, C. M. (2002). Gratitude and the science of positive psychology. In C. R. Snyder & S. Lopez (Eds.), *Handbook of positive psychology* (pp. 459–471). Oxford, UK: Oxford University Press.

Enright, R., & North, J. (Eds.) (1998). *Exploring forgiveness.* Madison: University of Wisconsin Press.

Fry, L. (2003). Toward a theory of spiritual leadership. *Leadership Quarterly, 14,* 693–727.

Fry, L. (2005). Toward a theory of ethical and spiritual well-being, and corporate social responsibility through spiritual leadership. In R. A. Giacalone, C. Jurkiewicz, & C. Dunn (Eds.), *Positive psychology in business ethics and corporate social responsibility* (pp.47–83). Greenwich, CT: Information Age.

Fry, L. W., Vitucci, S., & Cedillo, M. (2005). Spiritual leadership and army transformation: Theory, measurement, and establishing a baseline. *Leadership Quarterly, 16,* 835–862.

Gardner, H. (1983). *Frames of the mind: The theory of multiple intelligences.* New York: Basic Books.

Gardner, W. L., Avolio, B. J., Luthans, F., May, D. R., & Walumbwa, F. O. (2005). "Can you see the real me?" A self-based model of authentic leader and follower development. *Leadership Quarterly, 16,* 343–372.

George, B. (2003). *Authentic leadership: Rediscovering the secrets of creating lasting value.* San Francisco: Jossey-Bass.

Gibbs, N. (1995, October 2). The EQ factor. *Time, 146,* 60–67.

Goleman, D. (1995). *Emotional intelligence.* New York: Bantam Books.

Goleman, D. (1998). *Working with emotional intelligence.* New York: Bantam Books.

Goleman, D., Boyatzis, R., & McKee, A. (2002). *Primal leadership: Realizing the power of emotional intelligence.* Boston: Harvard Business School Press.

Haase, J. (1987). Components of courage in chronically ill adolescents: A phenomenological study. *Advances in Nursing Science, 9*(2), 64–80.

Hackman, J. R., & Wageman, R. (2005). A theory on team coaching. *Academy of Management Review, 30,* 269–287.

Hall, R. (1968). Professionalization and bureaucratization. *American Sociological Review, 33,* 92–104.

Harter, S. (2002). Authenticity. In C. R. Snyder & S. Lopez (Eds.), *Handbook of positive psychology* (pp. 382–394). Oxford, UK: Oxford University Press.

Hebl, J., & Enright, R. (1993). Forgiveness as a psychotherapeutic goal with elderly females. *Psychotherapy, 30,* 658–667.

Henderson, J., & Hoy, W. (1983). Leader authenticity: The development and test of an operational measure. *Educational and Psychological Research, 3,* 63–75.

Hill, P., Pargament, K., Hood, Jr., R., McCullough, M., Swyers, J., Larson, D., & Zinnbauer, B. (2000). Conceptualizing religion and spirituality: Points of commonality, points of departure. *Journal for the Theory of Social Behaviour, 30,* 51–77.

Hochschild, A. (1979). Emotion work, feeling rules, and social structure. *American Journal of Sociology, 85*, 551–575.

Hochschild, A. (1983). *The managed heart: Commercialization of human feeling.* Berkeley: University of California Press.

Janis, I. (1982). *Groupthink* (2nd ed.). Boston: Houghton Mifflin.

Kelley, R., & Caplan, J. (1993). How Bell Labs creates star performers. *Harvard Business Review, 71*(4), 128–139.

Lencioni, P. (2002). *The five dysfunctions of a team: A leadership fable.* San Francisco: Jossey-Bass & Wiley.

Locke, E. A. (2005). Why emotional intelligence is an invalid concept. *Journal of Organizational Behavior, 26*, 425–431.

Lopez, S., O'Byrne, K., & Peterson, S. (2003). Profiling courage. In S. Lopez & C. R. Snyder (Eds.), *Positive psychological assessment: A handbook of models and measures* (pp. 185–197). Washington, DC: American Psychological Association.

Lord, R. G., & Brown, D. J. (2004). *Leadership processes and follower self identity.* Mahwah, NJ: Erlbaum.

Luthans, F. (2002a). The need for and meaning of positive organizational behavior. *Journal of Organizational Behavior, 23*, 695–706.

Luthans, F. (2002b). Positive organizational behavior: Developing and managing psychological strengths. *Academy of Management Executive, 16*, 57–72.

Luthans, F., & Avolio, B. (2003). Authentic leadership: A positive development approach. In K. S. Cameron, J. E. Dutton, & R. E. Quinn (Eds.). *Positive organizational scholarship* (pp. 241–258). San Francisco: Berrett-Koehler.

Luthans, F., Luthans, K., Hodgetts, R., & Luthans, B. C. (2001). Positive Approach to Leadership (PAL): Implication's for today's organizations. *Journal of Leadership Studies, 8*(2), 3–20.

Luthans, F., Luthans, K. W., & Luthans, B. C. (2004). Positive psychological capital: Going beyond human and social capital. *Business Horizons, 47*, 45–50.

Luthans, F., Norman, S. M., & Hughes, L. (2006). Authentic leadership. In R. Burke & C. Cooper (Eds.), *Inspiring leaders* (pp. 84–104). London: Routledge, Taylor & Francis.

Luthans, F., & Youssef, C. M. (2004). Human, social and now positive psychological capital management: Investing in people for competitive advantage. *Organizational Dynamics, 33*, 143–160.

Mahoney, A., & Pargament, K. (2004). Sacred changes: Spiritual conversion and transformation. *Journal of Clinical Psychology, 60*, 481–492.

Mahoney, A., Pargament, K., Cole, B., Jewell, T., Magyar, G., Tarakeshwar, N., Murray-Swank, N., & Phillips, R. (2005). A higher purpose: The sanctification of strivings in a community sample. *International Journal for the Psychology of Religion, 15*, 239–262.

Marques, J., Dhiman, S., & King, R. (2005). Spirituality in the workplace: Developing an integral model and a comprehensive definition. *Journal of American Academy of Business, 7*, 81–91.

Martin, J., Knopoff, K., & Beckman, C. (1998). An alternative to bureaucratic impersonality and emotional labor: Bounded emotionality at the Body Shop. *Administrative Science Quarterly, 43,* 429–469.

Mattis, J. (2004). Spirituality (religiousness, faith, purpose). In C. Peterson & M. Seligman (Eds.), *Character strengths and virtues: A handbook and classification* (pp. 599–622). Oxford, UK: Oxford University Press.

Mauger, P., Perry, J., Freeman, T., Grove, D., McBride, A., et al. (1992). The measurement of forgiveness: Preliminary research. *Journal of Psychology and Christianity, 11,* 170–180.

Mayer, J., & Salovey, P. (1997). What is emotional intelligence? In P. Salovey & D. Sluyter (Eds.), *Emotional development and emotional intelligence: Educational implications* (pp. 3–34). New York: Basic Books.

Mayer, J., & Salovey, P. (2004). Social intelligence (emotional intelligence, personal intelligence). In C. Peterson & M. Seligman (Eds.), *Character strengths and virtues: A handbook and classification* (pp. 337–353). Oxford, UK: Oxford University Press.

Mayer, J., Salovey, P., & Caruso, D. (2000). Models of emotional intelligence. In R. Sternberg (Ed.), *Handbook of intelligence* (pp. 396–420). Cambridge: Cambridge University of Press.

Mayer, J., Salovey, P., & Caruso, D. (2001). *The Mayer-Salovey-Caruso Emotional Intelligence Test (MSCEIT).* Toronto: Multi-Health Systems.

McCullough, M. (2004). Forgiveness and mercy. In C. Peterson & M. Seligman (Eds.), *Character strengths and virtues: A handbook and classification* (pp. 445–459). Oxford, UK: Oxford University Press.

McCullough, M., Emmons, R., & Tsang, J. (2002). The grateful disposition: A conceptual and empirical typology. *Journal of Personality and Social Psychology, 82,* 112–127.

McCullough, M., Kilpatrick, S., Emmons, R., & Larson, D. (2001). Gratitude as moral affect. *Psychological Bulletin, 127,* 249–266.

McCullough, M., Pargament, K., & Thoresen, C. (Eds.) (2000). *Forgiveness: Theory, research and practice.* New York: Guilford Press.

McCullough, M., Rachal, K., Sandage, S., Worthington, E., Brown, S., & Hight, T. (1998). Interpersonal forgiving in close relationships II: Theoretical elaboration and measurement. *Journal of Personality and Social Psychology, 75,* 1586–1603.

McCullough, M., & Witvliet, C. (2002). The psychology of forgiveness. In C. R. Snyder & S. Lopez (Eds.), *Handbook of positive psychology* (pp. 446–458). Oxford, UK: Oxford University Press.

Miceli, M., & Near, J. (2005). Whistle-blowing and positive psychology. In R. A. Giacalone, C. Jurkiewicz, & C. Dunn (Eds.), *Positive psychology in business ethics and corporate social responsibility* (pp.85–102). Greenwich, CT: Information Age.

Miller, T. (1995). *How to want what you have.* New York: Avon.

Morris, J. A., & Feldman, D. C. (1996). The dimensions, antecedents, and consequences of emotional labor. *Academy of Management Review, 21,* 986–1010.

Organ, D. (1988). *Organizational citizenship behavior: The good soldier syndrome.* Lexington, MA: Lexington.

Pargament, K. (1997). *The psychology of religion and coping: Theory, research, and practice.* New York: Guilford Press.

Pargament, K. (2002). The bitter and the sweet: An evaluation of the costs and benefits of religiousness. *Psychological Inquiry, 13,* 168–181.

Pargament, K., Magyar, G., Benore, E., & Mahoney, A. (2005). Sacrilege: A study of sacred loss and desecration and their implications for health and well-being in a community sample. *Journal for the Scientific Study of Religion, 44,* 59–78.

Pargament, K., & Mahoney, A. (2002). Spirituality: Discovering and conserving the sacred. In C. R. Snyder & S. Lopez (Eds.), *Handbook of positive psychology* (pp. 646–659). Oxford, UK: Oxford University Press.

Peterson, C., & Seligman, M. (2004). *Character strengths and virtues: A handbook and classification.* New York: Oxford University Press.

Peterson, S., & Luthans, F. (2006). The impact of financial and nonfinancial incentives on business unit outcomes over time. *Journal of Applied Psychology, 91,* 156–165.

Putnam, R. D. (1995). Tuning in, tuning out: The strange disappearance of social capital in America. *Political Science and Politics, 28,* 664–683.

Reave, L. (2005). Spiritual values and practices related to leadership effectiveness. *Leadership Quarterly, 16,* 655–688.

Reis, H., & Gable, S. (2003). Toward a positive psychology of relationships. In C. Keyes & J. Haidt (Eds.), *Flourishing: Positive psychology and the life well-lived* (pp. 129–159). Washington, DC: American Psychological Association.

Salam, S. (2000). Foster trust through competence, honesty, and integrity. In E. Locke (Ed.), *Handbook of principles of organizational behavior* (pp. 274–288). Oxford, UK: Blackwell.

Salovey, P., Caruso, D., & Mayer, J. (2004). Emotional intelligence in practice. In P. A. Linley & S. Joseph (Eds.), *Positive psychology in practice* (pp. 447–463). Hoboken, NJ: John Wiley & Sons.

Salovey, P., & Mayer, J. (1990). Emotional intelligence. *Imagination, Cognition, and Personality, 9,* 185–211.

Salovey, P., Mayer, J., & Caruso, D. (2002). The positive psychology of emotional intelligence. In C. R. Snyder & S. Lopez (Eds.), *Handbook of positive psychology* (pp. 159–171). Oxford, UK: Oxford University Press.

Salovey, P., Mayer, J., Caruso, D., & Lopes, P. (2003). Measuring emotional intelligence as a set of abilities with the Mayer-Salovey-Caruso Emotional Intelligence Test. In S. Lopez & C. R. Snyder (Eds.), *Positive psychological assessment: A handbook of models and measures* (pp. 251–265). Washington, DC: American Psychological Association.

Seligman, M. E. P. (2002). *Authentic happiness.* New York: Free Press.

Sheldon, K., Davidson, L., & Pollard, E. (2004). Integrity (authenticity, honesty). In C. Peterson & M. Seligman (Eds.), *Character strengths and virtues: A handbook and classification* (pp. 249–271). Oxford, UK: Oxford University Press.

Shelp, E. (1984). Courage: A neglected virtue in the patient-physician relationship. *Social Science and Medicine, 18,* 351–360.

Snizek, W. (1972). Hall's professionalism scale: An empirical reassessment. *American Sociological Review, 37,* 109–114.

Stajkovic, A., & Luthans, F. (2003) Behavioral management and task performance in organizations: Conceptual background, meta-analysis, and test of alternative models. *Personnel Psychology, 56,* 155–194.

Subkoviak, M., Enright, R., Wu, C., Gassin, E., Freedman, S., Olson, L., et al. (1995). Measuring interpersonal forgiveness in late adolescence and middle adulthood. *Journal of Adolescence, 18,* 641–655.

Sutton, R. I. (1991). Maintaining norms about expressed emotions: The case of bill collectors. *Administrative Science Quarterly, 36,* 245–268.

Tsang, J., & McCullough, M. (2003). Measuring religious constructs: A hierarchical approach to construct organization and scale selection. In S. Lopez & C. R. Snyder (Eds.), *Positive psychological assessment: A handbook of models and measures* (pp. 345–360). Washington, DC: American Psychological Association.

Wiersma, U. P. (1992). The effects of extrinsic rewards in intrinsic motivation: A meta-analysis. *Journal of Occupational and Organizational Psychology, 65,* 101–114.

Worline, M. C. (2003). *Dancing the cliff edge: The place of courage in social life.* Unpublished doctoral dissertation, University of Michigan–Ann Arbor.

Worline, M., & Quinn, R. (2003). Courageous principled action. In K. S. Cameron, J. E. Dutton, & R. E. Quinn (Eds.), *Positive organizational scholarship* (pp. 138–157). San Francisco: Berrett-Koehler.

Worline, M., & Steen, T. (2004). Bravery (valor). In C. Peterson & M. Seligman (Eds.), *Character strengths and virtues: A handbook and classification* (pp. 213–228). Oxford, UK: Oxford University Press.

Worthington, E., Berry, J., Shivy, V., & Brownstein, E. (2005). Forgiveness and positive psychology in business ethics and corporate social responsibility. In R. A. Giacalone, C. Jurkiewicz, & C. Dunn (Eds.), *Positive psychology in business ethics and corporate social responsibility* (pp.265–284). Greenwich, CT: Information Age.

Worthington, E., Sandage, S., & Berry, J. (2000). Group interventions to promote forgiveness: What researchers and clinicians ought to know. In M. E. McCullough, K. I. Pargament, & C. E. Thoresen (Eds.), *Forgiveness: Theory, research and practice* (pp. 228–253). New York: Guilford.

Yamhure-Thompson, L., & Snyder, C. R. (2003). Measuring forgiveness. In S. Lopez & C. R. Snyder (Eds.), *Positive psychological assessment: A handbook of models and measures* (pp. 301–312). Washington, DC: American Psychological Association.

Zinnbauer, B., Pargament, K., Cole, B., Rye, M., Butter, E., Belavich, T., et al. (1997). Religion and spirituality: Unfuzzying the fuzzy. *Journal for the Scientific Study of Religion, 36,* 549–564.

Zinnbauer, B., Pargament, K., & Scott, A. (1999). The emerging meanings of religiousness and spirituality: Problems and prospects. *Journal of Personality, 67,* 889–919.

CHAPTER 8

Measurement and Development of PsyCap

Assessing the Return on Investment

With global competition heating up on the one hand, and the demand for increased accountability on the other, human resource researchers and practitioners have focused on and are trying to meet the challenge of assessing the investments in and dollar return from human resource development (e.g., Becker & Huselid, 1992; Boudreau, 1991; Cascio, 1991; Huselid, 1995). However, despite this spotlighted attention, debates regarding the reliability, validity, and utility of various approaches for quantifying the return on investment and value of human resources and their development are far from resolved (Latham & Whyte, 1994; Skarlicki, Latham, & Whyte, 1996; Whyte & Latham, 1997). Yet, the "bottom line" for our proposed PsyCap as presented in this book is that it must be reliably and validly measured, that it can be developed, and that it must have demonstrated performance impact. The investment in the PsyCap development of organizational participants must be able to show a dollars-and-cents return on that investment.

In this chapter, we present our recently developed and validated workplace-specific measure of PsyCap and the microintervention model that we have successfully used to develop PsyCap, and we also propose a simple, practical, but theoretically sound approach for assessing the return on investment in PsyCap development. The PsyCap measure and microintervention are based on chapters 2–5, which focused on efficacy, hope, optimism, and resiliency. For the assessment of the return on investment, we draw from the extensive body of knowledge on utility analysis. We provide some specific examples and propose alternative approaches to help minimize some of the potential pitfalls.

CHARACTERISTICS OF EXISTING PSYCAP MEASURES

Various instruments for measuring self-efficacy, hope, optimism, resiliency, and other potential positive psychological constructs have been designed, researched, and validated. Attention to these measures has greatly accelerated with the emergence of the positive psychology movement (e.g., see Lopez & Snyder, 2003). The following briefly summarizes the characteristics of the widely recognized published measures that we drew from in developing our PsyCap measure.

Scales Utilized

Multiple types of scales have been employed in measuring positive psychological capacities and strengths. For example, Bandura (1997) provides considerable theory and research that self-efficacy should be measured in terms of magnitude and strength. The magnitude dimension of self-efficacy is the level of task difficulty in which a person expects to be able to perform. It is measured by respondents' yes or no answers to a question of whether or not they can perform a specific task at a certain level, with the level gradually increased. The strength dimension of self-efficacy is the degree of certainty that a person possesses about the ability to perform at each level of difficulty, measured by the respondent's reported percentage of confidence, or what Bandura refers to as efficacy at each level (Bandura, 1997; Locke, Frederick, Lee, & Bobko, 1984; Stajkovic & Luthans, 1998b).

Recently, however, there is research supporting Likert-type continuous scales as being comparable to scales using the magnitude-strength approach in measuring self-efficacy. These Likert scales have been found to yield factor structures, reliability, and validity similar to the traditional magnitude-strength efficacy measures (Maurer & Pierce, 1998). For example, Parker's (1998) efficacy instrument utilizes a Likert scale relevant to the workplace and is the one that we draw from in constructing the efficacy component of our PsyCap questionnaire.

Length of Questionnaire

One of the primary criticisms of many valid and reliable positive psychological measures is the large number of items they incorporate (Lopez & Snyder, 2003). For example, Seligman (1998) provides a 48-item measure of optimism, while the Scheier and Carver (1985) instrument that we draw from for the optimism component uses only 12 items. Coupled with the necessity of measuring several predictors, outcomes, and control variables, most often administered in a single survey, the integration of a large number of long scales may cause such long survey measures to reduce voluntary response rates and the reliability of each measure. Moreover, science searches for the most parsimonious representation or solution, and in this case, it is to measure our selected PsyCap constructs with the least number of items necessary for reliability and validity—but no less.

Wording Context

The existing positive psychological measures have been developed and validated either very generically or in a broad spectrum of specific contexts. Most of these measures come out of clinical usage and are not directly applicable to the workplace (Lopez & Snyder, 2003). The exceptions are Parker's (1998) work role breadth self-efficacy scale, and Snyder (2000) provides a domain-specific hope scale that includes the workplace as one of six domains. On the other hand, resiliency scales are primarily oriented toward children and youth because, as we discussed in chapter 5, for many years interest in this psychological capacity has been almost solely aimed at clinical and developmental psychology (e.g., Masten, 2001; Masten & Reed, 2002). Thus, although there is a broad and deep literature to support the measures that we have drawn from to assess PsyCap, most of the evidence has not been accumulated in the workplace with normal working adults and thus needed first to have the items selected by a panel of experts on the basis of content and face validity and then have their wording adapted.

Theoretical Framework Supporting PsyCap Measurement

Beside the workplace-domain issue, there are also other limitations in the theoretical frameworks supporting some of the positive psychological measures that could affect PsyCap measurement. First, most of the scales that are frequently used to measure positive capacities and strengths were originally designed to measure the opposite end of the continuum, that is, negative psychological pathologies. The bipolarity-versus-independence issue of positive and seemingly opposite negative psychological capacities has received increased emphasis in positive psychological research (e.g., see Peterson & Chang, 2002, for a comprehensive review of this issue in relation to optimism). This theoretical issue still needs further exploration, but the measures we specifically draw from generally assume independent positivity.

Second, one of the most salient PsyCap inclusion criteria is that the psychological capacities should be state-like, and thus developmental, rather than just being stable, relatively fixed dispositional traits. Fortunately, some of the positive psychological measures of PsyCap make a clear distinction regarding this vital criterion. For example, Parker's (1998) measure, which we draw from in building our PsyCap questionnaire, assesses work role self-efficacy. By contrast, in Judge and Bono's (2001) core self-evaluation model, the trait of generalized efficacy is what is measured. Similarly, Snyder (2000) provides two different scales, a state hope scale (Snyder, et al., 1996) and a dispositional hope scale. For optimism (Scheier & Carver, 1985) and resiliency (Wagnild & Young, 1993), we adapt the items to make them as state-like as possible. Most important, the beginning instructions are to describe yourself "right now."

In most positive psychology measures, this distinction between stable dispositions and situational states is not clear. It is understandable that a psychometrically sound scale needs to show a certain level of stability over time. However, PsyCap presents a new challenge for researchers and practitioners, as its state-like variability is an integral component of the core construct rather than an artifact of measurement error. Striking a balance between stability and sensitivity to change and development is of key importance to understanding and assessing PsyCap and was recognized in constructing our PsyCap measure.

Finally, especially within positive psychology, many of the constructs are conceptualized and measured as outcomes in and of themselves (e.g., see our discussions in chapters 6 and 7 on other potential PsyCap constructs). Although it is desirable to have confident, hopeful, optimistic, resilient, creative, and wise organizational leaders and employees in and of themselves, of more value to PsyCap is the potential impact that these may have on work performance and attitudinal outcomes. Therefore, we conceive our PsyCap constructs more often as inputs. Although PsyCap research may show these positive capacities and although the core construct itself may also be an outcome of, say, authentic leadership, or even of moderators/mediators of trust or some other outcome, we generally portray PsyCap as antecedent to performance outcomes, as an investment in human resources. PsyCap should be of high interest to organizational leaders and decision-makers who allocate scarce resources (financial resources, as well as time and energy) to develop their people's high-potential strengths and psychological capacities. To the degree that we can show how investing in PsyCap provides a high return on development, the more likely that organizational leaders will begin to include PsyCap in their "standard" metrics for gauging organizational performance.

MEASURING PSYCAP IN THE WORKPLACE

As indicated, in developing our PsyCap Questionnaire (PCQ), we drew from recognized, published measures of efficacy (Parker, 1998), hope (Snyder, et al., 1996), optimism (Scheier & Carver, 1985), and resilience (Wagnild & Young, 1993). Each of these four standard scales are of varying numbers of items and points on Likert scales and degrees of being state-like and relevant to the workplace. In constructing the PCQ, based on content and face validity, six items were selected by an expert panel from each of the four standard measures, the wording was adapted as needed for the workplace and to be state-like, and responses were put into a 6-point Likert scale. The resulting 24-item PCQ is presented in the appendix to this book.

Although each of the standard scales that we drew from in constructing the PCQ has considerable psychometric support, we also conducted an extensive analysis on the PCQ per se. Both exploratory and confirmatory factor analysis and reliabilities across four diverse samples provided promising psychometric support for the PCQ (see Luthans, Avolio, Avey, & Norman, 2006). Obviously, there are a number of limitations with any questionnaire measure, and the PCQ is no exception. However, in our studies so far, we have been able to address these potential measurement issues and will discuss them further in this chapter.

EMPIRICALLY RELATING THE PSYCAP MEASURE TO WORK-RELATED OUTCOMES

Over the past few years, we have empirically analyzed the relationship of the individual efficacy, hope, optimism, and resiliency positive strengths and the overall core construct of PsyCap with desirable work-related outcomes such as performance, satisfaction, and commitment. This research effort has found a statistically significant relationship between the PsyCap predictor variables and outcomes. These results were obtained for rated performance, objective performance, and satisfaction outcomes.

Overall PsyCap, including using our recently developed PCQ measure, has consistently shown higher correlations with outcomes than any of the individual positive psychological capacities of efficacy, hope, optimism, or resiliency by themselves (e.g., see Luthans, Avolio, et al., 2006; Luthans, Avolio, Walumbwa, & Li, 2005). In other words, as we indicated in chapter 1, PsyCap does appear to have a synergistic effect; that is, the whole (PsyCap) may be greater than the sum of its parts (i.e., efficacy, hope, optimism, and resiliency). Furthermore, as potential macrolevel, contextual confounds (i.e., possible alternative explanations) such as industry, organization size, business unit size, and managerial span of control—as well as employee-level demographic variables such as age, gender, ethnic background, education, and tenure—are controlled for, more variability could be accounted for, yielding even higher explained variation (e.g., see Luthans, Avolio, et al., 2006; Youssef, 2004).

These encouraging results have been supported among diverse samples, such as engineers and technicians in a very large aerospace firm, executives in a logistics firm, nurses in a hospital, employees in an insurance services company, workers in a manufacturing company, fast-food franchise managers, entrepreneurs and small-business owners, information technology engineers, federal, state and local government employees, and many others, including across cultures, for example, Indian knowledge workers and Chinese factory workers. Although most of these studies are still in the process of being analyzed and published, and while the results vary somewhat, for the purpose of illustrations and examples in this chapter, we simply use 20% as the percentage of variation in outcomes explained by PsyCap. For practical purposes, we follow the recommendation that researchers and organizational decision-makers be encouraged to utilize the methods and statistical analysis that best fit their conceptual frameworks, data, assumptions, and needs (see Goldstein, 1986; Sackett & Mullen, 1993).

DEVELOPING PSYCAP IN THE WORKPLACE

In previous chapters, we have presented several approaches and specific guidelines for developing each of the PsyCap strengths. For example, in chapter 2, self-efficacy was said to be developed through mastery experiences, modeling and vicarious learning, social persuasion, and physiological and psychological arousal. In chapter 3, hope was said to be developed through goal-setting, participation, and contingency planning for alternative pathways to attain goals. Then in chapter 4, optimism was said to be developed through leniency for the past, appreciation for the present, and opportunity-seeking for the future. Finally, in chapter 5, resilience was said to be developed through asset-focused strategies such as enhancing employability, risk-focused strategies such as proactive avoidance of adversity, and process-focused strategies to influence the interpretation of adverse events. Several developmental approaches were also presented in chapters 6 and 7 with the other potential positive psychological capacities to help illustrate meeting the criteria for possible inclusion into future PsyCap.

Since our development of a reliable and valid measure of PsyCap and its demonstrated relationship to workplace performance and organizational participant satisfaction (see Luthans, Avolio, et al., 2006), we have also turned our research attention to PsyCap microintervention studies. These short, highly focused interventions use a pretest (the PCQ)–posttest (PCQ) control group experimental design. These microinterventions consist of 1- to 3-hour (the length depends on the size of the group and how many exercises and video clip examples are used) workshops generally following the PsyCap Intervention (PCI) model shown in figure 8.1 and the content summarized in figure 8.2. The participants' PsyCap in these early microintervention studies increased on average about 2%. Importantly, this statistically significant increase in PsyCap development has occurred in the experimental groups undergoing the PCI session but not in randomly assigned control groups undergoing a commonly used group dynamics, teaming exercise (i.e., "Desert Survival") under the same conditions with equivalent participants or matched control groups that did not receive the intervention, but who were measured before and after on the same variables.

The initial microintervention studies under highly controlled conditions (e.g., the random assignment to experimental and control groups)

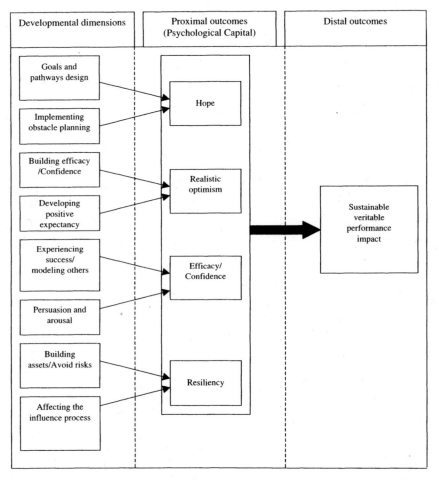

FIGURE 8.1 Psychological Capital Intervention (PCI)

Note: The PCI is intended to affect each state as well as the overall level of PsyCap for performance impact. *Source*: Adapted from Luthans, F., Avey, J. B., Avolio, B. J., Norman, S. M., & Combs, G. J. (2006). Psychological capital development: Toward a micro-intervention. *Journal of Organizational Behavior, 27*, 387–393.

FIGURE 8.2 Psychological Capital Intervention Content Summary

HOPE DEVELOPMENT

The hope construct was impacted and influenced by goals, pathways, and agency. Specifically, participants practiced generating work-related goals that were personally valuable and reasonably challenging and that included a clear beginning and end point. These goal characteristics generated sustained motivation, thus using goal components to increase agency. In addition, participants practiced generating multiple pathways to their work-related goals, and they identified obstacles that they should plan to encounter. After completing the exercise individually, each participant received feedback from the group on additional or alternative pathways that could be utilized and obstacles that could be expected. This practice increased each participant's pathway-generating skill and ability to identify and plan for obstacles, thus reducing the negative impact of obstacles on agency.

OPTIMISM DEVELOPMENT

Building efficacy in pathway generation and obstacle planning provided a foundation for the development of generally positive expectations. When participants were confident that they could identify and plan to overcome obstacles, their expectations of achieving their goals increased. Negative expectations that goals would not be accomplished were challenged as individuals began to see pathways to success and options on how to overcome obstacles. Group feedback increased positive expectations as individuals saw other group members also expect and plan for success. As participants' expectations of success increased, optimism both individually and within the group increased.

EFFICACY DEVELOPMENT

Participants practiced setting up stepwise techniques to accomplish goals. Then they explained each sub-goal (each step) to the group, and they answered questions about how each was to be accomplished. Task mastery for designing and pursuing goals was thus attained. Vicarious learning took place as each participant saw peers work toward their goals and heard success stories about how goals were attained. This stage included emotional arousal, which was influenced by positive expectations of achieving goals as well as the social persuasion by facilitator and group members by validating schedules and timelines, goals would be accomplished.

RESILIENCY DEVELOPMENT

Resiliency was increased by building awareness of personal assets in the form of talents, skills, and social networks. Participants were asked what resources they could leverage to accomplish a given goal. After creating the list of resources, the facilitator and peer group members identified additional resources participants did not include on their list. Participants were then encouraged to leverage these resources as necessary. Similar to planning for obstacles, participants were encouraged to identify in advance obstacles that could impede their progress. Whereas in the hope exercise the focus was on making plans to overcome these obstacles, in this exercise, the focus was on making plans to avoid the obstacles or to prevent them from becoming legitimate concerns. Finally, the influence process was impacted by each participant becoming aware of his or her initial thoughts and feelings when faced with adversity (i.e., confidence or despair, etc.) and choosing to focus on resilient thoughts based on their assessment of their resources and options to overcome adversity.

Adapted from Luthans, F., Avey, J. B., Avolio, B. J. Norman, S. M., & Combs, G. J. (2006). Psychological capital development: Toward a mico-intervention." *Journal of Organizational Behavior, 27,* 387–393.

were conducted with emerging adults (management students). These subjects are considered an important age group for development research in and of themselves (Arnett, 2000). Importantly, however, the same positive results (about 2% increase in measured PsyCap) have also been found in 2-to 3-hour microintervention studies with a broad array of managers and employees from a number of different types of jobs and organizations, and specifically with engineers and technicians in an aerospace firm (see Luthans, Avey, Avolio, Norman, & Combs, 2006, for more details on this PsyCap development research effort).

Based on this emerging empirical evidence, for the purpose of illustrations and examples in this chapter, we use 2% as the average potential increase in PsyCap through using our PCI 2- to 3-hour microintervention workshops. Although higher percentages have been reported in the literature on various human resource interventions in the workplace (e.g., see Hunter & Schmidt, 1983, for a review), we prefer to use this relatively conservative estimate based on our initial research to illustrate the potential gains that may result from developing PsyCap through short, highly focused microinterventions in the workplace.

ASSESSING THE RETURN ON PSYCAP INVESTMENT

Although in recent years there has been greatly increased demand for and attempted implementation of quantifying the impact of human resource investments, the approaches vary widely in terms of nature, depth, breadth, and complexity. We encourage review of this utility-analysis literature for background information and technical depth (e.g., see Brogden & Taylor, 1950; Cascio, 1991; Cascio & Ramos, 1986; Cronbach & Gleser, 1965; Hunter & Schmidt, 1983; Hunter, Schmidt, & Judiesch, 1990; Schmidt, Hunter, McKenzie, & Muldrow, 1979). We also acknowledge recent critiques of utility analysis that provide potential limitations and cautions, both regarding its conceptual validity and statistical reliability, as well as in terms of its practicality and credibility in applications to human resource management practice (e.g., Latham & Whyte, 1994; Whyte & Latham, 1997).

In this assessment, we chose to present a relatively simple, practical, but methodologically sound approach to assessing the potential return on PsyCap investment. The approach we use here is conceptually similar to that used in traditional utility analysis in human resource management. However, research has found that the complexity of traditional utility analysis may actually challenge the credibility of its results as perceived by managers, possibly even reversing its intended impact (Latham & Whyte, 1994).

In reaction to the criticism that you can "lie with statistics" or find any result that you want, decision-makers have sometimes reduced their support of otherwise promising human resource management investments when presented with very positive findings from complex utility analyses (Latham & Whyte, 1994; Whyte & Latham, 1997). As a result of this backlash, utility analysis has been recently simplified by management consultants and practitioners (e.g., Kravetz, 2004). We will present both the traditional and newer approaches to utility analysis and end the chapter by recognizing the potential limitations and pitfalls.

We present several hypothetical examples for calculating the financial impact that PsyCap could potentially have in some of today's largest and most prominent global firms, as well as in more typical medium and small firms. These examples offer alternative approaches based on objectives and data availability. As indicated, we assume 20% as the variability in outcomes explained by PsyCap, 0.45 as the correlation coefficient between PsyCap and outcomes (the square root of 0.2), and 2% as the increase in PsyCap that can be obtained in a short, developmental microintervention (i.e., our PCI approach briefly outlined in figures 8.1 and 8.2).

EXAMPLE 1: THE IMPACT PSYCAP MAY HAVE ON VERY LARGE GLOBAL FIRMS

To determine performance impact, objective data are very difficult to obtain (Dess & Robinson, 1984). However, in order to illustrate the financial impact that PsyCap may potentially have in the world's largest firms, we can use the publicly available sales revenue and profits of the top global companies on the *Forbes* list. Recent financial data on the top 10 are presented in table 8.1. As shown, the sales revenue results for these 10 companies range from $63–$285 billion, with a mean for these 10 of $156 billion and a standard deviation of $86 billion. Their profits range from $8–$25 billion, with a mean of $15 billion and a standard deviation of $5 billion.

One widely recognized way to estimate the average financial impact that PsyCap may potentially have in these huge, top ten global firms is to use

TABLE 8.1. Example 1. Sales Revenues and Profits of the Top Ten of the *Forbes* Global 2000 Companies

Forbes Global 2000 Rank	Company Name	Country	Industry	Sales ($Billion)	Profits ($Billion)
1	Citigroup	United States	Banking	108.28	17.05
2	General Electric	United States	Conglomerates	152.36	16.59
3	American International Group	United States	Insurance	95.04	10.91
4	Bank of America	United States	Banking	65.45	14.14
5	HSBC Group	United Kingdom	Banking	62.97	9.52
6	ExxonMobil	United States	Oil & gas operations	263.99	25.33
7	Royal Dutch/Shell Group	Netherlands/United Kingdom	Oil & gas operations	265.19	18.54
8	BP	United Kingdom	Oil & gas operations	285.06	15.73
9	ING Group	Netherlands	Diversified financials	92.01	8.1
10	Toyota Motor	Japan	Consumer durables	165.68	11.13
Mean				155.603	14.704
Standard deviation				86.466	5.118
SS$_{total}$				67288.08	235.7128

the following utility analysis equation (Hunter & Schmidt, 1983; Skarlicki, Latham, & Whyte, 1996):

$$U = NTr_{xy}SD_y,$$

where

> U = the dollar value of the outcomes that may be explained by PsyCap;
>
> N = the number of companies or units being assessed;
>
> T = the average duration of PsyCap's effect on outcomes;
>
> r_{xy} = the correlation coefficient between PsyCap and outcomes (i.e., the .45 correlation we are using in these examples);
>
> SD_y = the standard deviation of outcomes.

Assuming that we are examining only the average one of the ten companies in table 8.1 (N=1) and focusing on the contribution that PsyCap may have over the period of a single year (T=1), the potential financial impact PsyCap may have is calculated as follows:

> $U_{sales} = 1*1*0.45*86 = \$38.7$ billion;
>
> $U_{profits} = 1*1*0.45*5 = \$2.25$ billion.

In other words, as a gross example for illustrative purposes, the average of these top ten global companies may potentially have roughly $39 billion of its sales revenue and $2 billion of its profits explained by PsyCap.

By increasing the levels of PsyCap through a developmental intervention, there should be financial impact on these firms. Specifically, the following modified utility analysis formula can be used to estimate the impact that PsyCap development microinterventions may potentially have on the financial outcomes of the average of these very large firms:

$$\Delta U = NTr_{xy}SD_y(\Delta PsyCap),$$

where

> ΔU = the increase in the dollar value of outcomes due to PsyCap development;
>
> $\Delta PsyCap$ = the percentage increase resulting from a PsyCap developmental intervention.

Again, using our initial PsyCap intervention research findings of 2% from short 2- to 3-hour microinterventions as the estimate of ΔPsyCap in the calculations for the example above:

$$\Delta U_{sales} = 1*1*0.45*86*0.02 = \$774 \text{ million};$$
$$\Delta U_{profits} = 1*1*0.45*5*0.02 = \$45 \text{ million increase.}$$

This can be roughly interpreted as showing that regardless of what the existing level of PsyCap is in these ten very large global companies, they have the potential for increasing their sales revenues by several hundred million dollars and their profits by double-digit millions on an annual basis through PsyCap development microinterventions. Just as a 2% increase in market share of these global firms would result in a huge impact in their financial revenues, this analysis indicates that a similar 2% increase in PsyCap may also have a significant impact. In order to accurately assess net gains and return on PsyCap investment—or what we have called return on development or ROD (Avolio & Luthans, 2006)—intervention costs (e.g., the hourly costs of the participants away from their jobs and facilitator/training overhead costs) would have to be subtracted from the above figures. However, especially when compared to the rate of return on traditional economic capital, the ROD on PsyCap investment may be, relatively speaking, much greater (see Luthans, Avey, et al., 2006).

AN ALTERNATIVE METHODOLOGY FOR CALCULATING IMPACT

Obviously, we do not intend to imply that PsyCap is the only human variable that impacts performance. It is much more realistic to assume that there are a multitude of variables that should be controlled for in order to more accurately assess the contribution of PsyCap. Thus, the statistic of R^2 from a multiple regression model may be a more accurate way of estimating the utility of PsyCap. Again, for illustrative purposes, we can again assume 20% as an estimate of R^2. Regression models calculate as follow:

$$R^2 = SS_{explained} / SS_{total}$$

where,

$SS_{explained}$ = variability in outcomes accounted for by the regression
model;

SS_{total} = total variability in outcomes = $SS_{explained}$ + SS_{error}

Again using the sales and profit figures for the top 10 global firms in table 8.1, SS_{total} can be calculated. Assuming that PsyCap accounts for 20% of that total, $SS_{explained}$ can be calculated as follows:

sales $SS_{explained}$ = 0.2*67288.08 = 13458;
profits $SS_{explained}$ = 0.2*235.7128 = 47.

To obtain a rough estimate of the utility of PsyCap by this alternative method, we then divide the above figures by the number of companies (10) and calculate the square root of the resulting average:

U_{sales} = $\sqrt{13458/10}$ = \$36.68 billion;
$U_{profits}$ = $\sqrt{47/10}$ = \$2.17 billion.

These results are very similar to the results with the previous approach (i.e., example 1 above) to utility analysis. In other words, these two approaches to utility analysis are methodologically distinct from one another, but there is convergence between the results. These two analyses provide added support for each other. For simplicity, however, for the following examples of medium and small firms (i.e., not just the top global giants), we will just use the first approach. However, researchers and practitioners are strongly encouraged to compare and contrast the strengths and limitations of each approach to utility analysis in deciding which one to use.

EXAMPLE 2: THE IMPACT PSYCAP MAY HAVE ON MEDIUM-SIZED FIRMS

To provide a more complete picture, it is important to report the utility of PsyCap not only for the largest of today's organizations but also in high potential, medium-sized and small companies. Table 8.2 reports recent 12 months' sales data for the top ten companies on *Forbes'* "List of Mid-Cap Stocks." A mid-cap is defined in these data as a company with a market capitalization around \$1–\$4 billion. A total of 400 companies were identified to fit this size criterion.

TABLE 8.2. Example 2. Sales Revenues of the Top Ten *Forbes* 100 Mid-Cap Stocks

Forbes *100* Best Mid-Caps	Company Name	Industry	Sales ($Million)
1	Aéropostale	Casual apparel stores	1,008
2	William Lyon Homes	Homebuilding	1,837
3	Resources Connection	Accounting & human resources services	538
4	Unit	Oil & gas exploration	665
5	Engineered Support Systems	Military support equipment	976
6	Centene	Managed care organization	1,224
7	MDC Holdings	Homebuilding	4,350
8	Standard Pacific	Homebuilding	3,843
9	Oil States International	Oil & gas products & services	1,235
10	Education Management	Postsecondary degree programs	980
Mean			1,666
Standard deviation			1,333.65

As shown in table 8.2, sales revenues of these 10 mid-sized companies range from $538 million to $4.35 billion, with a mean of $1.7 billion and a standard deviation of $1.3 billion. To estimate the average utility of PsyCap in these 10 firms selected, we use the following equation, again assuming only the average single company ($N = 1$), a one-year period ($T = 1$), and our 0.45 correlation between PsyCap and performance and 2% as our PsyCap microintervention development increase:

$$U_{sales} = NTr_{xy}SD_y = 1*1*0.45*1.3 = \$585 \text{ million};$$
$$\Delta U_{sales} = NTr_{xy}SD_y(\Delta PsyCap) = 1*1*0.45*1.3*0.02 = \$11.7 \text{ million}.$$

In other words, this illustration indicates that for the average of these 10 mid-sized companies, PsyCap may explain $585 million of its revenue. However, even if these companies had commendable human resource management practices and their employees had a high level of PsyCap, the average of these mid-sized firms may still have the potential for increasing its sales revenues by about $12 million through short PsyCap development interventions.

EXAMPLE 3: THE IMPACT PSYCAP MAY HAVE ON SMALL FIRMS

Using a utility-analysis approach similar to that used for the large and medium firms, we drew from a recent *Forbes* "200 Best Small Companies" list to provide the data in table 8.3. As shown in table 8.3, sales revenues of these 10 smaller companies range from \$58–\$475 million, with a mean of \$279 million and a standard deviation of \$165 million. Using the same assumptions as the other two examples, the utility of PsyCap for the average of these 10 companies over a one-year period can be calculated as follows:

$$U_{sales} = NTr_{xy}SD_y = 1*1*0.45*165 = \$72.25 \text{ million};$$
$$\Delta U_{sales} = NTr_{xy}SD_y(\Delta PsyCap) = 1*1*0.45*165*0.02 = \$1.48 \text{ million}.$$

In other words, for the average of these 10 smaller companies, PsyCap can potentially explain about \$72 million of its sales revenue, and this amount may be increased by almost \$1.5 million through PsyCap development microinterventions.

EXAMPLE 4: WHEN PERFORMANCE DATA IS IRRELEVANT OR UNAVAILABLE

Even in the absence of objective performance measures, an estimate of the utility of PsyCap return on investment and development can still be made. For example, Kravetz (2004) suggests that "the cost of keeping an employee

TABLE 8.3. Example 3. Sales Revenues of the Top Ten *Forbes* 200 Best Small Companies

Forbes's 200 Best Small Companies	Company Name	State	Industry	Sales ($Million)
1	Cognizant Technology Solutions	NJ	Computer services	465
2	Headwaters	UT	Energy	462
3	Lannett	PA	Drugs	58
4	Amedisys	LA	Healthcare	183
5	Cytyc	MA	Medical products	334
6	Shuffle Master	NV	Leisure	78
7	Orleans Homebuilders	PA	Construction	475
8	Ceradyne	CA	Aerospace & defense	136
9	St. Mary Land & Exploration	CO	Oil & gas	388
10	Biosite	CA	Medical products	206
Mean				279
Standard deviation				165.2

on the payroll" is a conservative estimate of the dollar value of that employee's productivity. The reasoning is very simple—unless employees are at least contributing what they are costing, the organization would not keep them on the payroll. This employee cost includes not only salary but also government-mandated and additional benefits, plus a share of overhead costs, such as facilities space, technological processes, equipment, and other indirect expenses. Kravetz (2004) estimates that these additional costs usually range from 75–250% of an employee's salary. He suggests that for utility-analysis purposes, the total cost of keeping an employee on the payroll (and thus the contribution made) should be set at about twice the employee's direct salary.

Applying this rule of thumb, we can then estimate the utility of PsyCap contribution and the value of its development using the following slightly adapted formulas:

$$U_{productivity} = NTr_{xy}(2S);$$
$$\Delta U_{productivity} = NTr_{xy}(2S)(\Delta PsyCap),$$

where

$U_{productivity}$ = the dollar value of employee productivity (contribution) that can be explained by PsyCap in this case;

$\Delta U_{productivity}$ = the increase in the dollar value of productivity (contribution) due to increased PsyCap through its development;

N = the number of employees;

T = the average tenure;

S = the average salary.

For an example, say that we have an organization that employs 300 employees, who, on average, earn an annual salary of $50,000 and stay with the organization for five years. With these conservative assumptions, then using Kravetz's (2004) rule of thumb for estimating productivity or contribution (i.e., twice the average salary) and the 0.45 relationship between PsyCap and performance, utility of PsyCap can be calculated as follows:

$$U_{productivity} = 300*5*0.45*2*50,000 = \$67.5 \text{ million.}$$

Furthermore, again using the 2% increase in PsyCap based on our short development interventions, the change in productivity (contribution) in this example can be calculated as follows:

$$\Delta U_{productivity} = 300*5*0.45*2*50,000*0.02 = \$1.35 \text{ million.}$$

It should be noted that these results are close to those using traditional utility analysis for small companies (see example 3). We expect that, over time, organizations that effectively employ high-performance work practices in general (e.g., see Pfeffer, 1998) and PsyCap investment, development, and management in particular can potentially experience considerable performance impact and competetive advantage. Specifically, we would propose that the return on investment in PsyCap would be much higher than has been obtained from traditional economic and financial capital.

To provide research support for this assertion, we can draw from actual data of 74 engineering managers (\$100,900 average annual salary) in a high-tech manufacturing firm who went through our 2.5-hour psychological capital intervention (see the PCI model in figure 8.1 and the content summary in figure 8.2). These research study participants had a 0.33 correlation between their level of PsyCap and performance. They also had a 1.5% increase in PsyCap as a result of the microintervention development session. We then calculated a 270% return on development (ROD) (see Luthans, Avey, et al., 2006). This return on PsyCap development is based on \$73,919 of increased contribution using the utility analysis formula above over just a one-year period (74*1*0.33*2*\$100,900*0.015), minus the high 2.5 hourly wage rate (\$50/hour) of these managers (times two for the additional benefits/indirect costs) and the estimated facilitator/training overhead costs (\$1,500) for conducting the microintervention (PCI). This total cost of \$20,000 for the PCI (74*2.5*\$50/hour*2 + 1,500) is used to derive the 270% ROD (73,919–20,000/20,000). This result, from a real example and using actual data, of course, is much higher than traditional economic and financial capital has typically been able to return.

This return on investment in PsyCap from this sample of engineering managers can be seen to be even more dramatic if we are able to have the same effect from our PsyCap development intervention on all the employees of this very large high-tech firm. It has about 170,000 employees that average \$62,500 in wages and salaries. Using the same utility analysis (and assuming the same results obtained in our study of the sample of engineering managers from this very large firm) yields over $100 million in contribution, with an ROD of well over 200%, depending on the size of the training groups.

By using the Kravetz (2004) rule of thumb (i.e., two times salary to measure contribution), the higher up the salary scale a group of managers or employees rank, the more likely that developing this group's PsyCap will have substantial results and contribution to the organization's performance. Furthermore, developing these highly paid employees will not only leverage their contribution and performance but may also have a cascading, trickle-down effect on their associates' PsyCap—and, consequently, their impacts as well (Avolio & Luthans, 2006; Luthans & Avolio, 2003).

Using an extreme example to make a point, a 2% increase in the PsyCap of Terry Semel, CEO of Yahoo and the highest paid CEO in 2004 (total compensation was $230.6 million), by himself, may have the potential of increasing Yahoo's annual performance by about $2 million. With this extreme example, we do not intend to imply that this leader by himself will have such a dramatic impact on performance from a small increase in his PsyCap. Instead, we are simply suggesting that the higher up the individual is in any organization, the greater the potential cumulative impact (through others in terms of a cascading or social contagion effect) that an increase in PsyCap may have (see Luthans & Avolio, 2003; Avolio & Luthans, 2006).

POTENTIAL LIMITATIONS AND PITFALLS

Although the above analysis of PsyCap measurement, relationship with performance, and return on development is quite promising to date, there are also several potential limitations and pitfalls that need to be recognized. We classify these potential limitations and pitfalls into three categories: those that can impede the reliable and valid measurement of PsyCap, those that can threaten the accuracy of performance assessment and impact, and those that can occur in estimating and calculating the return on PsyCap investment.

Pitfalls in Measuring PsyCap

Earlier in this chapter, we presented some of the potential internal, external, and overall construct-validity challenges that the measurement of

PsyCap may present. Being true to the PsyCap criteria of focusing on the positive (rather than negative), workplace-specific (rather than generic or other contexts), and developmental states (rather than relatively fixed, dispositional traits) that are related to performance (rather than being outcomes in and of themselves), our newly developed and validated PsyCap Questionnaire (PCQ) shown in the appendix directly addresses such concerns (see Luthans, Avolio, et al., 2006, for a detailed analysis).

In addition, Podsakoff, MacKenzie, Lee, and Podsakoff (2003) summarize several potential biases in using surveys for measuring any psychological variables, including PsyCap. These biases include consistency, social desirability, leniency, acquiescence, transient mood states, and item ambiguity. Despite their positivity, the most commonly used PsyCap scales have not been found to be significantly influenced by such biases (e.g., see Snyder, 2002). However, we recommend controlling for potential biases such as social desirability when measuring PsyCap, and we have routinely done so in our studies. Short instruments to do this are now available, such as Reynolds's (1982) short version of the classic Marlowe-Crowne Social Desirability Scale (Crowne & Marlowe, 1960), which has been supported by recent research (Loo & Thorpe, 2000) to be even more valid and reliable than the original long version. Furthermore, as our research progresses on PsyCap, there is a need to conduct meta-analyses using confidence intervals that will help with such potential error and bias issues.

Other ways in which our PsyCap measure takes into consideration and combats some of the potential biases are the inclusion of reverse-scored items, multiple administrations of the scale at different points in time, using randomly assigned control groups for intervention studies, and the use of well-developed and tested items that are adapted from established, standardized measures from positive psychology. Nonetheless, other potential threats still exist. For example, Podsakoff and colleagues (2003) suggest that the use of a common scale format and fixed anchors may increase common method biases. However, we have not found significant differences between the factor structures yielded by the scales of our new PCQ instrument and those from the literature for measuring the various PsyCap capacities (Luthans, Avolio, et al., 2006).

Moreover, shorter scales can cause more consistency due to answers to previous items continuing to be present in the respondent's short-term memory. This can be further increased by the lack of intermixing of items that measure the various PsyCap capacities. Intermixing of items and varying the scales and anchors are possible. On the other hand, there are tradeoffs, particularly in organizational behavior research, where lengthy instruments have been found to significantly reduce response rates.

Clearly, any survey measure such as our PCQ will have its limitations. For the future development and refinement of measuring PsyCap, we propose to move toward a triangulation strategy. Specifically, one can use questionnaire surveys (the PCQ), observation, and interviews to triangulate around what an individual's PsyCap score ends up being, based on all three sources (e.g., see Berson & Avolio, 2004, for an example of how to use triangulation to estimate leadership behavior). Only through the use of such multi-methods can we eventually reduce to a minimum the bias inherent in surveys that may artificially increase (or decrease) PsyCap scores.

Pitfalls in Measuring Performance

One of the most problematic issues facing organizational behavior research in general is the collection of objective performance data. Performance measures may be nonexistent, too subjective, outdated, infrequent, inadequate, or not voluntarily made available. When objective performance measures are not directly available, using multiple measures may be able to compensate, even if some of these supplemental/substitute measures are subjective (Dess & Robinson, 1984). Moreover, Chakravarthy (1986) shows that, even when present, traditional performance measures are often insufficient, and he highlights the utility of incorporating satisfaction measures, which have been clearly demonstrated to relate to performance (see the meta-analysis of Judge, Thorensen, Bono, & Patton, 2001). Harter, Schmidt, and Hayes (2002, 2003) also support the use of composite measures of performance, including productivity and profitability, as well as turnover and customer satisfaction.

In our research, we have found that integrating various measures of performance (e.g., objective quality and quantity data, financial and sales data, supervisors' evaluations, self-reported assessments, and merit-based salary information), as well as administering validated measures of attitudinal outcomes (e.g., job satisfaction, intention of quitting, organizational commitment), to provide a more complete picture of performance (Luthans, Avolio, et al., 2006; Youssef, 2004). To avoid common source biases, outcome assessments can be obtained from a different source (e.g., organizational data or the respondent's manager) or from the respondents themselves, but at a different point in time, in a different location, or through a different medium. Anonymity should be ensured, which can present a hurdle in relating each respondent's predictor to outcome data. However, various procedural and statistical approaches have been found to be effective in such situations (Podsakoff, et al., 2003).

It is important to remember that supervisory performance appraisals of individuals may appear objective but still be based on subjective premises. The most objective measures of performance are those based on actual "hard data" (e.g., productivity numbers or sales made). Obviously, other issues such as technology may enter into these objective data as well. However, supervisory ratings that are commonly utilized in performance appraisals are usually influenced by a number of variables, such as the rated employee's organizational citizenship behaviors (Schmidt & Hunter, 2000), as well as a multitude of perceptual and attributional biases that may influence the supervisor's rating. However, even with these potential problems, such outside ratings are still considered preferable to self-ratings.

Another significant but generally overlooked issue regarding the measurement of performance is getting the right range and dimensions of performance. For example, we would suggest that the PsyCap measure is more likely to predict a broader range of performance criteria given the nature of the constructs that comprise this instrument. Specifically, constructs such as efficacy, hope, optimism, and resiliency are likely to predict in the upper ranges of human performance by their very nature, especially measures that tap into durability and sustainability. Thus, if the performance measure captures "typical" performance ranges in organizations, then the PsyCap index may very well underpredict because the top end of the performance range is not available. We propose the need to examine performance not only under ordinary but also extraordinary conditions before we can settle on the metarelationship of PsyCap to performance.

An example from the transformational leadership literature can illustrate this point about the need to examine performance ranges. Beng-Chong and Ployhart (2004) reported that the validity of the transformational leadership scale went from .3 to .6 when predicting typical versus extraordinary performance. Since the transformational leadership scale was designed to predict performance beyond expectations, it is not surprising that it predicts extraordinary performance much better than just typical performance. We believe the same problem with how organizations measure performance may exist for the studies that have been completed to date focusing on PsyCap. Future research needs to test this proposition of better prediction of high levels of performance.

Pitfalls in Measuring the Return on PsyCap Investment

Beside the possible measurement problems associated with PsyCap and performance, the work of Podsakoff and colleagues (2003) can also contribute to addressing the potential pitfalls in conducting utility analysis when assessing the return on PsyCap development interventions in terms of the impact on performance and attitudinal outcomes. One primary concern would be that common method biases may result in small or nonexistent relationships that are found and exaggerated, but strong and true relationships are not uncovered or are diminished.

Most of our initial research results on PsyCap were obtained through studies in which common method biases were minimized, both procedurally and statistically. However, Cote and Buckley's (1987) extensive, multidisciplinary analysis suggests that even if there were some common method biases, our preliminary results that PsyCap has a significant impact on the variance in performance and satisfaction may actually have a higher true variance. However, as discussed earlier, strong PsyCap measurement instruments, diversified outcome measures and sources, and controlling for potential confounds are factors that we feel have contributed to the reliability and validity of our studies to date.

More specifically in relation to the utility calculations, one of the most frequently cited difficulties is the estimation of SD_y, the standard deviation of the outcome of interest. Our calculations in the above examples are no exception. Beside the limitations of outcome data scarcity and relevancy, various assumptions such as randomness and normality may not necessarily apply across situations. For example, our illustrative cases of utility analysis did not utilize random samples of companies. However, researchers and practitioners can ensure that these assumptions are met by utilizing company-specific, longitudinal data. Such data can constitute either a random sample of outcomes or, ideally, a complete data set of outcomes over time for each of the organizations being studied (i.e., the y-population). Such future research can facilitate the use of more realistic estimates of SD_y, particularly in intervention research, where such data are infrequently reported (Hunter & Schmidt, 1983).

Moreover, PsyCap is by definition a malleable state. This state-like criterion implies its potential for development and thus variability not only across respondents but also within respondents over time. Although PsyCap variability and developmental potential are conceptually and practically desirable, they represent challenges to our currently available methodologies. We have utilized randomly assigned control groups in our intervention research designs as a way to manage such challenges. At least in the basic research, we feel that such classic, as well as innovative, design steps must be taken to scientifically evaluate the impact of PsyCap development programs.

Finally, an important challenge in assessing the impact of PsyCap is choosing the appropriate level of analysis for the outcomes being assessed. Statistically, individual-level outcomes are the simplest to relate to PsyCap since it is also measured at the individual level. However, such outcomes are not always available, and they may not necessarily be of highest priority or significance to organizations. On the other hand, the utilization of important group and organizational-level outcomes, such as the sales and profits figures used in the utility analysis examples above, may be of the highest interest to organizations. For example, Harter and colleagues (2002) and Peterson and Luthans (2003) utilized business-level outcomes to assess the impact of employee engagement and leader hope, respectively. However, aggregation may not always be statistically possible or justifiable, particularly with the high within-group variability expected in future PsyCap research.

In conclusion, in order to meet the criteria and to differentiate from almost all human resource management approaches through the years, PsyCap must show performance impact. In this chapter, we have attempted to demonstrate such PsyCap impact on performance and ROD, as well as how it can be done as validly as possible in the future.

FUTURE IMPLICATIONS AND DIRECTIONS FOR PSYCAP RESEARCH AND PRACTICE

As we conclude the book, we offer a few final remarks and advice for those who are interested in integrating PsyCap within their future research agenda or for the more effective practice of human resource management and development.

- Unlike most innovations, where early adopters must assume a high level of risk and tolerate possibly dismal or negative returns (at least in the short term), we have shown in this chapter that PsyCap as presented in this book offers unique "upside" potential for a low-risk, low-cost, and very high return on investment.
- Our hope is that this book will stimulate further research and application that will refine our understanding of PsyCap and its development processes. Moreover, in light of the recent criticisms of quantitative research in general and utility analysis in particular, we encourage the use of classic research designs; and we also are concerned that we do not simply dismiss insignificant or unexpected empirical findings as "errors" without further investigation and keeping an open mind. For example, meta-analytic findings have enhanced our understanding of potential moderators for the efficacy-performance relationship (e.g., see Stajkovic & Luthans, 1998a). Similarly, emerging, alternative statistical techniques such as structural equation modeling can further support PsyCap as a higher order construct that synergistically encompasses and is manifested not only through self-efficacy, hope, optimism, and resiliency, but also through other positive constructs such as those suggested in chapters 6 and 7.
- As we look downstream, one of the big challenges is connecting the growth in work on PsyCap to the authentic leadership development (ALD) process. We expect that ALD will drive PsyCap growth, and vice versa. Demonstrating how each can contribute to the other's growth over time will become an important research agenda item.
- Looking into growing PsyCap in teams and larger collectives such as organizations will also engage a significant part of the future research agenda.
- We have only begun to scratch the surface on how PsyCap develops in other cultures, as well as the nature of its impact on performance in those other cultures. We envision a great deal more work being done in cross-culturally applying PsyCap in different contexts across the globe.

- Finally, in line with the "big picture" perspective that we encouraged you to maintain at the beginning of this book, we emphasize that even as more PsyCap theory-building and research emerges, it is important to maintain a broad, cross-disciplinary perspective in the study of human behavior in general and PsyCap in particular. Various synergies are likely to exist as research across life domains is integrated. Much can be learned from transferring knowledge not only from positive psychology, positive organizational scholarship, and positive organizational behavior, but also from education, clinical psychology, sports, health care, and other social settings to the workplace, and vice versa. A broader perspective can also facilitate the integration of cross-cultural dimensions, the understanding of which is vital for competitiveness *and* positive collaboration in today's global environment.

REFERENCES

Arnett, J. J. (2000). Emerging adulthood: A theory of development from the late teens through the twenties. *American Psychologist, 55,* 469–480.

Avolio, B., & Luthans, F. (2006). *The high impact leader.* New York: McGraw-Hill.

Bandura, A. (1997). *Self-efficacy: The exercise of control.* New York: Freeman.

Becker, B. E., & Huselid, M. A. (1992). Direct estimates of SD sub y and the implications for utility analysis. *Journal of Applied Psychology, 77,* 227–233.

Beng-Chong, L., & Ployhart, R. E. (2004). Transformational leadership: Relations to the five-factor model and team performance in typical and maximum contexts. *Journal of Applied Psychology, 89,* 610–621.

Berson, Y., & Avolio, B. J. (2004). Linking transformational and strategic leadership: Examining the leadership system of a high-technology organization in a turbulent environment. *Leadership Quarterly, 15,* 625–646.

Boudreau, J. W. (1991). Utility analysis in human resource management decisions. In M. D. Dunnette & L. M. Hough (Eds.), *Handbook of industrial and organizational psychology* (2nd ed., Vol. 2, pp. 621–745). Palo Alto, CA: Consulting Psychologists Press.

Brogden, H. E., & Taylor, E. K. (1950). The dollar criterion: Applying the cost accounting concept to criterion construction. *Personnel Psychology, 3,* 133–154.

Cascio, W. F. (1991). *Costing human resources: The financial impact of behavior in organizations* (3rd ed.). Boston: PWS-Kent.

Cascio, W. F., & Ramos, R. A. (1986). Development and application of a new method for assessing job performance and behavioral/economic terms. *Journal of Applied Psychology, 71,* 20–28.

Chakravarthy, B. S. (1986). Measuring strategic performance. *Strategic Management Journal, 7,* 437–458.

Cote, J., & Buckley, R. (1987). Estimating trait, method, and error variance: Generalizing across 70 construct validation studies. *Journal of Marketing Research, 24,* 315–318.

Cronbach, L. J., & Gleser, G. C. (1965). *Psychological tests and personnel decisions* (2nd ed.). Urbana: University of Illinois Press.

Crowne, D. P., & Marlowe, D. (1960). A new scale of social desirability independent of psychopathology. *Journal of Counseling Psychology, 24,* 349–354.

Dess, G. G., & Robinson, Jr., R. B. (1984). Measuring organizational performance in the absence of objective measures: The case of the privately held firm and conglomerate business unit. *Strategic Management Journal, 5,* 265–273.

Goldstein, I. L. (1986). *Training in organizations: Needs, assessment, development, and evaluation.* Monterey, CA: Brookes/Cole.

Harter, J., Schmidt, F., & Hayes, T. (2002). Business-unit-level relationship between employee satisfaction, employee engagement, and business outcomes: A meta-analysis. *Journal of Applied Psychology, 87,* 268–279.

Harter, J., Schmidt, F., & Hayes, T. (2003). Well-being in the workplace and its relationship to business outcomes: A review of the Gallup studies. In C. Keyes & J. Haidt (Eds.), *Flourishing: Positive psychology and the life well-lived* (pp. 205–224). Washington, DC: American Psychological Association.

Hunter, J. E., & Schmidt, F. L. (1983). Quantifying the effects of psychological interventions on employee job performance and work-force productivity. *American Psychologist, 38,* 473–478.

Hunter, J. E., Schmidt, F. L., & Judiesch, M. K. (1990). Individual differences in output variability as a function of job complexity. *Journal of Applied Psychology, 75,* 28–42.

Huselid, M. A. (1995). The impact of human resource management practices on turnover, productivity, and corporate financial performance. *Academy of Management Journal, 38,* 635–672.

Judge, T. A., & Bono, J. E. (2001). Relationship of core self-evaluations traits—self-esteem, generalized self-efficacy, locus of control, and emotional stability—with job satisfaction and job performance: A meta-analysis. *Journal of Applied Psychology, 86,* 80–92.

Judge, T. A., Thoresen, C. J., Bono, J. E., & Patton, G. K. (2001). The job satisfaction-job performance relationship: A qualitative and quantitative review. *Psychological Bulletin, 127,* 376–407.

Kravetz, D. (2004). *Measuring human capital: Converting workplace behavior into dollars.* Mesa, AZ: KAP.

Latham, G. P., & Whyte, G. (1994). The futility of utility analysis. *Personnel Psychology, 47,* 31–46.

Locke, E., Frederick, E., Lee, C., & Bobko, P. (1984). Effects of self-efficacy, goals and task strategies on task performance. *Journal of Applied Psychology, 69,* 241–251.

Loo, R., & Thorpe, K. (2000). Confirmatory factor analyses of the full and short versions of the Marlowe-Crowne social desirability scale. *Journal of Social Psychology, 140,* 628–635.

Lopez, S., & Snyder, C. R. (Eds.). (2003). *Positive psychological assessment: A handbook of models and measures.* Washington, DC: American Psychological Association.

Luthans, F., Avey, J. B., Avolio, B. J., Norman, S. M., & Combs, G. J. (2006). Psychological capital development: Toward a micro-intervention. *Journal of Organizational Behavior, 27* 387–393.

Luthans, F., & Avolio, B. (2003). Authentic leadership: A positive development approach. In K. S. Cameron, J. E. Dutton, & R. E. Quinn (Eds.), *Positive organizational scholarship* (pp. 241–258). San Francisco: Berrett-Koehler.

Luthans, F., Avolio, B., Avey, J., & Norman, S. (2006). Psychological capital: Measurement and relationship with performance and satisfaction (Working Paper No. 2006–1). Gallup Leadership Institute, University of Nebraska–Lincoln.

Luthans, F., Avolio, B. J., Walumbwa, F. O., & Li, W. (2005). The psychological capital of Chinese workers: Exploring the relationship with performance. *Management and Organization Review, 1,* 249–271.

Masten, A. S. (2001). Ordinary magic: Resilience process in development. *American Psychologist, 56,* 227–239.

Masten, A. S., & Reed, M. J. (2002). Resilience in development. In C. R. Snyder & S. Lopez (Eds.), *Handbook of positive psychology* (pp. 74–88). Oxford, UK: Oxford University Press.

Maurer, T. J., & Pierce, H. R. (1998). A comparison of Likert scale and traditional measures of self-efficacy. *Journal of Applied Psychology, 83,* 324–329.

Parker, S. (1998). Enhancing role breadth self-efficacy: The roles of job enrichment and other organizational interventions. *Journal of Applied Psychology, 6,* 835–852.

Peterson, C., & Chang, E. (2002). Optimism and flourishing. In C. Keyes & J. Haidt (Eds.), *Flourishing: Positive psychology and the life well-lived* (pp. 55–79). Washington, DC: American Psychological Association.

Peterson, S., & Luthans, F. (2003). The positive impact of development of hopeful leaders. *Leadership and Organizational Development Journal, 24,* 26–31.

Pfeffer, J. (1998). *The human equation.* Boston: Harvard Business School Press.

Podsakoff, P., MacKenzie, S., Lee, J., & Podsakoff, N. (2003). Common method biases in behavioral research: A critical review of the literature and recommended remedies. *Journal of Applied Psychology, 88,* 879–903.

Reynolds, W. (1982). Development of reliable and valid short forms of the Marlowe-Crowne social desirability scale. *Journal of Clinical Psychology, 38,* 119–125.

Sackett, P. R., & Mullen, E. J. (1993). Beyond formal experimental design: Towards an expanded view of the training evaluation process. *Personnel Psychology, 46,* 613–627.

Scheier, M., & Carver, C. (1985). Optimism, coping, and health: Assessment and implications of generalized outcome expectancies. *Health Psychology, 4,* 219–247.

Schmidt, F. L., & Hunter, J. E. (2000). Select on intelligence. In E. Locke (Ed.), *The Blackwell handbook of principles of organizational behavior* (pp. 3–14). Oxford, UK: Blackwell.

Schmidt, F. L., Hunter, J. E., McKenzie, R. C., & Muldrow, T. W. (1979). Impact of valid selection procedures on work-force productivity. *Journal of Applied Psychology, 64,* 609–626.

Seligman, M. E. P. (1998). *Learned optimism.* New York: Pocket Books.

Skarlicki, D. P., Latham, G. P., & Whyte, G. (1996). Utility analysis: Its evolution and tenuous role in human resource management decision making. *Revue Canadienne des Sciences de l'Administration, 13*(1), 13–21.

Snyder, C. R. (2000). *Handbook of hope.* San Diego: Academic Press.

Snyder, C. R. (2002). Hope theory: Rainbows in the mind. *Psychological Inquiry, 13,* 249–275.

Snyder, C. R., Sympson, S. C., Ybasco, F. C., Borders, T. F., Babyak, M. A., & Higgins, R. L. (1996). Development and validation of the state hope scale. *Journal of Personality and Social Psychology, 70,* 321–335.

Stajkovic, A. D., & Luthans, F. (1998a). Self-efficacy and work-related performance: A meta-analysis. *Psychological Bulletin, 124,* 240–261.

Stajkovic, A. D., & Luthans, F. (1998b). Social cognitive theory and self-efficacy: Going beyond traditional motivational and behavioral approaches. *Organizational Dynamics, 26,* 62–74.

Wagnild, G., & Young, H. (1993). Development and psychometric evaluation of the resilience scale. *Journal of Nursing Measurement, 1*(2), 165–178.

Whyte, G., & Latham, G. (1997). The futility of utility analysis revisited: When even an expert fails. *Personnel Psychology, 50,* 601–610.

Youssef, C. M. (2004). *Resiliency development of organizations, leaders and employees: Multilevel theory building and individual-level, path-analytical empirical testing.* Unpublished doctoral dissertation, University of Nebraska–Lincoln.

PsyCap Questionnaire (PCQ)

BELOW ARE STATEMENTS that describe how you may think about yourself right now. Use the following scales to indicate your level of agreement or disagreement with each statement.

(1 = Strongly disagree, 2 = disagree, 3 = somewhat disagree, 4 = somewhat agree, 5 = agree, 6 = strongly agree)

1. I feel confident analyzing a long-term problem to find a solution.
2. I feel confident in representing my work area in meetings with management.
3. I feel confident contributing to discussions about the company's strategy.
4. I feel confident helping to set targets/goals in my work area.
5. I feel confident contacting people outside the company (e.g., suppliers, customers) to discuss problems.
6. I feel confident presenting information to a group of colleagues.
7. If I should find myself in a jam at work, I could think of many ways to get out of it.
8. At the present time, I am energetically pursuing my work goals.
9. There are lots of ways around any problem.
10. Right now I see myself as being pretty successful at work.
11. I can think of many ways to reach my current work goals.
12. At this time, I am meeting the work goals that I have set for myself.

13. When I have a setback at work, I have trouble recovering from it, moving on.**(R)**
14. I usually manage difficulties one way or another at work.
15. I can be "on my own," so to speak, at work if I have to.
16. I usually take stressful things at work in stride.
17. I can get through difficult times at work because I've experienced difficulty before.
18. I feel I can handle many things at a time at this job.
19. When things are uncertain for me at work, I usually expect the best.
20. If something can go wrong for me work-wise, it will.**(R)**
21. I always look on the bright side of things regarding my job.
22. I'm optimistic about what will happen to me in the future as it pertains to work.
23. In this job, things never work out the way I want them to.**(R)**
24. I approach this job as if "every cloud has a silver lining."

Source: Luthans, F., Avolio, B., Avey, J., & Norman, S. (2006). Psychological capital: Measurement and relationship with performance and satisfaction (Working Paper No. 2006–1). Gallup Leadership Institute, University of Nebraska–Lincoln. Items adapted from Parker, 1998; Snyder, et al., 1996; Wagnild & Young, 1993; Scheier & Carver, 1985.

Note: R indicates reverse scoring. These 24 items were used in conducting reliability and validity analyses of the PCQ. If the PCQ is used for research purposes, and if it is adpated or altered in any way, permission must be obtained from the authors by writing to gli@unl.edu.

Index

Academy of Management, 187
After Action Reviews (AARs), 53
age and wisdom, 153
agency and hope, 66, 69, 78, 79, 81
aggressive humor, 165–166
ALD. *See* authentic leadership development
appreciation for the present, 102, 106
approach-coping techniques, 126
asset-focused strategies for resiliency, 124–125
assets necessary for resiliency, 21, 116–117, 131
attention
    as antecedent for flow, 163
    as positive reinforcer, 47–48
attributional style of optimism, 90–92
authenticity, 18, 49, 175, 192–195
authentic leadership development (ALD),
    22, 56
    and balanced processing, 152
    defined, 193
    future research on, 232
    and hopeful managers, 73, 79
    and optimism, 99
    and resiliency, 119, 130–132
    and wisdom, 154
autotelic personality, 161
avoidance-coping techniques, 126
Avolio, B. J., 118–119, 152, 154, 166, 193

Badran, M., 50–51
balanced processing, 152
Baltes, P., 154
Bandura, A.
    on collective efficacy, 50
    on conceptual challenges to studying
        efficacy, 55–56

on development of efficacy, 43
on inhibitors of efficacy, 53–54
on measurement of efficacy, 208
on probability of individual success, 33
social cognitive theory of, 16, 39, 47,
    176
Bar-On, R., 185–186
Bass, B. M., 52, 127, 189
Beng-Chong, L., 229
"Berlin Wisdom Paradigm," 152
"Best Places to Work," 49, 76
Bono, J. E., 210
broaden-and-build theory, 166
Buckley, R., 230
Burns, J. M., 127

Caplan, J., 184
career resiliency, 5, 98, 127–129
Carver, C., 209
Center for Creative Leadership on
    emotional intelligence, 184
Chakravarthy, B. S., 228
Chang, E., 95
coaching
    in building of mastery experiences, 44
    from hopeful managers, 73
    as risk-management strategy, 125
cognitive strengths, 145–174
coherence, sense of, 20
Collard, B. A., 127–128
collective efficacy, 49–52, 54, 56, 131
competitive advantage from PsyCap, 3–4, 7
    hope providing, 72
    optimism providing, 103
conceptual framework of PsyCap, 21

confidence to succeed, 33–61
  See also self-efficacy
Conner, D., 124
conservation of resources (COR) theory, 23
constructive opposition, 198
coping
  and humor, 165
  vs. resiliency, 135
  and spirituality, 190
corporate culture
  and authentic leaders, 22, 49
  and gratitude, 180
  leadership's role in setting, 49
  nurturing hope in, 75–78, 79
  nurturing wisdom in, 156
Cote, J., 230
courage, 18, 175, 196–200
Cowan, P. A., 118
creativity, 18, 149–151, 167
cross-cultural applications of PsyCap, 25, 57, 68, 81
Crumpler, C. A., 181
Csikszentmihalyi, M., 160, 162

"damage model" of being at risk, 118
Daniels, D., 149
debriefing, importance of, 40–41
DEC (Digital Equipment Corp.), 136
deterioration of PsyCap over time, 23
developing
  of authenticity, 195
  of efficacy in managers and employees, 43–49
  of hope in managers and employees, 68–72
  of optimism in workforce, 100–103
  of PsyCap in workplace, 213–216
  PsyCap's recognition of, 21
  of resiliency in workforce, 124–126
  wisdom open to, 153–154
Digital Equipment Corp. (DEC), 136
disaster dynamics, 136
discrepancy reduction, 38
distractions preventing flow, 163–164
diversity and tolerance, 156
domain-specific nature of self-efficacy, 36, 41, 55
downsizing, effect of, 5, 97, 128, 135, 182

Duchon, D., 188
duress and courage, 198

efficacy. *See* self-efficacy
EI. *See* emotional intelligence
Emmons, R. A., 178, 181
emotional intelligence (EI), 18, 183–186
emotional strengths as potential PsyCap, 148, 157–158
employees, developing PsyCap in. *See* developing
employment environment of today, 5–6, 14, 97, 122–123, 127
empowerment and hope, 69
engagement vs. subjective well-being, 158
enriched jobs, 74
entrepreneurial thinking, 125–126
EQ-i (Emotional Quotient Inventory), 185
explanatory style of optimism, 90–92, 95, 98–99
external influences on self-efficacy, 37
extrinsic motivators in workplace, 150

false efficacy, 53–54
false hope, 78, 80
feedback
  constructive feedback as risk-management strategy, 125
  and organizational resiliency, 133
  positive feedback to develop self-efficacy, 47–48, 53
fit
  of cognitive and affective strengths with PsyCap, 145–147
  importance in human resource management, 14
  of socially-oriented and higher-order strengths with PsyCap, 176–177
  and strategic alignment, 71
flattened structure of organizations, 98
flexibility as qualifier of optimism, 94–96, 107
flow, 18, 160–165
  measurement of, 164
  performance impact of, 164–165
  potential problems for, 163–164
  state-like nature of, 161
  in workplace, 162–163
forethought, 39

forgiveness. *See* gratitude and forgiveness

Fredrickson, B., 149, 166

Fry, L., 188, 191, 192

future PsyCap research and practice, 22–25
  and higher order positive capacities, 200
  and hope, 80–81
  and measurement of PsyCap, 231–233
  and optimism, 106–108
  and potential PsyCap, 168, 200
  and resiliency, 137–139

Gallup Organization areas of research and practice, 158–159, 162

Gardner, H., 183–184

goal-setting
  See also "stretch" goals
  and hope, 68
  regoaling, 78

Goleman, D., 184

Gorman, C., 117

gratitude and forgiveness, 18, 178–183
  definition of forgiveness, 179
  definition of gratitude, 178–179
  satisfying PsyCap criteria, 181–183

Graves, C. W., 149

Hackman, J., 74

Hamel, G., 131, 134, 137

happiness vs. subjective well-being, 158

hardiness, 20

Harter, J., 158, 228, 231

Harter, S., 192

Hayes, T., 158, 228, 231

Henderson, J., 194

Herzberg, F., 12

higher order positive capacities, 186–187

high-performance work practices (HPWPs), 7

Hill, P., 187

Hobfoll, S., 25

hope, 17, 63–85
  and cultural differences, 25
  defined, 17, 66–67
  developing in managers and employees, 68–72
  example of, 64–65
  false hope, 78, 80
  future research and practice on, 80–81
  and goal-setting, 68

hopeful employees, 73–74
  and involvement, 69
  of leaders or managers, 68, 72–73
  measurement of, 210
  nurturing culture of, 75–78, 79
  personal reflections exercise on, 64
  potential pitfalls for, 78–79
  relationship between hope and performance, 67–68
  and resources, 70–71
  and reward systems, 69–70, 74, 79
  and stepping, 69, 79
  and strategic alignment, 71
  and "stretch" goals, 17, 69, 79
  and training, 71–72

Horne, J., 132, 134

Hoy, W., 194

HPWPs (high-performance work practices), 7

human capital
  development of, 124, 131
  as foundation for PsyCap, 20–21

humor, 18, 165–167

"imaginal" experiences in place of training or coaching, 47

improvement possibilities and self-efficacy, 36–37

individuation and courage, 198

innovation, 197

intrinsic motivators in workplace, 150

involvement
  and courage, 198
  of workforce, 69

Judge, T. A., 210

Kelley, R., 184

Kohler, G., 167

Kunzmann, U., 154

leadership
  and collective efficacy, 52, 56
  hopeful leader, effect of, 68, 72–73
  and humor, 166
  and optimism, 99–100
  PsyCap and developing leaders, 22
  resiliency of, 126–127, 129–130
  self-efficacy as substitute for, 56–57

leadership (continued)
   self-efficacy of leaders, 57
   setting of organizational culture by, 49
   and spirituality, 188
   transformational leadership, 127
Leadership Quarterly (2005) on spirituality, 187
leniency for the past, 101–102, 106
Likert scales to measure self-efficacy, 208
limbering for resiliency, 133
Locke, E., 53–54
Luthans, F., 68, 119, 154, 184, 193, 231

MacArthur Foundation national study of successful midlife, 159
Maddi, S. R., 124
managers
   See also leadership
   developing efficacy in, 43–49
   developing hope in, 68–72
   elimination of middle management, effect of, 98
   hopeful managers, effect of, 68, 72–73
   support from, 70–71
Marlowe-Crowne Social Desirability Scale, 227
Masten, A., 111–112, 116–117, 124–126
mastery as basis for self-efficacy, 36, 44–45
Mayer, J., 184
Mayer-Salovey-Caruso Emotional Intelligence Test (MSCEIT), 185–186
McCullough, M., 182, 191
means efficacy, 37
measurement criterion of positive organizational behavior, 13, 21–22
measurement of PsyCap, 21–22
   See also PsyCap Questionnaire (PCQ); return on investment from PsyCap; *individual components of PsyCap*
   characteristics of existing measures, 208–211
   empirical relationship to work-related outcomes, 212–213
   future research and practice on, 231–233
   potential pitfalls of, 226–230
   questionnaire length, 209
   scales utilized, 208–209

theoretical framework supporting, 210–211
wording context, 209
in workplace, 211–212
mentoring. *See* coaching
microintervention studies, 14–15, 22, 213–216
micromanagement, effects of, 74
Miller, T., 181
modeling
   to develop self-efficacy, 39–40, 45–47, 53
   of hopeful managers, 73
   and humor, 167
morality and resiliency, 119
MSCEIT (Mayer-Salovey-Caruso Emotional Intelligence Test), 185–186
multiple intelligences, 183

negativity
   contrasting with positive psychological capacities of PsyCap, 24
   exclusion from PsyCap, 148
   extrapolating from negative to positive, 12
   in today's employment environment, 6, 8–9
   and unrealistic optimism, 95

observational cognitive processing, 39–40
O'Hare, P., 166
Oldham, G., 74
opportunity seeking for the future, 102–103, 106
optimism, 17, 87–110
   and cultural differences, 25
   defined, 17, 90–94
   of employees, 96–99
   as explanatory or attributional style, 90–92, 95, 98
   future research and practice on, 106–108
   of leaders, 99–100
   measurement of, 210
   in organizations, 103–104
   personal reflections exercise on, 88–90
   potential pitfalls of, 105–106
   realism and flexibility as qualifiers of, 94–96, 101, 107
   state-like and developmental properties of, 100–103

traditional perspectives of, 93
unidimensionality of, 93, 106
organizational behavior theory, 6, 162
See also positive organizational behavior
(POB)
organizational culture. *See* corporate
culture
organizational learning, 49–50
organizational resiliency, 130–134
Orr, J., 132, 134

Pargament, K., 190
Parker, S., 208–210
pathways and hope, 66, 69, 71, 78–79, 81
PCI (PsyCap Intervention), 14
PCQ. *See* PsyCap Questionnaire
performance
relationship with creativity, 151
relationship with emotional intelligence,
184
relationship with flow, 164–165
relationship with hope, 67–68
relationship with resiliency, 122–123
relationship with self-efficacy, 16, 42–43,
54
relationship with spirituality, 188–189
relationship with wisdom, 157
performance appraisals, 229
pessimism, 91–92
See also optimism
pitfalls of, 105
unidimensionality of, 93, 106
Peterson, C., 95
Peterson, S. J., 68, 231
physiological condition and self-efficacy,
48–49, 53
playfulness in workplace, 167
Plomin, R., 149
Plowman, D. A., 188
Ployhart, R. E., 229
POB. *See* positive organizational behavior
Podsakoff, P., 227, 230
POS. *See* positive organizational
scholarship
positive affectivity, 157–158
positive feedback to develop self-efficacy,
47–48, 53
positive identity, 180
positive labeling, 179

positive organizational behavior (POB),
10–16
background of, 9
criteria meeting psychological capacities,
16–18
defined, 10–11
distinguished from positive
organizational scholarship, 10, 16
and emotional intelligence, 185
measurement criterion of, 13, 21–22
performance impact criterion of, 15–16
positivity criterion of, 11–12
PsyCap's relationship to, 10
state-like criterion of, 13–15
theory- and research-based criteria of,
12–13
positive organizational scholarship (POS)
background of, 9–10
distinguished from positive
organizational behavior, 10, 16
and organizational resiliency, 131
positive performance impact of, 16
positive psychology, 9–10
bipolarity-versus-independence issue of,
210
and courage, 196
and creativity, 151
and gratitude and forgiveness, 178
and resiliency, 124
and spirituality, 187, 191
trait-like constructs of, 14–15
valid measurement criterion of, 13
and wisdom, 152–154
positivity
criterion of POB, 11–12
downward and upward effects of, 22–23,
49
need for, 8–9
traditional constructs of, exclusion from
PsyCap, 148
Posttraumatic Growth, 123
Posttraumatic Stress Disorder, 122–123
potential PsyCap, 145–174
affective and emotional strengths, 157–
158
authenticity as, 192–195
classifications of constructs of, 147–149
courage as, 196–200
creativity as, 149–151

Salovey, P., 184–185
Sandau-Beckler, P., 119
Sarbanes-Oxley Act of 2002, 97
Scheier, M., 209
Schmidt, F., 158, 228, 231
Schneider, S. L., 96, 101–102, 106
selective optimization with compensation (SOC) theory, 23
self-awareness, 126, 130, 154
self-determination theory, 193
self-development and authentic leaders, 22
self-efficacy, 16–17, 33–61
    See also collective efficacy
    characteristics associated with, 38
    contagion effects of, 56
    and cultural differences, 25
    defined, 16, 38–39
    development in managers and employees, 43–49
    domain-specific nature of, 36, 41, 55
    false efficacy, 53–54
    fluctuations in, 23
    future research and practice on, 55–57
    influence of others on, 37
    of leaders, 57
    as leadership substitute, 56–57
    magnitude dimension of, 41
    mastery experiences to develop, 36, 44–45
    measurement of, 208–210
    modeling to develop, 39–40, 45–47, 53
    as open to development, 43
    other factors affecting, 41
    personal reflections exercise on, 34–35
    positive feedback to develop, 47–48, 53
    and possibility of improvement, 36–37
    potential pitfalls of, 53–55
    practice or mastery as basis for, 36
    and psychological and physiological arousal, 48–49, 53
    and social capital, 21
    social persuasion to develop, 47–48, 53
    state-like nature of, 43
    strength dimension of, 41
    success as factor in, 41, 44
    supporting cognitive processes of, 39–41
    transferability among domains, 43, 55
    variable nature of, 37–38
    vicarious learning to develop, 45–47

    and well-being, 48–49
    and work performance, 16, 42–43, 54
self-help literature, 12
self-reflective processing, 39–40
self-regulation, 39–40, 126, 154, 163
Seligman, M., 9, 90, 96, 98–99, 209
sense of coherence, 20
Shatte, A., 123–124
Shelp, E., 198
situational similarity and modeling, 45
Snyder, C. R., 17, 66, 78, 80–81, 209–210
social capital
    development of, 125, 131
    as foundation for PsyCap, 20–21
    and self-efficacy, 21
social learning theory process, 47
    See also Bandura, A.
social persuasion to develop self-efficacy, 47–48, 53
social positive capacities, 176–178
SOC (selective optimization with compensation) theory, 23
spirituality, 18, 175, 187–190
    defined, 187–188
    in organizational behavior and leadership, 188–189
    relevancy to PsyCap, 189–190
    in terms of PsyCap criteria, 190–192
state-like nature of PsyCap, 13–15, 210, 231
State-Trait Cheerfulness Inventory, 167
Staudinger, U., 157
stepping and hope, 69, 79
strategic alignment and hope, 71
strengthening for resiliency, 133
strengths-based management approach, 9, 162
"stretch" goals
    and hope, 17, 69, 79
    and self-efficacy, 44
success as factor in self-efficacy, 41, 44
SWB (subjective well-being). *See* well-being
symbolizing, 39

teams. *See* collective efficacy
Torrance Test of Creative Thinking (TTCT), 150
training
    and hope, 71–72
    and self-efficacy, 45–46

trait-like capacities vs. state-like capacities, 13–14
transformational leadership, 127, 129
trigger moments or events, 96, 114, 131–132, 138, 154
trust issues of employees, 128, 193
Tsang, J., 191

Vaillant, G., 124
Välikangas, L., 131, 134, 137
values
    promoted by courage, 196–197
    role in resiliency, 119–120, 132, 136
    role in wisdom, 156
van Thriell, C., 167
vicarious learning to develop self-efficacy, 45–47
Vinton, K. L., 166
vulnerability factors, 117

war-for-talent perspective, 3, 4–7, 24
Waterman, J. A., 127–128

Waterman, R. H., 127–128
waypower and hope, 66, 78, 81
well-being
    alignment of PsyCap with, 24
    and efficacy, 48–49
    subjective well-being (SWB), 18, 158–160
whistle-blowing, 197, 199
willpower and hope, 66, 78, 81
wisdom, 18, 151–157
    measurement and performance impact of, 156–157
    as meta-heuristic of development, 154–156
    open to development, 153–154
    state-like nature of, 153–154
    theoretical perspectives of, 152–153
wit vs. humor, 165
Wolin, S., & Wolin, S., 118–119, 124
workplace performance. See performance
World War II and field of psychology, 8–9
Worline, M. C., 133, 196, 198, 199